That Should Still Be Us

How Thomas Friedman's Flat World Myths Are Keeping Us Flat on Our Backs

Martin Sieff

WILEY

John Wiley & Sons, Inc.

For general information about our other products and services, please contact our Customer Care Department within the United States at (800) 762–2974, outside the United States at (317) 572–3993 or fax (317) 572–4002.

Wiley also publishes its books in a variety of electronic formats and by print-on-demand. Some content that appears in standard print versions of this book may not be available in other formats. For more information about Wiley products, visit us at www.wiley.com.

ISBN 978-1-118-19766-0 (hardback); ISBN 978-1-118-22813-5 (ebk); ISBN 978-1-118-24063-2 (ebk); ISBN 978-1-118-26535-2 (ebk)

Printed in the United States of America

10 9 8 7 6 5 4 3 2 1

For Debbie Yavelak Sieff . . .

*And for the Industrial Generations of
Belfast, Northern Ireland,
and
Carteret, New Jersey,
Who Built a Better World*

*And for our Fathers,
Simon Sieff and Dimitri Yavelak*

Contents

Introduction

Thomas Friedman and Michael Mandelbaum's book *That Used to Be Us* starts out with an anecdote, as all Thomas Friedman books must. While attending the 2010 World Economic Forum summer conference in China, Friedman was deeply impressed by the new Beijing South Railway Station, a huge modern building covered with solar panels and with high-speed trains coming and going. It was built, he calculated with wonder, in only eight months. He compared that with the escalators in his local train station in Bethesda, Maryland, outside Washington, DC, that had been undergoing repairs for nearly six months.

"A simple comparison made a startling point," he and Mandelbaum wrote. "It took China's Teda Construction Group thirty-two weeks to build a world-class convention center from the ground up—including giant escalators in every corner—and it was taking the Washington Metro crew twenty-four weeks to repair two tiny escalators of twenty-one steps each." (The escalators in question, one should note, are not "tiny," as triple Pulitzer Prize winner Friedman and his coauthor wrote. I go through this station myself half a dozen times a week. They are among the longest in the United States with about a hundred steps each.

For Friedman and Mandelbaum, this was the perfect example of how China will beat us: with a sense of urgency and scale. Americans are willing to settle for less these days, they said. Of course, they could have used the exact same example as an argument against his thesis: the Chinese expect to be ferried around in overly expensive government trains while American workers are hardy enough to walk up stairs to work if they have to. That's the trouble with anecdotes.

But what is the real reason why it will take the Washington Metropolitan Area Transit Authority (WMATA) twenty-four weeks (at best) to repair the

Bethesda Metro escalators? The first reason is that the WMATA is a miserably managed mess. Maintenance, one of the most important functions of any advanced industrial economy, has been documented throughout the Washington area Metro system as a bad joke.

The second and main reason is that America's own domestic industrial base is a pale shadow of its old self. It is far more difficult to get spare parts and especially hard to find the skilled engineers necessary to keep older machinery working smoothly. Why is that? Because successive US administrations for thirty years have done exactly what Friedman has ceaselessly urged them to do—maintain free trade with the rest of the world, especially China, and refuse to protect America's old-fashioned traditional manufacturing base.

Memo number one to Messrs. Friedman and Mandelbaum: if you insist on focusing US government efforts on high-tech research and development and refuse to protect low-tech, far-from-cutting-edge traditional industries, you can expect endless delays in getting spare parts for your Metro rail escalators, your buses, the wonderful new high-speed-train systems, and everything else you fantasize, because you no longer have the broad industrial base to produce those spare parts and basic systems yourself.

And that is likely also the real reason why China was able to build its new super railway station in only eight months: it's capable of producing most, if not all, of the components for anything it wants to build right there in its own factories. And it has the foreign currency on hand to easily afford to buy the rest overseas.

And why is that? Because the Chinese, like the Germans, have very sensibly protected their own industrial economy from potentially destructive foreign competition.

And where did they learn to act in this manner, which is so different from the idealized flat world of Friedman's endless siren songs? They learned it from us because *that used to be us.*

Friedman and Mandelbaum tell another story, of a company called Endo-Stim, as an example of how the future will work. That story says a lot more about their real concerns than the broken escalators of the Bethesda Metro station. EndoStim is a company in St. Louis developing a treatment for acid reflux. It's a very small yet very international company. The CEO's "head office is an iPad." It's not clear from their story how many people work for EndoStim, but it appears it's no more than a handful, all highly educated and highly international. It's not clear that their product will ever make it to market, but that's not the point. What matters to Friedman and Mandelbaum is that it's "lean" and not filled with workers. One thing you quickly learn reading Friedman and Mandelbaum is that they really do hate ordinary American workers. They say, "You've heard the saying 'As goes General Motors, so goes America.' Fortunately, that is no longer true. We wish the new GM well, but thanks to the hyper-connecting of the world our economic future is no longer tied to its fate. The days of a single factory providing 10,000 jobs for one town are fast disappearing. What we need are start-ups of every variety, size, and shape. That is why our motto is 'As EndoStim goes, so goes America.'"

A paragraph later they write, "While rescuing General Motors will save some old jobs, only by spawning thousands of EndoStims—and we do mean thousands—will we generate the good new jobs we need to keep raising this country's standard of living."

And here we have the core of Thomas Friedman's prescription for America. First, we let China and South Korea have all those high-paying old-fashioned jobs making cars. We don't need them. Second, we retrain all those auto workers as doctors, engineers, and MBAs. Then we get those Asian countries to start venture capital funds to pay for thousands of start-ups that may or may not bring products to market. Everybody wins!

Well, no. China wins! South Korea wins! Japan wins! But America loses! America loses! America loses!

America loses because most of the well-paying industrial jobs in China, South Korea, and Japan are not in Friedman's cutesy little enterprising high-tech start-ups. Friedman and Mandelbaum express their cavalier sloppiness on facts and even math when they write, a bit further, "The same forces empowering EndoStim and [a similar company] Eko are also empowering one- and two-person firms that can go global from anywhere. We can see this in the multibillion-dollar come-out-of-nowhere 'apps' industry. . . . An industry that did not exist in 2006 will be generating $38 billion in revenues within a decade."

Those $38 billion are presented with such astonishing fake authority. There is simply no way to be that confident and that specific about such a hypothetical income stream. Even if it were true, against just the $1.4 trillion added to the national debt in three short years by President Obama, or compared to the continuing $500 billion annual US trade deficit with the rest of the world, that $38 billion figure is just peanuts. *Peanuts.*

It's also ironic whenever Friedman and Mandelbaum celebrate smart phone technology. Smart phone innovation has been locked up by heavily protected advanced industrial economies. Also, these devices require the use of rare earths, more than 90 percent of which per year are mined in China. So boosting investment in Friedman's beloved smart phones will only add to the trade deficit (http://economicsintelligence.com/2011/03/02/the-strange-logic-of-the-iphones-economics/). How many of these wonderful new apps are being programmed in India?

Most maddeningly, Friedman and Mandelbaum complain that, no kidding, the big problem with kids today is that they spend more time playing with their smart phones than doing homework. Well hell, someone has to buy those $38 billion in apps he hopes we'll be programming, right?

If *The World Is Flat* was Thomas Friedman's 1.0 wisdom of globalization and free trade, and *Hot, Flat, and Crowded* was his 2.0, then, of course, *That Used to Be Us* is the 3.0 upgrade. But really, it's just Friedman 1.2, with Mandelbaum's input, with probably more bugs added than fixed. Like the famous Bourbon kings of France and Spain, Friedman has forgotten nothing false and remembered nothing true. His supposed 3.0 upgraded arguments here are just the same old lies, fantasies, and sloppy, easily disproven clichés we've seen in his previous books.

I always despised Pangloss, Voltaire's naive optimist who thought that everything, even the 1755 Lisbon earthquake that killed scores of thousands of innocent people, was all for the best. (Voltaire despised Candide's adviser Pangloss, too; that's why he wrote the book.) The whole point of writing this book is to address the grave crises that America now faces. But the clichéd, fact-free solutions that Friedman and Mandelbaum peddle in *That Used to Be Us* are the very things that have led the United States into this awful mess.

So where does Friedman, with Mandelbaum, now identify the main areas of crisis? They concentrate on the following areas:

- "[We] as a country have failed to address some of our biggest problems—particularly education, deficits and debt, and energy and climate change."
- "[We] have stopped investing in our country's traditional formula for greatness."

I'm sure you're thinking that it is only in this abbreviated form that they look vague and meaningless. If you've ever read a whole book by Friedman you know that vague, meaningless, and contradictory are his hallmarks.

What America used to be, and isn't anymore, is cooperative, competitive, and clever. I couldn't agree more. *That Used to Be Us* offers, as a solution, solar power, software, and sympathy. Those things are all nice, but they are no more likely to cure what ails us than an aspirin is to cure cancer.

They take plenty of cheap shots of their own—especially at the Tea Party movement. At one point the authors actually chortle that Friedman "wittily" refers to them as a "tea kettle"—letting off lots of noise and steam but producing nothing worthwhile.

There isn't a single acknowledgment that the Tea Party movement is expressing a genuine concern about the mushrooming financial deficits and government spending binges: Friedman and Mandelbaum give not a hint of acknowledgment that they might be right to demand wholesale cuts in government spending.

The authors like to write about big thinkers and courage, but they see neither in the Tea Party's policy prescriptions. In times of crisis, a real-life courageous Democratic president such as Franklin Roosevelt in 1933, as well as a real-life courageous Republican one such as Warren Harding in 1921, slashed federal spending by 20 percent or more. Friedman and Mandelbaum fail to add that balancing the federal budget used to be us.

Friedman's supposedly "brilliant . . . tea kettle" slur for the Tea Party movement expresses an underlying truth that is the opposite of what he imagines. As the Book of Proverbs says, a parable in the mouth of fools always backfires.

Steam is enormously powerful. Using steam power before anyone else had developed it, the British people built the greatest empire the world had ever known. For about a century it directly controlled a quarter of the population, resources, and territories of the entire globe. The Romans, the Russians, the Chinese, and the Mongols never came close to doing that. And the British did it all with the steam produced by "tea kettles" that Friedman despised. Therefore if the Tea Party movement really is like a tea kettle, it is capable of producing enormous power.

And for more than a hundred years, the steam power of "tea kettles" built the colossus of industrial America, too.

So when Friedman sneers that the Tea Party participants are "only" kettles, he is unwittingly paying them an enormous compliment: the anger they represent may have the power to transform American politics and achieve great things; they have already had much more of an impact than any middle-of-the-road vanity independent candidate has had.

Friedman clearly thinks of himself as prescient, but he didn't see them coming. Instead, he dismisses them as unrealistic, vague, and not worth the attention millions of people pay them. It seems like there might be another witticism about a kettle in there, this time with a pot and the color black.

The Tea Party is as welcome a development as H. Ross Perot's third-party candidacies were in 1992 and 1996. It doesn't matter that he didn't win, and it doesn't matter if the Tea Party never replaces the Republican Party. They are bringing a crucial issue vital to the survival of the Republic to the forefront of political discourse. That is exactly what Perot did. Ironically, it is also the kind of independent, special-issue third-party movement that Friedman and Mandelbaum actually call for in the last, supposedly "rousing," chapter of their book.

Ironically, Friedman and Mandelbaum pay lip service to Perot's constructive third-party campaigns, too (despite absolute disagreement on the issue both obsess over, free trade). They even acknowledge the valuable role that third-party political movements have played in forcing the two old behemoths—Republicans and Democrats—to change their policies and nature in times of challenge.

Although Friedman and Mandelbaum advocate creation of a third-party movement, nowhere in their book do they spell out what they have in mind. But speaking at the Aspen Institute in Colorado in 2011, Friedman was more explicit: he expressed the desire for New York mayor Michael Bloomberg to lead such a movement.

As it happens, I am a great admirer of Mayor Bloomberg in many areas (but not on international trade policy). He is a titular Republican who is distrusted by almost all Republicans and respected by many (though far from all) Democrats. I believe he would be far more fiscally intelligent and responsible at home, and far more sensibly cautious in foreign affairs, than either Barack Obama or George W. Bush.

But if Friedman and Mandelbaum convinced Mayor Bloomberg to lead a third-party challenge in 2012, the result could be the last thing they want: a victory for the conservative Republicans. For Mayor Bloomberg would attract almost no votes from the Republican-conservative base. His appeal would be entirely to Democrat-liberals. He would therefore split President Obama's liberal base and ensure the election of the Republican candidate.

And if the Tea Party participants were to split from the GOP and run their own presidential candidate, that would guarantee President Obama's reelection for the same reason. They would split the conservative Republican base and leave the liberal Democratic one untouched.

Over the past generation, the creation of narrative has become central to American politics. Translated into honest English, it means that all any politically street-smart candidate has to do to get into the White House is create a plausible fairy tale about himself or herself that people will love and that will be enough to get him or her into the White House. It worked for presidents George W. Bush and Obama.

One narrative Obama successfully peddled—which it appears he bought wholesale from Thomas Friedman—is that part of America's economic revival will come from green jobs. It would be nice to have more green jobs but it's not the solution to any of our problems in the near term. The opposite is the truth: Friedman's obsession with creating green jobs and using green energy is stripping America of all its competitiveness, resilience, and power. As this book will prove, green energy will make us more dependent on the Middle East and China than ever before. There isn't remotely enough of it and there never will be.

Friedman and Mandelbaum actually admit their prejudice: they are obsessively opposed to any continued use of fossil fuel as energy sources, even though China and India are now investing in fossil fuel energy on a far vaster scale than the United States ever has. Friedman and his collaborator actually write, *"Higher American fuel bills will ultimately be for the good of the country."* (italics added)

Read that last sentence again. I am not making it up.

As I document in this book, the wind and solar technologies Friedman and Mandellbaum favor will certainly remain marginal for the next few decades and probably will always stay that way.

The corn-ethanol and biomass technologies favored by the scientifically illiterate Bush II administration were never more than bizarre jokes that made a handful of people rich.

We will also see that Friedman and Mandelbaum are so blinded by ideology, they can't recognize that the extraction of natural gas from clay shale formations has already become the answer to their prayer of a new clean "miracle fuel" that could sharply cut America's dependence on imported oil. They couldn't recognize the importance and value of natural gas, especially when it was staring them in the face.

Friedman and Mandelbaum sneer at fracking, the new technology of horizontal mining for oil and natural gas using chemical-hydraulic cocktails. Yet fracking is a real technology that will deliver enough proven energy reserves to power this country and Canada for at least fifty years and probably 250 years.

The pattern of energy reliance in developing scientific-industrial societies over the past five hundred years is very clear: paradigm breakthroughs and advances in utilizing new and more power and energy-intensive fuels occur at least once a century, and usually every fifty years.

That should give us plenty of time to develop genuine successor energy sources, especially if as a global species we finally get our population levels under control by humane means.

Wind power utilized for trade and projecting power through sailing ships became a crucial global power source at the beginning of the sixteenth century. In the early seventeenth century, whale oil became a major source for light in Western Europe. Wood, often burned as charcoal, played an increasing role through the seventeenth and the first half of the eighteenth centuries. It was then displaced by coal for heating and to generate industrial steam power. From 1859 on, oil became a crucial source for heating and light after being distilled into kerosene. From the beginning of the twentieth century, electrical power generated by coal- and later oil-fueled power stations dominated the advanced world. From the 1960s on, they have been supplemented, though never displaced, by nuclear power plants.

As energy analyst Robert Bryce points out in his book *Power Hungry*, there was a consistent logic behind all these changes. Every new fuel source was chemically far more effective and concentrated in its power and energy densities than the fuel it superseded.

But solar and wind power, hydrogen, and biomass are not advances on current fuels. They are not cost-efficient; they are more expensive; and none of them is based on a mature, reliable technology. They represent major retreats down the power-energy density scales rather than advances on them.

Of course, if you just read Friedman and Mandelbaum, you'd never know any of that. They don't quote a single oil, coal, or natural gas expert in their entire book.

Over the past thirty years, liquefied natural gas has grown in importance. But within the past three years, natural gas extracted from clay shale formations by the use of the new fracking technologies has emerged decisively as the cheap, easily available, and low-carbon emission fuel of the twenty-first century.

Friedman and his collaborator repeat Friedman's tired old obsession with solar and wind power development. But remember the hard chemistry-based wisdom of Robert Bryce: "On an average day by itself the (medium-sized) Cardinal Mine (in Kentucky), which has about 400 people on its payroll, produces about 75 percent as much raw energy as all of the wind tunnels and solar panels in the United States."

The Cardinal Mine also produces what is the most essential product to keep America competitive in the global market place: inexpensive energy.

And what is the position of Friedman and Mandelbaum about inexpensive energy to revive the American economy? *They're against it.*

Nothing will change the fact that most of the world economy will be about growing, mining, manufacturing, and shipping everyday things, mostly using existing technologies and energy sources. These sectors aren't going to go away; they are going to become bigger and more important than they ever have been because the market for these goods and services has never been bigger. It consists already of seven billion people—and it is still growing. According to Friedman, if we can't outcompete, it's only because we didn't want it badly enough.

Friedman and Mandelbaum rose to their eminence and power during the Cold War era, when the horrific consequences of unlimited free trade policies had not yet fully devastated the American people. Their narrative is therefore simple: we lost our way after the Cold War when we didn't have an evil empire to fight anymore.

There is just one problem with this narrative: it's a fairy tale; it isn't true.

We really "lost our way" with the Kennedy Round of tariff cuts in the early 1960s. By 1970 the US economy, under President Richard Nixon, had already moved into an annual trade deficit with the rest of the world. Things got far worse under President Ronald Reagan, as even Friedman and Mandelbaum elsewhere acknowledge. But what this means should be very clear: as a nation, the American people didn't lose their way in the new world after the Cold War; they lost their way in the thirty years before it ended.

Friedman and Mandelbaum have never grasped this central point: the Greatest Generation cohorts who controlled the presidency for thirty-two years starting with John F. Kennedy and ending with George Herbert Walker Bush threw America's economic defenses wide open and led it down the path to ruin. These seven presidents and their sixteen successive congresses achieved many admirable things: they won the Space Race, put Americans on the Moon, funded half a century of high-tech growth, passed the Civil Rights Act, and finally ended segregation. Eventually they even won the Cold War. The last of them, President George Herbert Walker Bush, even guided America and the world peacefully through the Collapse of Communism.

But the Greatest Generation presidents also abolished the trade tariff walls that had protected American industry for a century. They passively allowed millions of good-paying industrial jobs to hemorrhage to north-eastern Asia (and not even to China). They imposed tens of thousands of crushing new restrictions on the American domestic economy. They allowed the US steel industry to be reduced to a pale shadow of its former greatness. They allowed American shipbuilding to virtually disappear. They allowed the annual federal deficit to spiral to unprecedented heights (this was Reagan's contribution).

The seven Greatest Generation presidents also overcommitted the United States to be the policeman of the world, a role that Friedman and Mandelbaum, predictably, want it to carry on forever.

Friedman and Mandelbaum are defeatists throughout their book. They claim to be optimists, but their best-case scenario is as frightening as any horror movie.

They claim that America's old industrial strength can never be restored. That is just plain wrong. The policies that worked so well for China (and Japan, South Korea, Taiwan, Malaysia, and Germany as well) also can work for us. After all, those policies used to be our policies—*they used to be us*.

Friedman and Mandelbaum actually celebrate the death of America's manufacturing sector. On page 60 they write that their Flat World "was great at enabling Boeing to make part of its 777 jetliner with a team that included designers in Moscow, wing manufacturers in China, and control electronics producers in Wichita."

They are celebrating this. They are literally pointing to how exciting it is that we don't have to bother with making all this stuff anymore.

But we do have to bother making it.

Occasionally, however, brief, remarkable flashes of truth and honesty break through Friedman and Mandelbaum's endless confusion and gloom. On page 95 they actually admit, "It is vital that we retain as much manufacturing in America as possible." Even then, their only reason for admitting this is that they claim "more innovation will come from the bottom up, rather than just from the top down."

Are Friedman and Mandelbaum so ignorant of the history of engineering, technology, and applied science that they do not realize that this has always been the case for hundreds of years?

The tremendous industrial and technological breakthroughs in eighteenth-century England, nineteenth-century Germany, and nineteenth- and twentieth- century America came overwhelmingly *from the ground up*. As I document in this book, *industrial innovation always comes best from a vast, secure, and expanding industrial base.* That happened in Japan half a century ago and it's happening in China today, as Dan Breznitz and Michael Murphee have documented in their book *Run of the Red Queen.*

Of course, it took an Indian businessman, P. V. Kannan, to point out this elementary truth to a suitably awestruck and open-mouthed Friedman in *The World Is Flat.*

"Kannan's observation points to one of the most important reasons that America needs to keep high-skilled manufacturing at home. So many innovations come from engineers and workers who are actually handling the product, seeing what goes wrong, and anticipating the next breakthrough improvement."

Two paragraphs later he says, "when a factory moves offshore now it takes with it not just the jobs of today but also, perhaps, the jobs of tomorrow."

Wow! Really? After a quarter century of celebrating the stripping of American industry to the rest of the world, it's a bit late in the day for Friedman to recognize *that*.

Here is what Friedman and Mandelbaum claim as their central arguments about America's past and future: our political leaders disagree on too much; kids today need to put down their smart phones and start training themselves to design smart phones; wind and solar will power our nonindustrial economy; and wanting to save or create good-paying Middle America jobs manufacturing useful Middle American staples is an old-fashioned way of thinking.

Three assumptions underlie these insipid conclusions. First, we're losing to China, but that's no reason to spend another minute thinking about China. Second, there's nothing we can do to mitigate the destructive aspects of globalization. Third, American workers are a bunch of lazy jerks and don't deserve what they have anyway.

Friedman and Mandelbaum blithely assert as early as page 12 of their book: "Our problem is not China, and our solution is not China." They are engaging in more simple blatant untruths.

America is running a $270 billion-plus deficit every year with China, so it should be obvious that our immediate problem is China. And since China flatly refuses to let US industrial exports compete on anything like a fair playing field in its own domestic economy, obviously the problem is China. And since China keeps its yuan/renminbi artificially pegged 35 percent to 40 percent below its realistic rates of exchange against the US dollar, obviously our problem is China.

But since China's policies are not evil, but merely wise and sensible on behalf of its own 1.3 billion people, *our solution really is China, too.* All we have to do is copy China's international trade, industrial, and protectionist policies. Then we will not ruin or even seriously damage China. Nor should we want to. But we will reestablish the United States as a great, stable, prosperous, and confident industrial nation again. After all, those policies that are now working so well for China used to be our policies too: *they used to be us.*

Friedman and Mandelbaum also openly admit their hatred of using all fossil fuels, even when China, India, and other countries are using them on a far greater scale than the United States does. It is no wonder, therefore, that they conclude that the inevitable impact of globalization was that "Americans had to run even faster—that is, work harder—just to stay in place."

There are, of course, exceptions to this rule: Friedman and Mandelbaum clearly aren't working harder than they did before; the superficiality and sloppiness of their book prove that.

There is not a single idea in their new book that has not already been worked to death in Friedman's previous books. And there is not a single acknowledgment of any "damned" facts, facts that, as the writer Charles Fort noted ninety years ago in his iconoclastic work *The Book of the Damned*, are "damned" by reigning authorities because inconvenient facts fly in the face of established belief systems.

That remains true today: the success of fracking and protectionism, and the reality of China's currency manipulations, protectionism, and expansion of fossil fuel use fly in the face of Friedman's flat-world theology. But the true facts say otherwise. The world is still round. As Galileo is reputed to have said after being forced to publicly deny that the Earth goes around the Sun, *"Eppur si muove"* (Yet it moves).

Friedman and Mandelbaum also offer a dangerous, utterly untrue complacency that China can't rely on its domestic labor and capital-competitive advantages for much longer. They write, "China cannot go on relying heavily on its ability to mobilize cheap labor and cheap capital and on copying and assembling the innovations of others."

Of course, they don't explain why that would not be true. It is only their pious wish; it is certainly not a realistic forecast.

Some futurists!

Instead, as I document in this book, China can rely upon its "Red Queen" industrial strength for decades, probably at least a century, as Dan Breznitz and Michael Murphee document in their recent book.

Real industrial innovation doesn't come from the antiseptic, spotlessly clean high-tech labs of Intel; *it comes from the noise, dirt, fire, and greasy oil of the industrial workplace.*

If there's one thing Friedman hates, it's people who get their hands dirty for a living. Can't we get rid of those people? Reading Friedman and Mandelbaum, one has to conclude that their overriding "idea" is to make every American worker (except, of course, themselves) more and more insecure and unsecure. Their minds are completely closed to imposing any protective tariffs to protect American domestic industry. They never utter a sentence of protest about China's deliberate undervaluing of its own currency by 35 percent to 40 percent—the measure that more than any other has devastated American domestic manufacturing over the past decade.

Here's something Friedman quotes approvingly that might make any reader put down the book and have a beer to calm himself or herself. It's from a *Wall Street Journal* op-ed, "Is Your Job an Endangered Species?", that ran on February 17, 2011, by Andy Kessler, a former hedge fund manager: "Forget blue-collar and white-collar. There are two types of workers in our economy: creators and servers. Creators are the ones driving productivity—writing code, designing chips, creating drugs, running search engines.

Servers, on the other hand, service these creators (and other servers) by building homes, providing food, offering legal advice, and working at the Department of Motor Vehicles. Many servers will be replaced by machines, by computers and by changes in how business operates."

You could only write something this asinine if you've never had to figure out where a leak was coming from, why a car is making a certain sound, why your cow is unhappy, guess if something is libelous or not, find a tax shelter under recently changed tax laws, or encounter a customer with a problem that's never come up before. Ironically, hedge funders are more and more being replaced by trading programs and high-speed computers. I hope Kessler doesn't consider himself more creative than the poor doctor who will someday have to figure out how to pull his head out of his ass.

There is also a genuinely disgusting undertone to Friedman and Mandelbaum's arrogant lecture on page 29 that "Americans will have to save more, consume less, study longer, and work harder than they have become accustomed to doing in recent years."

Typically Friedman and Mandelbaum are totally ignorant of the reality known firsthand to hundreds of millions of Americans of the past two generations: *Americans have been studying longer and working harder for fewer rewards since the early 1970s.* And the reason for that state of affairs is the refusal to protect the real interests of the American people and the domestic economy because of the blind worship of Friedman's favorite false god, the idol of unlimited free trade.

Friedman and Mandelbaum even get the current economic crisis wrong at the most essential point. On page 31 they write, "There is a difference between the challenge of the economic crisis and the four long-term challenges that America faces. The deep recession of late 2007 to 2009 was what economists call a 'cyclical event' . . . the economy, and the country, will eventually recover."

This may be the most egregious of all the wrong things Friedman with or without Mandelbaum has ever written. *No one* thinks our problems now are disconnected from what's been slowly plaguing us for a few decades, even though there are many disagreements about what those problems are and how to solve them.

But this is not a simple debating point. Friedman claims to be a red-blooded, all-American patriot.

But Friedman's books are filed with a genuine distaste, even hatred, for the ordinary American workingman and -woman. Every one of them has to get a PhD or display unbelievable prodigies of entrepreneurial initiative and success to make it in his world. He has been ruthless and relentless for decades in celebrating the destruction of millions of American jobs, and he refuses to contemplate the most obvious and proven effective measures to protect them. He insists on imposing massive increased energy burdens on 310 million Americans in the face of abundant fuel resources at home. *He burns the well-being and happiness of scores of millions of families on the altar of his clean, pure, spotless high-tech visions.*

Friedman even seems to have a fear of heavy industry. He never visits any mines, oil wells, steelworks, or shipyards. He talks to billionaire CEOs — the only people he clearly thinks worthy of his attention. He loves to talk to taxi drivers on the way to international meetings, but you never see him put on a hard hat and actually visit an oil refinery, a coal mine, a steelworks, or a Du Pont chemical plant to see what goes on there.

Occasionally Friedman revealingly lets his "Aw, shucks, I'm just a good guy like everyone else" act slip. On pages 130–131 he and Mandelbaum revealingly expose their real feelings.

There Friedman and Mandelbaum recount something that happened to the former CEO of Hewlett-Packard Carly Fiorina after she said, "There is no job that is America's God-given right anymore." That was read, correctly, as her saying that American companies had no reason to prefer American workers to foreign workers. A local editorial shot back that we should start offshoring CEO jobs, since qualified CEOs in other countries will work for far, far less. It also came back to haunt her when she ran for the Senate years later in 2010 as a Republican. Incumbent senator Barbara Boxer, a Democrat, beat her in a walk.

Thomas Friedman has never shown a moment's real compassion for the hundreds of millions of Americans who have suffered grievously from the failed and infantile policies he has urged on them for decades. He's the kind of bleeding heart who will always bleed to the last drop of anyone else's blood. But he and Mandelbaum did show compassion for Fiorina over her truly contemptible statement. "It is not a good sign when bluntly speaking the truth turns into a negative political advertisement that harms a candidacy," they write in *That Used to Be Us.*

Friedman may claim to be a liberal, but his applauding of offshoring here puts him to the far right of Milton Friedman. Of course, in nineteenth-century terms, Milton Friedman was a classic liberal, too.

What is most disgusting about Thomas Friedman, Carly Fiorina, and their endless ideological cheering chorus is the contempt they have for ordinary Americans and for their own country and society. They have no true patriotism at all. They have no true loyalty to the well-being of the American people at all. They worship at the altars of merciless false goods of intellectual vacuity and vanity that are not supported in any way by the historical record.

Friedman's hatred of the industrial workplace drives him into bizarre fantasies. He and Mandelbaum on page 136 of their book quote at length *Wired* magazine editor Chris Anderson's malarkey about the DIY revolution in manufacturing: people will be able to make things one at a time or in small batches!

It wasn't clear to anyone when Anderson announced this how this was different from the way we did things 150 years ago before the economies of production and scale made possible by the Industrial Revolution. This is more childish nonsense. It is meaningless. The economies of China, Japan, Germany, South Korea, Taiwan, India, and all other major countries simply do not function this way. And they are not moving in this direction.

We live in a world of more than seven billion people. Mass production and economies of scale are even more important to maintaining market share and establishing market dominance in any economy than they were to John D. Rockefeller and Henry Ford a century ago.

Friedman in his series of books by himself and now with Mandelbaum is blind to this essential fact. But this book will document it. The American people do not live in a flat world. They never have. They have to abandon the false myths that have led them along the road to ruin. And they have to learn the true nature of the economic world they live in if they want to survive.

ONE

Seven Billion

A World of Winners, Losers, and Growing Dangers

There are seven billion human beings living in the world today. Half a century ago there were less than half that number—only three billion. The two-billion figure was only reached in 1930. It had taken a hundred years for the world population to double to that level from 1830. In the past fifty years, global population has been increasing eight times as fast as it did from 1830 to 1930.

A world of seven billion people creates its own realities; you cannot get away from that. Seven billion people need food. They need jobs. They need more oil, coal, and gas to warm their homes, power their cars, and run their electric power plants. When you complain about gas prices soaring to more than $4 a gallon, you are facing the reality of a world with seven billion people. When inflation boosts the costs of your groceries at the supermarket every week, ultimately you are paying that extra money because you are in competition with seven billion other people.

When millions despair of living a decent life at home, they will travel thousands of miles to try to find a better life somewhere else. And they will go wherever they can.

A world of seven billion people forces millions of people to emigrate and look for new jobs every year. Emigrations on that scale are always dangerous.

Massive droughts have afflicted sub-Saharan Africa for much of the past two decades. As result, millions of people have fled the region and sought new lives in Europe or North America.

Huge emigrations are always chaotic. And the emigrations are always from poor, so-called developing countries to rich, prosperous ones. But if you don't want your own country and its way of life to be submerged by a tsunami of immigrants, you've got to have strong borders and hundreds of thousands of troops to defend them. If you don't, you'll get swamped. That, too, is the meaning of a world of seven billion people.

Some 95 percent of annual population growth is in poor countries. This poses a huge threat to rich countries. The United States and the twenty-seven nations of the European Union already face growing crime and security problems from the rising deluge of immigrants, most of them illegal, every year. Border security has become a major political issue for the state governments of Arizona, New Mexico, California, and Colorado. But no US administration or Congress has dared to confront the issue of what would really be needed to defend the southern land border of the United States from a deluge of multiple millions of illegal immigrants from Mexico and Central America. Since the 1990s, illegal immigration has outpaced legal immigration (which also is growing), but it is still not viewed by Washington as a problem in need of solving. Friedman's plan, it appears, is to keep attracting software developers and hope the rest of the economy gets so bad it loses its appeal to all but the poorest immigrants.

Eventually we will stop listening to Friedman, the economy will improve, and the answer to the questions of illegal immigration and land border security will be simple: it will take American soldiers—perhaps hundreds of thousands—to guard the border with Mexico.

The think tank geniuses and newspaper pundits of Washington won't like that idea. Protecting the American people along their own land border isn't glorious. Washington intellectuals such as Paul Wolfowitz, who eagerly and recklessly commit America's power and wealth around the world, wouldn't be seen dead doing it. Wolfowitz and his friends would much rather "help" the rest of the world improve the country they live in. So they come up with new cockeyed, crazy schemes to "build democracy" in Iraq or create a "stable, pro-American nation-state" in Afghanistan, where no central government has ever succeeded since Alexander the Great stumbled into the place twenty-three hundred years ago. President Barack Obama and the tribe of "tough" (in their imaginations) liberal internationalists advising him still think they can do it. But Obama, like George W. Bush before him, is no Alexander, and the liberal internationalists urging him on are no Macedonian phalanx of warriors.

Both Friedman and Mandelbaum are even forced to admit in their book that they both enthusiastically urged the US government to invade Iraq in 2003. Thousands of American soldiers and an estimated nine hundred thousand Iraqis have died so far because of that catastrophic policy, but Friedman has never paid any penalty for urging it so forcefully. Neither have any of his fellow armchair warriors. Wouldn't it be wonderful to live in a world where pundits who had been so vocally and openly wrong lost their jobs and their audiences? Thomas Friedman was shamefully wrong about invading Iraq in 2003, and he is disastrously wrong about his open-immigration, free-trade, flat-world policy prescriptions for the United States now. The future of the state National Guards of the United States is not to police Iraq or Afghanistan but to police, patrol, and protect the northern side of the Rio Grande.

President George W. Bush made a big political point of sending ten thousand National Guard forces for a few months to police the southern border. But what he did was so minor it was farcical; a mere drop in the ocean.

The US-Mexico land border is one of the longest in the world, stretching 1,969 miles. It logs 350 million legal crossings in both directions every year. At least one million illegal immigrants are estimated to successfully cross it each year. The European Union nations face a comparable problem dealing with their flood of immigrants every year from the impoverished countries of North Africa and sub-Saharan Africa.

If the world were flat, such immigrations would be peaceful and constructive, and the new immigrant populations would be quickly and harmoniously absorbed into their host societies, which would rapidly become more prosperous due to the many new, productive hard workers.

But as this book repeatedly documents, Thomas Friedman is wrong. The world is not flat. It never has been. There have always been winners and losers. Nations and their populations either rise in security, power, and general prosperity, or they fall. Ultimately, in a finite world with potentially infinite population growth, all issues of trade and immigration are a zero-sum gain. If someone wins, someone else is going to lose.

Over the past forty years, America has been losing—big time. In a world of seven billion people and growing, if the United States does not defend its borders and its domestic business and industry, it is going to lose a lot more.

• • •

In 2005, *The World Is Flat* was a best seller embraced by liberal Democrats and conservative Republicans. Friedman argued—and still argues—that the sophistication of modern communications and the scale of modern air travel mean that there is no point in national borders and national restrictions on imports because goods and services are going to flow freely anyway. He argued that any attempt to restrict the free interchange of ideas, goods, and services or to cut down on immigration patterns would only harm the countries trying to practice it.

At first sight this idea appeared attractive and convincing. Extreme examples of isolation are self-defeating. The most isolated societies in the world are usually the poorest and most miserable. The more foreign direct investment any country can attract, the faster its economy can grow and the higher the standard of living will be for its people. All of this is true—up to a point.

It also is true that countries need to get "wired in" to the global economy as fully as possible to attract more investment and run their agriculture and industries more efficiently. If you don't know the trends in different countries, you can't know what they want and you won't know what to sell to them.

But the flat world that Tom Friedman and his many allies have preached goes a lot farther than investing in education, or getting wired up on the Internet. Underlying Friedman's idea is a utopian fantasy, assuming that only good things will spread freely through a flat world. But in the real world that more than seven billion people now live in, a lot of bad things can—and do—spread freely.

Flat-world theory argues that allowing free trade is not a zero-sum game where one side has to lose when the other side gains. It argues that the mutual exchange of goods and services eventually benefits everyone. So if American industrial workers lost good-paying jobs in the Pittsburgh steel industry in the 1980s or in the Detroit auto industry in the 2000s, they will still benefit from far-better-paying jobs in the long run as new sectors of the economy open up. Or, at least, lots of other Americans will.

Thomas Friedman and friends didn't invent this idea. It is a tenet of classical free liberal economics. It goes back in part to Adam Smith in the late eighteenth century and much more to David Ricardo fifty years later. Therefore, *classical free-trade theory was developed before electricity was discovered or any modern industry was invented.* Yet this doesn't bother its many supporters. They are happy to squeeze today's world into a view that was developed when people could read at night only by candles and spluttering oil lamps and where the total population of the world was less than 1 billion people.

In fact, as we shall see, international free trade was always a zero-sum game. Its beautiful diagrams and graphs have nothing to do with the real world, for pure free trade between nations has never existed.

Even in the nineteenth century, the "golden age" of classical liberal free-trade economics, nations that protected their industries, such as the United States and Germany, rose; nations that naively believed in free trade fell.

Free-trade zones within and between nations can work, but only if there is a level playing field to begin with. But in reality, there are always some countries that have prevented unlimited imports from flowing into them from other countries.

In the long run, these protected countries always do better than pure free-trade countries. The industries of protected economies have secure home markets and larger, more secure profits. This means that they can develop economies of scale and then export lots of their own goods and services to other societies that don't have protective tariffs. They usually can export lots of goods at cheaper prices, which is how South Korea and Japan undermined and replaced great American industries such as shipbuilding, steelmaking, automaking, and televisions with their own.

It isn't just national industries that can be rapidly wiped out when a country's leaders buy into Friedman's ideas. Diseases can spread far more easily across a flat world where travel and immigration controls are minimized. As we learned on September 11, 2001, terrorists travel across entire oceans and continents far more easily in a flat world. Osama bin Laden, hiding in the mountain caves of Afghanistan, was able to send a gang of conspirators halfway around the world to the United States to hijack four airliners and kill nearly three thousand people.

Friedman's theory also assumes that an interconnected world would reduce the dangers of conflict and war. As we shall see, this is a very old idea, and it has always been proved to be disastrous nonsense. Even Friedman had second thoughts about this—sort of. He had to recognize that there were more people alive today than there ever had been in all of recorded history. That is why he called one of his books *Hot, Flat, and Crowded.*

The world is certainly crowded, and it's getting hotter. But even then, Friedman couldn't admit that it isn't flat and never has been. In fact, a crowded world guarantees an unflat one. Too many people automatically means more conflicts, more divisions between large groups, more fights over resources, and—ultimately—more wars.

Government bureaucracies and the endless, mind-numbing jungle of Washington think tanks are fond of issuing "briefing papers." Think tanks, government agencies, and other interest groups make the correct assumption that the attention span of politicians and government leaders is so short and superficial that they will not bother to look at anything longer than a single page. In real time, America's leaders and media pundits have a shorter attention span than any hive of well-organized insects.

This guarantees that far more stupid decisions will be made than sensible ones. People need to have the patience and the attention span to read detailed documentation and counterarguments before they can make mature judgments. But with ever more ways of getting news, if you can't make your point in the first twenty-second sound bite or in the headline, if you aren't predicting doom, if you aren't claiming you've found something new and revolutionary, or if you aren't willing to prove to the audience only the things they already "know," you've lost them.

Briefing papers therefore have devolved into simplified, strident assertions. They unconsciously confirm the cynical judgment of human nature that carried Adolf Hitler and Josef Goebbels so far: if anything, good or bad, is shouted often enough, people will mindlessly believe it regardless of the facts.

That is not true of ordinary people only. It is even more true of governing elites, precisely because they tend to be more insulated from the dirty realities of soaring supermarket food prices, growing crime and grime in the streets, and the erosion of the American middle class. But all these things are the natural consequence of maintaining open borders and free trade in a world of seven billion people (that figure was officially reached on October 31, 2011).

American liberals assume the world is full of well-meaning, unselfish people who just need to be understood. Conservatives think that as long as we walk tall and have someone like Ronald Reagan or George W. Bush to talk tough to the world, no one will dare to invade us or declare war on us. A respected military analyst, a retired US Army colonel, Col. Douglas Macgregor, has just published a study arguing that nuclear war and other major wars between or among nations such as the United States, China, and Russia are unthinkable in the twenty-first century. Wanna bet?

American liberals think that no one wants to invade us. American conservatives think that no one will ever dare to invade us. They're both wrong. They're both living in Dreamland.

Libertarians are even worse. They think it is immoral to have a strong government that can and will put soldiers on the borders and police in the streets to protect ordinary people. And they don't realize that the United States is going to need hundreds of thousands of its own soldiers to guard its borders; otherwise we will go under, like the Roman Empire and so many other great nations before us.

Jesus took a very different view of human nature. The twenty-fourth chapter of the Gospel of St. Matthew contains his famous Olivet prophecy. It is one of the most succinct and brilliant policy briefing papers on national security ever written. The Olivet prophecy is a national security survival guide for the American people in the twenty-first century.

The Olivet prophecy is called that because it was delivered to Jesus's disciples while they were all sitting on the Mount of Olives overlooking the city of Jerusalem. In it, Jesus predicts that the era before he returns as the Messiah will be a time of "wars and rumors." Then he adds, "These things must come to pass, but the end is not yet." In other words, wars and rumors of wars would never disappear before his second coming. Nearly two thousand years have passed, and Jesus hasn't returned yet. Wars show no sign of disappearing, either. They are as numerous as ever.

For nearly two thousand years, these words have been misapplied to almost every war that has ever been fought in the Western world. There have always been "wars and rumors of wars." And as Jesus said, that isn't going to change just because a handful of deluded pundits have spent the past thirty years crying "The world is flat."

The twentieth century brought this trend of wars to a new level of scale and bloodshed. At least 250 million people—a quarter of a billion—died violently in war.

Many were civil wars, fought by governments that brutally murdered their own people. The genocide of the Jewish people in Europe in World

War II by the Nazis, of the Ukrainian people by the Soviet Communists in the famine-genocide of 1929–1932, and of the Armenian people in the Ottoman Empire's "Final Solution" during World War I, all fell into that category.

Those genocides were carried out in the first half of the twentieth century, and they were all carried out by strong governments. But in the second half of the twentieth century, more people died because of weak government, or no government at all, than because governments were too strong.

More than ten million people have died in the Congo, formerly known as Zaire, the largest nation of central Africa, in the past twenty years. "Pray for the strength of the government," the wise old Jewish rabbi Hanina warned two thousand years ago, "because if it was not for the fear of it, men would swallow each other alive." Traditional Christian and Muslim religious law and teachings also emphasize the crucial importance of respecting and maintaining government to protect the lives and well-being of ordinary people.

A world of seven billion people does not mean that the long-awaited Christian or Jewish Messiah is going to come tomorrow. But it does confirm Jesus's pessimistic and unflinching insight into the human condition. Wars and rumors of wars are going to continue. And as we shall see, no one has ever succeeded in preventing them by trying to make the world flat.

Two world wars were fought in the first half of the twentieth century. We should all hope and pray that another one won't be fought in the first half of the twenty-first. But no one except the most blind of fools can take that hope for granted. A world of seven billion people creates enormous pressures. Major nations are already moving to lock up the natural resources of the world for the next hundred years. They are in competition with each other. This world of growing economic competition is not smooth, unified, and flat. It is a cracked world. Enormous dividing lines and tensions are opening between different nations, cultures, and civilizations. Our world is cracked.

A new set of cracks is now splintering the Arab world and neighboring Iran. In the first three months of 2011, popular revolutions for democracy toppled long-established governments in Tunisia, Egypt, and Libya and rocked the governments of Syria, Yemen, and Bahrain.

The Arab world is split. Most of its governments, which are long-established, set in their ways, and generally autocratic, are also privately pro-Western. The fast-growing, impoverished majorities of their populations want more democracy. But they simultaneously tend to support far more extreme political and Muslim religious movements. The gap between the standards of living of hundreds of millions of people across the Middle East and the populations of North America, Europe, and northeastern Asia is growing all the time. This doesn't make the world more flat, of course; it makes it far more divided. It is another growing crack.

The terrorist attacks on the United States on September 11, 2001, were cheered throughout the Arab world. That should have served notice to the West that the world wasn't getting flatter, it was getting more sharply divided.

The newsprint and media websites of America are filled with obsessive pontificating about the Arab world. A far more serious split goes unnoticed: the split between the Orthodox Christian Slav world and the Protestant-Catholic-secular worlds of Europe and North America. This gap started to open, though almost nobody in Washington realized it, in 1998 when the United States bombed Serbia to force the Serbs out of the Muslim-majority province of Kosovo.

The bombing campaign worked. The Serbs had no answer to the high tech of the US Air Force. President Bill Clinton and his two "muscular liberals," Secretary of State Madeleine Albright and Ambassador Richard Holbrooke, proclaimed that Right had vanquished Might. But the Serbs seethed. And so did their traditional ally Russia.

Worse was to come. Over the next decade the George W. Bush administration expanded NATO (the North Atlantic Treaty Organization) to include three former Soviet republics—Latvia, Estonia, and Lithuania.

Bush's father, President George H. W. Bush, had solemnly promised the Russians during the collapse of communism that the United States would never take advantage of Russian weakness to extend NATO into central and eastern Europe. The elder Bush was a man of his word. But his two immediate successors, Bill Clinton and George W. Bush, did not honor that commitment. The Russians felt they had been betrayed. Since Russia now has the most powerful thermonuclear arsenal on Earth, there are potentially extremely dangerous consequences to making Russian leaders and their people believe they have been betrayed or played for fools.

In the first decade of the twenty-first century, Russia has steadily built up a global power constellation of forces independent of and potentially very hostile to the West. On June 15, 2001, President Vladimir Putin of Russia and President Jiang Zemin of China met in Shanghai with the presidents of four former Soviet republics in Central Asia. Together they formed the Shanghai Cooperation Organization (SCO), also known as the Shanghai Pact. Only a tiny handful of foreign policy specialists bother to know anything about it. The popular American media pay it no attention even though it is potentially the most powerful military alliance ever created.

The SCO includes 1.5 billion people—more than 20 percent of the human race and two of the world's top three military thermonuclear powers, Russia and China. It is openly dedicated to keeping the Eurasian heartland "multipolar"—that is diplomatic code for saying that Russia and China, the SCO's leaders, are determined to push the United States out of Asia.

Every year SCO nations hold ambitious joint military exercises. They are routinely described as "antiterrorist" exercises, but they are open preparations for much more ambitious joint military actions.

Themes of the exercises have included tackling problems of amphibious landings against hostile, defended shores. That would be an obvious warm-up to a Russian-backed Chinese invasion of Taiwan. The SCO also protects Russia's rear in the event of any future conventional war between Russia and NATO or the United States.

The exercises also include practicing the interoperability of command and control communications systems between the armed forces of Russia and China. The armed forces of Russia and China over the past decade have successfully practiced far more practical cooperation than the armed forces of the United States and Britain ever did up to 1941.

During the long decades of the Cold War and the decade of Russian weakness that followed the disintegration of the Soviet Union, the prospect of a military clash between the Soviet Union or Russia and the West was considered to be inconceivable. Both US and Soviet leaders reacted with great concern over the 1962 Cuban Missile Crisis and took great care to ensure they never came as close to any danger of even conventional military conflict again. Most Washington pundits imagine that is still the case. They are wrong. They were proved wrong in August 2008, when Russia invaded the former Soviet republic of Georgia in the Caucasus.

Georgia wasn't a NATO member. That was just as well, because if it had been, the United States would have been bound by treaty to go to war with Russia to defend it. But the Bush II administration had favored Georgia's entry into NATO, and they supported its erratic leader, President Mikheil Saakashvili. The Russian government couldn't stand Saakashvili, and eventually it invaded the country. In forty-eight hours Russian forces had conquered a third of it.

The success of the Russian tank forces flew in the face of the so-called experts on the Russian military in the West. They had long claimed that the Russian army couldn't fight, that it was worthless and wouldn't last five minutes against US armed forces.

This might have been true if the Russians were ever stupid enough to fight the full mass of US armed forces head on. But they don't have to. As of October 2011, US armed forces are still bogged down in Iraq. A final withdrawal is scheduled before the 2012 presidential election, but it will take many years for the US armed forces to recover from its exhausting, long commitment there. US forces still remain caught up in Afghanistan and obliged to defend commitments around the world. No one in the Obama administration, or the US Department of Defense, takes the possibility of Russian military action against US allies seriously. Why should they, since they've been assured that the world is flat?

But the world isn't flat. Russia is a different nation and a different civilization from the rest of Europe and the United States. The Russian people have become bitter and cynical in the two decades since the fall of the Soviet Union. They are far more ready to support their government if it invades weak neighboring nations sympathetic to the West than any of Washington's Beltway geniuses imagine.

Russia also now has a larger thermonuclear arsenal than the United States. It spends a far higher percentage of its Gross Domestic Product every year on its armed forces, especially on its strategic thermonuclear missile forces, than the United States does. One of the most dangerous Cracks in the World is the one between Russia and its allies on one side and the West on the other.

While total global conflicts have been declining for the past two decades, we're a long way from a perfect peace, and it's hard to imagine that this is a permanent situation. If the world were flat, civilized behavior would be spreading across it like a benign, rose-colored inkblot. But that isn't happening. Sub-Saharan Africa, the Middle East, and the northern half of Mexico are being covered instead by a spreading bright red color—the stain of innocent spilled blood.

At least ten million people died in a succession of civil wars and inter-tribal bloodbaths in Congo, the largest nation of central Africa. Hundreds of thousands have died in what humanitarian agencies describe as a genocide in Darfur in western Sudan. Global climate change has made many sub-Saharan nations virtually uninhabitable. This has triggered enormous population movements. Millions of people a year try to enter wealthy nations of Europe by any way they can.

Mexico had a population of 15 million in 1910. It has a population of 111 million today. With a population of more than 20 million, Mexico City probably is the most heavily populated urban area on Earth. This enormous population growth is the natural consequence of a world of seven billion people.

Globalization and the creation of NAFTA (the North American Free Trade Agreement) in 1994 were supposed to create a new era of prosperity for Mexico. Instead, the US appetite for drugs has boosted the ruthless Mexican drug cartels. They have become a regional power stronger than the Mexican government. The US-Mexico border region, like vast tracts of Africa, is becoming a valley of death. At least twenty thousand people have died in the past five years since Mexican president Felipe Calderon rashly declared war on the drug cartels.

The Mexican government is now far weaker than it was when President Calderon took power in November 2006. But if the Mexican government collapses, the United States could face not just a valley of death but also a full-size cauldron of carnage on its southern border.

The Mexican Revolution of 1910–1917 caused the death of one million of the country's fifteen million people. A comparable crisis today could kill ten million people and send twenty million more flooding north in an unstoppable human torrent to flood the southwestern regions of the United States. What good would Friedman's complacent lectures about the need for free trade, open borders, and unlimited immigration be then?

The escalating crisis inside Mexico gets almost no coverage in the US national media. The latest obscure twists of Israeli and Palestinian domestic politics command infinitely more attention. But the crisis in Mexico in our own backyard is crucial for the future security and well-being of the American people: not only is the world less flat in Iraq and Afghanistan than it was ten or fifteen years ago, it is far less flat in America's backyard as well.

Any citizen in Phoenix or Tucson knows that simple truth. Border security is now a priority political issue in Arizona and other border states. Tell people reeling from the threat of the Mexican drug cartels down there that the world is flat and you'll get at best a horselaugh and maybe a horsewhipping. People in Arizona and other border states want tighter border controls because they've seen what happens when they don't get them. They know the world isn't flat. They see the new crack in the world that has opened along the Rio Grande.

Friedman and Mandelbaum's immigration-policy prescriptions are also lazy, sloppy, and potentially lethal for this country. No great nation or civilization has ever survived the swamping of its borders by millions or tens of millions of illegal immigrants who flood in far too fast for them to be absorbed by and integrated into the existing culture.

The Western Roman Empire tried Friedman and Mandelbaum's "generous," "farsighted," and "visionary" policy of open borders full of fresh, vigorous "entrepreneurial" talent in the fourth century AD. Its elite army was annihilated by those enlightened future entrepreneurs (they were indeed very enterprising and entrepreneurial) at the Battle of Adrianople in 379. Within thirty-one years the city of Rome was sacked by Alaric the Goth.

The Eastern Roman Empire, by contrast, maintained strict policies of protectionism and tight control over immigration that Friedman would certainly have wept crocodile tears over for its "shortsighted, tragic, self-defeating selfishness." It flourished for another eight hundred years (till 1204) and survived for more than a thousand years (till 1453) after the Western Roman Empire went under.

America can certainly benefit from attracting the best and the brightest from the rest of the world through discriminating and intelligent visa policies. But this would come to only a few hundred thousand people in total every year.

America's legendary immigration gates slammed shut in 1924 for more than forty years because of a racist backlash against the "wrong kind" of Europeans—Catholic, Jewish, Slavic, swarthy Mediterranean—supposedly flooding in. That policy proved to be a death sentence for millions of Jewish and Slavic victims of Adolf Hitler and his evil, genocidal Third Reich. (Stalin had locked the borders of the Soviet Union so that almost no one could escape *his* genocide.)

Yet during those forty years, America, as even Friedman and Mandelbaum acknowledge, still benefited enormously from the influx of a few thousand refugees from Hitler. After World War II, in Operation Paper Clip, Harry Truman even cynically approved the rescue of thousands of Nazi German scientists, many of whom had knowingly been involved in using slave labor. Wernher von Braun, the main designer of the Saturn V rocket that won the race to the Moon for the United States, had been a member of the SS.

This welcome for brilliant scientific talent, regardless of its race, religion, or political creed, served the American people tremendously well. But it did not require the influx of millions more new people every year.

Just think about this: during the four decades when mass immigration was cut off, the United States still found the room to welcome Albert Einstein, Enrico Fermi, nuclear physicist Leo Szilard, Edward Teller (the father of the thermonuclear, or hydrogen, bomb), Francis Crick (who mapped the DNA double helix), Wernher von Braun, Saturn V rocket engineer Josef Blumrich, Andrew Grove (the founder of Intel), John von Neumann (the developer and the *real* father of the computer), Henry Kissinger, Zbigniew Brzezinski, Madeleine Albright, architect Ieoh Ming Pei, and master physicists Subrahmanyan Chandrasekhar, Richard Feynman, and Hans Bethe.

And during those four decades, from 1924 to 1965, without the scores of millions of high-tech, business-starting, entrepreneurial immigrants whom Friedman insists we need to welcome every year, the US industrial economy recovered from the Great Depression and developed, from scratch, the modern radio, television, washing machine, nuclear, antibiotics, radar, computer, information technology, space flight, satellite, and aviation industries. The US industrial economy remained the undisputed global leader in automobiles, electrical power generation, coal mining, steelmaking, shipbuilding, and chemicals during these years.

The United States was able to do all this because its vast, prosperity-generating industrial base was protected from unfair foreign competition by the great tariff walls that Abraham Lincoln and William McKinley had erected and that Franklin Roosevelt, Harry Truman, and Dwight Eisenhower maintained.

It was far more important to create new and better job and career opportunities for the children of the immigrants who were already here than to swamp the country with unlimited access for too many new ones.

Today, by contrast, if we follow Friedman and Mandelbaum's prescription for unlimited immigration combined with unlimited free trade and no tariff or tax-break protection for American industry, the result will be inevitable: the total destitution of the vast middle class and prosperous working class that has been the strength and pride of America—they will be destroyed forever. Of course, Friedman, Mandelbaum, and their friends will still be able to get lots of illegal immigrants to cut their lawns and look after their children at bargain-basement wages.

To repeat the essential point, industrial America was able to absorb thirty-two million immigrants in seventy-two years from 1860 to 1932 (the flow really ended in 1924) because it had a protected industrial economy that generated enough jobs to support them. Unprotected, vulnerable, twenty-first-century, postindustrial, free-trade America can no longer generate those jobs.

Therefore the endless flood of immigrants across our southern border is no guarantee of continued prosperity. It is a guarantee of future destitution and ruin for them and for America's existing population.

Most of all, the world is getting less flat every day because a world of seven billion people creates intense economic competition between and among nations and power blocs struggling to tie up natural resources for themselves.

Russia is increasing its military power in the Arctic because global climate change is melting the ice covering the Arctic Ocean. That means all the oil, diamonds, gold, and other mineral riches under the Arctic Ocean seafloor will be fair pickings for whoever controls them. Don't think the Russians won't be prepared to resort to force to assure their control over such priceless real estate. That means a crack in the world has already opened in the freezing depths of the Arctic Ocean.

The equation is a simple one: the world's population is growing exponentially, but the available agricultural and energy resources of the world are not. Therefore, the competition to control those limited resources is certain to get more intense.

Put in its simplest terms, more people mean more wars and more likelihood of misunderstandings and rivalries breaking out and setting off new wars. Human nature hasn't changed. The forces that made Jesus's Olivet prophecy true for nearly two thousand years are still true today. Nation doesn't rise against nation and kingdom against kingdom in a flat world, but that's still the way to bet when the world is round.

If the world was really getting flatter, as Friedman claims, trading barriers between nations and blocs would be coming down all over the place. Friedman, indeed, argues that this is a great, irreversible process. Even if we don't like it, there's nothing we can do about it, so it's a waste of time to try. How can you fight history?

This argument has been repeated so often that 99 percent of the national politicians in America now mindlessly repeat it. They might as well be battery-cage chickens mindlessly laying the same kinds of eggs endlessly on command.

There is only one problem with the argument: it just isn't true.

Over the past decade, the most notorious trade-limiting cartel in the world, the Organization of Petroleum Exporting Countries (OPEC), has revived and gone from strength to strength.

In December 1998 the global price of oil plunged to $10 per barrel. Saudi Arabia and other leading OPEC nations feared they were faced with ruin. So then Crown Prince Abdullah bin Abdel Aziz of Saudi Arabia swallowed his pride and negotiated a production-limiting pact with his country's archrival, the Islamic Republic of Iran.

All the free-trade pundits in the US press sneered that the pact was like King Canute telling the tide to retreat: it couldn't possibly work because it went against the classic principles of international free trade and a free marketplace.

But within four years, global oil prices had trebled. Their sharp rise was a major motivation for Bush administration policymakers to push ahead with ordering the second Iraq war to topple Saddam Hussein in March 2003. Surely the United States would then be able to impose or negotiate favorable deals to control the oil wealth of Iraq with its grateful new leaders.

That never happened. Instead, as we'll see in the next chapter, over the past seven years China, not the United States, has snapped up the most important oil concessions in Iraq. And the price of oil has remorselessly continued to climb. As a result, the market leverage of OPEC has become much stronger.

OPEC is not the only far-from-level cartel restricting world trade and benefiting mightily from using the market leverage it can impose. Japan, South Korea, and, most of all, China continue to heavily protect their domestic economies. At the same time, they all continue to flood the unprotected US domestic market with their own manufactured goods. And Uncle Sap—sorry, Uncle Sam—continues to get deeper into debt paying for all those imports.

As a result, in January 2010 the Economist Intelligence Unit in London listed heavily protectionist China and India as two of the world's top-ten fastest-growing economies. Yet both nations treat the idea of international free trade as a pathetic joke, and their economic success stories prove they are right to do so.

Mercosur, the Southern Common Market of Latin America, was founded in 1991 among Argentina, Brazil, Paraguay, and Uruguay. It is a classic example of a sensible limited free-trade agreement among countries at comparable stages of economic development. Such countries then work together to protect themselves from too much foreign competition.

Mercosur has stimulated trade among its four member nations. Bolivia, Chile, Ecuador, Colombia, Peru, and even Venezuela have negotiated associate member status with it.

Mercosur is a big success precisely because it is a regional grouping. It has not sacrificed its powers to boost the abstract idea of global free trade. It has very sensibly focused on protecting and promoting the economic interests of its member states. That is why Mercosur has made the world less flat, too.

In July 2010, Russia and two other former Soviet republics, Belarus and Kazakhstan, created a new Customs Union of their own. American and British free- trade pundits dismissed it as a pathetic and certainly doomed attempt to deny the universal power of globalized free trade.

The Russians and the Kazakhs have been laughing all the way to the bank ever since. Russia is the world's largest exporter of oil and natural gas combined. Kazakhstan is a rapidly rising global producer and exporter of both energy sources. The Energy Information Administration of the US government predicted in November 2010 that by 2019 Kazakhstan would be one of the three biggest oil exporters in the world.

This means that when the Russians and the Kazakhs coordinate their oil production and export tax policies, they have even more leverage over world markets. Then they can make even more lucrative deals for their oil and gas exports. And, of course, that is exactly what has happened.

The Kazakhs used the political cover of the Customs Union and Russia's protection to slap a new export tax on the oil piped out of their country. It raised at least $1 billion in additional revenue in the first year it was applied. Already, two more former Soviet republics—giant, industrialized Ukraine and mountainous, remote, little Kyrgyzstan— have said they want to jump on the bandwagon of the new Customs Union, too.

The Customs Union, like OPEC and Mercosur, shows that free-trade policies are not inevitable; they can be resisted and reversed. Countries usually make a lot more money when they do so.

One nation above all others has rejected international free trade and is determined to prevent the world from ever becoming flat. Its policies have been so successful that they have already made this nation the front-runner to dominate the world in this century. That nation, of course, is the one that Friedman admires above all others but doesn't understand at all. It is the rising dragon: China.

TWO

Rising Dragon

China Really Is the Solution

During the twenty years following the fall of the Berlin Wall, I explored and covered a very different world from that of the prestigious conferences and awestruck high-tech executives, bankers, and prestigious academics who provide the anecdotes and the admiring audience that Thomas Friedman peoples his books with.

In 1995 I sipped tea in Moscow with a rising Russian fascist who knew the details of modern American history far better than any American politician, columnist, or think tank pundit I had ever met. Viktor Alksnis's American political hero was President Theodore Roosevelt. Alksnis ended up as an influential adviser to the Russian government of Vladimir Putin.

Alksnis was described by *New York Times* writer David Remnick as "the black colonel." Meeting him, I got a clear foretaste, a foreshadowing, of the reviving, strong, tough, and potentially ruthless Russian state that has reemerged over the past decade under the dynamic leadership of former president and current prime minister Vladimir Putin. For Putin and Alksnis, as for the leaders of China, the world of the twenty-first century is not flat.

I witnessed hundreds of thousands of terrified, traumatized Muslim refugees displaced from their homes by militant non-Muslim neighbors in one of the endless, obscure, and complicated ethnic wars that still burn across the Caucasus region of what used to be the southern Soviet Union. They learned the hard way that the new, post-Soviet world wasn't flat at all.

I saw how India and China were taking very different paths from the United States to becoming global superpowers. And I learned why it was absurd to imagine, as Thomas Friedman has relentlessly claimed for decades, that rising prosperity would convert China into a peaceful democracy before our eyes.

I saw dictatorships that succeeded, ranging across the world and following the example of China. And I saw successful democracies such as Japan and South Korea that prospered in the world by protecting their home markets and industries from foreign competition. I also saw new democracies that were bound to fail. Iraq and Afghanistan were obvious examples.

The rulers and business leaders of Japan, South Korea, Taiwan, and China laughed at the free-market lectures of Ronald Reagan and Margaret Thatcher privately. They publicly paid lip service to those ideas to con American politicians and diplomats into keeping US markets wide open for their lucrative exports. And they laughed all the way home to the bank.

I also saw that Google, Microsoft, Facebook, and their creators do not create real wealth for millions of people. Hyundai, Honda, Toyota, Mitsubishi, and the rising corporations of China do that.

The idea that the United States, an enormous continent-size nation of 310 million people, can remain wealthy, stable, and strong when it allows its long-established industries to wither and die is simply ridiculous. It's a big lie. It's a false prophecy. It makes the false prophets who peddle it wealthy and revered as sages. There's just one problem with their answer: it isn't true. The real reasons behind the rise of China come from those hard realities. They reveal a very different world from the cozy, benign (for everyone except the American people) one that Tom Friedman imagines in *The World Is Flat* and its successors.

Far from eagerly embracing free trade, over the past decade China has launched an enormous and exceptionally successful global campaign to suppress it.

For more than a hundred years, when people referred to "the Workshop of the World," the industrial fulcrum of the planet, they meant Pittsburgh, Pennsylvania. Today, they mean Guangdong, formerly known in the West as Canton, on the southeastern coast of China.

From 1980 to 2010, China became the largest industrial manufacturing nation in the world. Its rise was as fast and successful as the rise of industrial America a century before it. This should be no surprise, for China's rise was directed by the same policies and principles that protected and encouraged the rise of American industry a hundred years ago.

Thomas Friedman and his flat-Earth free traders tell us that industrial manufacturing is passé. They endlessly preach that the future lies with gleaming high-tech and software IT development. But how many jobs has Facebook created? Or Twitter?

The Chinese know that a world of seven billion people needs steel, pipelines, cars, ships, television sets, washing machines, screwdrivers — you name it. Producing all the utensils of modern life creates value-added manufacturing. That is where the jobs are and that is where the profits are.

Near the end of their book, Friedman and Mandelbaum write, "We don't need to imitate China. And China's fate, whatever it is, will not determine ours." That's like saying that whatever happened to your spouse won't determine your fate. China and the United States are as intertwined as the double helix in DNA. We're like two peas in a pod, but China made the pod and we borrowed the money from them to buy. What's especially myopic about this is that the vague prescription immediately following this foolish bit of analysis is actually dead on: "What we need is not novel or foreign. What we need instead is to understand our own history. We need to adapt the formula, the priorities, and the practices that are embedded in that history and culture."

If only Friedman and Mandelbaum understood that American history and achievement was based on the building of an industrial behemoth, and that China's current success and future prospects are based on doing that too. All these things used to be made in the industrial Northeast and Midwestern states of the United States including Ohio and Michigan. Joel Garreau, writing in *The Nine Nations of North America*, published in 1980, accurately described this core industrial region as "The Foundry." Now all those industrial products are made in the industrial Southeast of China. But China's industries are protected from any significant foreign competition — just as America's were from 1862 to the Kennedy round of tariff cuts in the early 1960s.

China is a member of the World Trade Organization, just as the United States is. But that hasn't stopped China from operating the most protectionist policies on Earth. (It hasn't stopped Japan and South Korea from doing the same thing.) The Chinese routinely keep their currency, the *renminbi* (also called "the *yuan*," the way we call our currency "the dollar"), artificially low. That is why the State Bank of China has been so patient for so long in holding hundreds of billions of US Treasury bonds.

Chinese policy for more than thirty years has been to keep the dollar high and the renminbi low so that the terms of trade automatically undercut US manufacturing all across the board. From 1860 to 1968, the US dollar had the same competitive advantage against the pound sterling, the currency of Britain.

China has been shameless in its protectionist policies. If Thomas Friedman was right, this should have doomed China's economic competitiveness. If the people who argue that protectionist policies mean global isolation were right, then China should be an isolated pariah among world nations.

But neither of those things has happened. On April 26, 2011, China Business News reported that foreign direct investment (FDI) in China grew 32.9 percent year-on-year in March 2011, to $12.52 billion for that month. That averages out at an extra $150 billion per year in new FDI flooding into China every year.

Why is all that investment flooding into such a heavily protectionist and, for that matter, nondemocratic society? Don't all those businessmen listen to Thomas Friedman and his colleagues?

No, they don't. They look at where the strongest economies in the world are, where the most economic growth is, and where they can therefore expect to get the most secure and biggest returns on their investment. And that is in heavily protectionist China.

China has other lessons for America, too. The Chinese do not believe in global warming. Or, rather, they do not believe that they are risking their country and their people's future by vastly increasing their carbon emissions.

One new coal-fired power plant opens in China on average every month in the year. India is constructing new coal-powered plants almost as fast. China's nuclear power plant program is the most ambitious the world has ever seen. The Chinese plan to open five hundred new ones in the next thirty years.

A regular staple of Thomas Friedman columns has been how China invests so much in solar power and other alternative energies. Friedman has convinced both Republican and Democratic administrations in the

United States to plow billions of dollars a year into alternative energy, "clean" energy research.

But what Friedman doesn't write is that China isn't betting all its chips *or even most of them* on clean energy. Like everyone else, the Chinese still dream of some enormous technological breakthrough that will deliver cheap fusion or solar energy on demand. But they aren't stupid enough to make that fantasy the basis of their energy policy. They are investing far more heavily in the regular Big Four sources of energy—coal, oil, natural gas, and nuclear.

There are certainly enormous disparities of wealth in China between rich and poor and between its booming southeastern coastal regions and the far poorer heartland. Industrial America 120 years ago had the same problems.

China could easily go through upheavals over the next ten to twenty years that would make the Great Depression in the United States look like a hiccup. But even if that happens, China will rebound stronger than ever, just as the United States did from the Great Depression.

Like 1930s America, China today can fall back on an enormous industrial infrastructure that will rapidly revive after the economic storm passes. The United States had that industrial safety net eighty years ago: it doesn't anymore. If we don't wake up right now, our children and grandchildren could be paying the price of that loss for generations to come.

The United States is democratic and free. China is neither of those things. Americans believe that their political freedom is essential to produce their prosperity. History in fact teaches the opposite dynamic.

Political freedom is most reliably generated when a country has a large, stable middle class. And it takes a strong central government that isn't democratic yet to maintain the policies that will raise prosperity and create a strong middle class. Once you have a strong middle class, democracy will follow. The people in the middle class will push hard, and usually with success, to make their country a democracy. But prosperity has to come first.

Creating democracy before you create prosperity and a stable middle class never works. It puts the cart before the horse.

I earned these lessons under the shadow of the Kremlin twenty-three years ago while communism was collapsing around me.

I could hardly believe my ears. It was November 1989 and I was in Moscow accompanying a delegation of senior *Washington Times* editors. They were eager to gloat over the coming Collapse of Communism with their own eyes.

We were in the shabby, very much the worse for wear, unpretentious little office of the chief ideologist of the Institute for the Study of Systems of Socialism. His name was Andranik Migranian. Today he is a wealthy and successful man, running a think tank in New York, and has been consulted by Russian leaders for more than twenty years. And he was, at least in those days, an enthusiastic admirer of Margaret Thatcher.

"Now I really believe that communism is on its last legs," *Washington Times* managing editor Wes Pruden said to me. "One of the top Communist professional ideologists in Moscow is publicly singing the praises of Margaret Thatcher."

For all his stature in Russia and his practical professional success, Migranian remains almost unknown to the American media. His influence in the halls of Congress, the White House, and the State Department is zero. In those days he was an enthusiastic champion of democracy for Russia. But he believed that it would take at least twenty years, maybe more. A free market would have to be created first. Migranian argued passionately that the worst way to create democracy was to create it instantly from a standing start.

That's the same mistake the United States has made in Iraq and Afghanistan. It's the mistake we—following Thomas Friedman—are making in assuming that the Arab Spring will create any stable, Western-style democracies in the Middle East. It's the mistake Friedman and the presidents naive enough to believe him have made in sacrificing American jobs to build the Chinese economy. They all believe in Instant Democracy. Just add the hot water, like instant coffee, and it will come.

Back in 1989, Migranian already knew that idea was rubbish. He had studied world history. He knew all about the birth of successful democracies and free markets across Europe, North America, and Asia going back hundreds of years. And his conclusions were simple:

First, you cannot create a successful democracy if a successful free market and a large middle class enjoying basic propertied rights and the rule of law do not already exist.

Second, the system of checks and balances in any democratic society allows existing protected interest groups to prevent a free market from emerging. So there is no free market to generate the overall rising levels of prosperity and optimism across society that any democracy needs to survive and flourish.

Third, it takes a tough, centralized authoritarian government or a strong, self-confident oligarchy to create the conditions for a free market to emerge. Only a strong central government can impose a free market and prevent the less efficient elements of society from blocking it.

However, once the free market is created and starts to function, a new, wider, stronger middle class will emerge. Over a period of one to three generations—from about twenty to a hundred years—democracy will emerge. It won't be easy, there may be years of frustration, of struggle, and of learning. But when democracy does come, as it has to nations ranging from Poland to South Korea, it's the real thing. It works.

Think about it: if Migranian is right, then Thomas Friedman, Charles Krauthammer, Peter Beinart, and the entire, endlessly chattering tribes of neoconservatives and neoliberals are all wrong. You cannot expect democracies to emerge fully formed whenever a repressive or even mildly authoritarian but just plain corrupt government falls to revolution and popular protests. Back in Moscow in 1989, I already recognized the original, radical nature of what Migranian was saying. I often thought of his ideas during the next twenty years when I traveled widely across Europe, the Middle East, and Asia for the *Washington Times* and United Press International. I personally witnessed where new democratic societies were emerging and where they obviously were not.

I also recognized that Migranian's model perfectly explained the conditions under which Britain emerged to global greatness as the first major industrialized nation in the eighteenth century. It also explained the pattern of how successful democracies emerged in most other major countries as well.

Migranian's model explained why democracy collapsed in Weimar Germany in the 1930s. For fifteen years after the end of World War I, the long-suffering German people were hit by one national calamity after another. An idealistic weak and ineffective democracy discredited the whole idea of democracy among the German people. Instead, the failed Weimar experiment prepared the way for them to accept the monstrous dictatorship of Adolf Hitler. Their parents would never have swallowed Hitler's evil lies in the stable, tolerant, and largely democratic imperial Germany before 1914.

In the years that followed, Migranian incurred the rage of Russian liberal democrats. They accused him of being a secret fascist. But the course of Russian history in the 1990s and early 2000s proved him to be a prophet.

Under the hapless guidance of US president Bill Clinton, Vice President Al Gore, and Secretary of the Treasury Lawrence Summers, Russia embarked on an enormous privatization program. It sounded great.

But in reality this meant that control of the vast resources of the Russian Federation — even without the other fourteen former Soviet republics still the largest country in the world — fell into the hands of a tiny group of enterprising buccaneers. They became known in the West as Russia's new oligarchs.

Over the past decade some of those oligarchs have fallen. Quite a few have fled Russia. They have been replaced by new oligarchs known as the *siloviki*. These new guys have close ties to the circle of current Russian prime minister Vladimir Putin.

But Russia never developed a truly free market. And it didn't develop a successful democracy either. Migranian expected this. Back in November 1989, he prophesied to me and to the visiting *Washington Times* editors that Russian democracy under Boris Yeltsin would fail. Yeltsin, he said, was going to create a weak, liberal democratic government. It would bungle the creation of real free market. The new political system would be weak and unsuccessful. It would throw Russia's 150 million people into dire poverty. Its failure would discredit true democracy. Everything worked out exactly the way he said it would.

Migranian also predicted that China, by contrast, would go from strength to strength in its economic and global power. But he insisted that China wouldn't go democratic for generations, if ever. Far from hastening democracy, the protests of millions in Tiananmen Square would scare its rulers and hundreds of millions of their supporters around the country into cracking down hard, he predicted. That, too, is exactly what happened.

No one in the West predicted that at the time. Liberal and conservative columnists alike in the United States endlessly lectured China. Thomas Friedman and his friends smugly predicted that by crushing the great prodemocracy demonstrations in Tiananmen Square, China's leaders were bound to fail and fall. Today they're stronger than ever.

China, Friedman and his friends claimed, would fall apart. Its people would not accept the fact that they had been robbed of democracy. Some idiots even believed that China might split apart in a civil war.

Migranian's interpretation of history explains why China has prospered in developing a free market under an authoritarian system when Russia, which was certainly more democratic in the 1990s, failed miserably. In Russia, democracy meant chaos and corruption. We've seen the same fiasco in Iraq since 2003.

China is certainly filled with corruption. But its tough authoritarian and neofeudal government structure has maintained stability. Foreign direct investment continues to flood in.

Does this mean that democracy in China is just around the corner? Thomas Friedman has been preaching for years that raising the standard of living in China will automatically lead to the mellowing of its government. Then the new middle class will demand and establish democracy. Even Migranian's model suggests that this may eventually happen.

There's just one problem: Friedman's bright idea ignores all of China's horrific modern history.

I documented the history of China over the 140 years from 1840 to 1980 in my book *Shifting Superpowers*. It was a nightmare from the seventh circle of hell. It was a bloodbath so big it even dwarfed the ghastly history of Eastern Europe in the twentieth century.

Probably 150 million people died from war, violence, disease, and starvation in China during those 140 years. They died in the Taiping Rebellion from around 1850 to 1865 (death toll at least 20 million, possibly double that). They died in the Era of Anarchy and Warlords from 1911 to 1937 following Sun Yat-sen's ludicrous attempt to create perfect Western democracy from scratch on the fall of the Qing (Manchu) Dynasty. Thomas Friedman would have loved Sun Yat-sen and the peaceful Chinese Revolution of 1911. If he were writing a hundred years ago, he would have claimed that revolution proved his thesis that Chinese democracy was here to stay.

Francis Fukuyama would have loved the Chinese Revolution of 1911, too. Clearly, if democracy could topple the 267-year-old Qing Dynasty, it could topple anything. History was clearly over.

Well, no. Not exactly. As Zbigniew Brzezinski said to me in a 1994 phone conversation, after the End of History comes—More History. And that is just what the Chinese people got in the 65 years from the proclamation of their democracy in 1911 to the death of Mao Zedong in 1976: they got—More History.

The Japanese invasion and rape of China from 1937 to 1945 killed at least 10 million people—serious estimates go as high as 20 million. At least 750,000 people probably died in the Japanese military drive up to the Yangtze River Valley to Nanking in the summer of 1937 alone.

Then Mao Zedong took over: his massacres, repressions, and simply bungled policies during his 28 years in power from the end of 1948 to his death in 1976 were another Holocaust. Some 300,000 to 500,000 Chinese soldiers were killed fighting the US Army in the Korean War from 1950 to 1953. Estimates of the number of people who died in the bungled polices of Mao's Great Leap Forward from 1959 to 1962 are still rising. They were certainly higher than 20 million. They could even have been higher than 40 million. The heritage of those generations of horror haunts the Chinese people today. It explains why there was a national consensus of support and relief for the tough governments of Paramount Leader Deng Xiaoping and his immediate successor, President Jiang Zemin. It explains why Deng and his successors were widely supported when they crushed the 1989 democracy demonstrations. Most Chinese people believed this was vital to preserve their precious economic growth, peace, and stability.

Few Western pundits who applauded the 1989 Beijing demonstrators knew that similar mass protests for democracy had exploded across China on May 4, 1919. Those were far more influential and successful. But they led to thirty years of anarchy and civil war, to mass starvation, despair, foreign invasion, and slavery. Compared with the unbelievable horror of those years, even Mao's communism looked good at first. Of course, that soon set off its own cycle of suffering and horror.

The modern history of China also explains why successive Chinese governments fear, police, and seek to repress popular new religious movements such as the Falun Gong. Western critics of China today do not know anything about the Taiping Rebellion of the 1850s. They know nothing about the movement that created the fascist dictatorship of Chiang Kai-shek, today known in China as Jiang Jieshi, in 1926. (Chiang's government was responsible for at least 10 million deaths in the next 22 years.) Even China's Communist Revolution sprang from secret societies, religious cults, and underground political movements in the 1920s. That's why China's government hates and fears the Falun Gong. They can't risk ignoring it.

Anyone who rules China has to take those kinds of things seriously; they know that tens of millions of innocent people may die if they do not. The entire modern history of China has taught them that lesson.

China's leaders therefore still believe we live in a world where they need to preserve every possible advantage. They won't risk democracy. And they won't risk opening China to real free trade. They will never open China to unlimited free and fair competition with the United States. Why should they? They don't believe that the world is flat.

In 2010, the American foreign affairs magazine *Foreign Policy* produced a special feature highlighting the major energy deals China had made over the previous five years to lock up global resources long-term around the world. Some of the details are listed below.

In May 2010, the China Investment Corporation paid $817 million to buy a 45 percent share of a Penn West Energy Trust project in Canada, worth up to 50,000 barrels per day. It also paid $435 million for a 5 percent stake of Penn West. Canada has the world's second-largest oil reserves, bigger than Saudi Arabia's. But it is hungry for foreign investment to develop the vast potential of the Alberta oil sands. Also in Canada, in August 2009, Petrochina paid $1.9 billion for a 60 percent stake in two properties controlled by Athabasca Oil Sands Corporation.

In April 2010, Sinopec purchased a 9 percent stake in Syncrude Canada for $4.65 billion. *Foreign Policy* explained that Syncrude was the world's largest producer of crude from oil sands and therefore a priceless resource to extract oil from the western Canadian shales.

In 2006, the Chinese state-owned Eximbank generously approved a $3 billion loan to Angola, and all it asked for—and got—in return was a regular supply of oil. The Chinese support allowed the Angolan government to boost its annual budget spending from about $12 billion to $25 billion and to thumb its nose at the Washington-based International Monetary Fund.

In May 2010, the Chinese state company Sinochem purchased 40 percent of Brazil's offshore Peregrino oil field for $3.07 billion.

In February 2009, the China Development Bank approved a $10 billion loan to Brazil's Petrobras Company to finance much of its new prospecting operations; in return Petrobras sent 200,000 barrels of oil per day, or 73 million barrels per year, to China. *Foreign Policy* noted that China is now Brazil's biggest trade partner and that Brazil controls the fifteenth-largest oil reserves in the world—and that's not counting large prospective reserves in Brazilian territorial waters of the South Atlantic. In May 2010, the enormous China National Offshore Oil Corporation (CNOOC) approved the $3 billion purchase of Argentina's Bridas Group, giving it a 40 percent stake in Pan American Energy. *Foreign Policy* noted that Bridas controlled 23 oil and gas production blocs in Argentina and Bolivia and was looking for more. Major US oil companies have generally ignored Argentina, and much of its long coastline has not been adequately prospected with modern technology, the journal noted.

Under the noses of the Obama administration, China has even been locking up major oil fields in Iraq. In October 2009, the China National Petroleum Corporation (CNPC) joined with British Petroleum (the same people who brought you the Deepwater Horizon environmental catastrophe in the Gulf of Mexico) to exploit the Rumaila super oil field. Production there is expected to max out at about 100,000 barrels per day, or 36.5 million barrels per year. CNPC also is investing $15 billion in infrastructure to export the Rumaila field oil and refine it. In January 2010, PetroChina confirmed that it had bought a 37.5 percent stake in Iraq's Halfaya oil field, which has at least 4.1 billion barrels of oil. In May 2010, CNOOC joined with a Turkish company to control and extract the output of Iraq's Missan oil field for the next twenty years. No wonder therefore that *Foreign Affairs* concluded that "China is snapping up tons of Iraqi fields."

Foreign Affairs also reported that China has invested at least $20 billion in Sudan. Little problems for the West like the Sudanese government's virtual genocide against black Christian tribes in the Darfur region haven't bothered Beijing at all. On the contrary, China has also been supplying weapons to the Sudanese Army for use in Darfur and elsewhere.

China also has close relations with President Hugo Chavez of Venezuela, arguably the most implacable and hostile national leader the United States has ever faced in Latin America.

Chavez has failed spectacularly to successfully court American and other major Western oil companies, but now he's laughing all the way to the bank. In May 2010, the China National Petroleum Corporation approved a $20 billion loan to Venezuela's PDVSA Corporation to extract ultimately 3 billion barrels of oil from Venezuelan fields.

Venezuela has the sixth-largest oil reserves in the world, but its poor history of management and the anti-Western policies of Chavez have left it a notorious underperformer in developing its oil potential and attracting foreign investment—or at least that was the case until the Chinese came along.

Nigeria's oil reserves are almost as large as Libya's, making Nigeria's the tenth-largest in the world, but like Venezuela, the most populous nation in Africa is a notorious underachiever in developing its oil industry. But that, too, is beginning to change. In May 2010, the China State Construction Engineering Corporation agreed to finance construction of $23 billion worth of new oil refineries there that would eventually produce 750,000 barrels of oil per day or more than 270 million barrels per year.

The Chinese haven't neglected the oil reserves of Russia, either. In February 2009, China approved a loan of $25 billion to two of the biggest Russian oil corporations, Rosneft and Transneft, to buy 15 million metric tons of Russian oil per year. Eventually 241,000 barrels of oil per day, or close to 90 million barrels per year, will be piped to China. So huge was the deal that *Foreign Affairs* calculated it would account for as much as 10 percent of China's annual oil imports.

China is even locking up the natural gas reserves of Australia. In August 2009 CNOOC paid a colossal $41 billion to buy liquefied natural gas from Queensland for a full two decades. *Foreign Affairs* calculated that as a result of the deal, 3.6 million metric tons of liquefied natural gas would be sent by tanker to China every year. It was the biggest trade agreement in Australian history.

Nor do the Chinese have any time for American sanctions against Iran. Indeed, their support of Iran threatens to make US efforts to leverage economic pressure on the Islamic republic irrelevant. In October 2004 the Chinese state oil company Sinopec closed a $70 billion agreement with Iran for liquefied natural gas. In all, 250 million tons of liquefied natural gas will be shipped or pumped to China by 2040.

Will the vast oil reserves of Iran, Iraq, Sudan, Brazil, Argentina, and even Canada and Australia be easily available to the United States after these deals? Of course not; China has already locked them up.

Is this the interdependence and the open flow, to and fro, of goods and services that Thomas Friedman predicted? Of course it isn't.

Friedman naively follows the simplistic, totally fictional theory that China will allow open, free, and fair competition in trade and production with the United States. In *The World Is Flat* he writes, "As the Chinese economy opens up to the world and reforms, the wages of Chinese knowledge workers will rise up to American world levels. Ours will not go down to the level of a stifled, walled-in economy."

Reread that paragraph. Then reread it again. It is hugely important. It is simply not true. I suspect that Friedman is an honest man and truly believes this. But how could he possibly think this is true? There is absolutely no empirical evidence to support it. Is there anyone who has a job in the real economy who actually believes that such a thing could be true?

The Chinese economy has not opened up to the world. It is getting far more protectionist, not less. The wage levels of China's workers are not rising to American levels. And America's economy is rapidly falling to Third World standards, with its middle class shrinking and under unparalleled economic attack.

The American economy is being stifled not because it is protectionist and "walled in," but because it is free trade and wide-open vulnerable to all its competitors, *just the way Thomas Friedman has preached that it should be.*

The Tea Party movement in the United States has been repeatedly slandered. Tea Partiers have been accused of being fascist, racist, irresponsible, xenophobic, and isolationist. Maybe it will become some or all of these things. Maybe it won't. But it just began as an understandable and generally sensible and constructive grassroots effort by concerned middle-class Americans. All they want is to take back policymaking from policies and leaders they are beginning to recognize are impoverishing them.

By contrast, the widely acclaimed and supposedly "statesmanlike" and "responsible" Friedman continues to advocate policies that have already ravaged the lives and well-being of hundreds of millions of Americans. The policies he still preaches will reduce the American people to complete ruin if they are continued.

Note also Friedman's clichéd assertion that the US economy will become "stifled" if it becomes "walled in." The US economy today is already being stifled — but for exactly the opposite reasons that Friedman claims. It continues to lose jobs hand over fist to foreign competitors. These competitors pay their workers far less than American workers would make. But even if China paid its workers as much in real terms as American workers make, China would still swamp US manufacturers. It would still drive them out of business with the help of Walmart, its main Trojan horse in the US economy.

That is because China continues to keep the value of the renminbi, its official international trading currency, pegged artificially low to the US dollar. By this simple action, China ensures that it doesn't matter how much its own workers make, or how many pay cuts American workers swallow; American workers in their millions will continue to be robbed of their jobs. That is because the Chinese industrial economy is protected and the US economy isn't — not anymore.

Friedman is blind to this simple fact. It contradicts his basic thesis. Friedman continues to blame American businessmen and workers for factors they have no control over.

The Chinese government is not being evil in keeping its currency artificially low and protecting its domestic industries; it is being smart.

US governments used to be smart, too. In a later chapter we shall see how President Franklin Roosevelt responded to the Great Depression. He devalued the dollar to make it more competitive in world markets. He wanted to reflate the depressed domestic US economy. It worked a lot better than anything presidents George W. Bush and Obama have tried.

We also shall see how Abraham Lincoln, the most revered of all American presidents, made the United States a heavily protected, tariff-enclosed industrial economy in the 1860s. His policies worked brilliantly for more than a hundred years until they were fecklessly abandoned by free-trade idealists.

History, I like to think, is like a good martini: it comes with a twist. The Greater East Asia Co-Prosperity Sphere that the military rulers of 1930s Japan dreamed of creating is now a reality—but it serves China, not Japan.

The United States fought a bitter war that cost 106,000 American lives against Japan in World War II. But in the twenty-first-century world, that Co-Prosperity Sphere has been created after all, right under America's nose. It was set up without a whisper of complaint from presidents George W. Bush and Barack Obama, and their less than stellar secretaries of state Condoleezza Rice and Hillary Clinton.

What was the Greater East Asia Co-Prosperity Sphere? General Hideki Tojo and his colleagues in the military clique that led Japan in the 1930s and 1940s had a simple idea. They believed that their small but heavily industrialized and bursting-at-the-seams island nation desperately needed to control the oil and natural resources of Southeast Asia to survive and prosper.

The war, according to Tojo and his friends, had to be fought to seize these resources from the European colonial powers of Britain, France, and the Netherlands. Otherwise they would be forever denied to Japan.

Viewed from the Japanese perspective, the surprise attack on the US Navy's battle fleet in Pearl Harbor on December 7, 1941, was not the cause of the war but a necessary consequence of it. Its purpose was to prevent the US Navy from steaming to the aid of the European empires.

Today the Co-Prosperity Sphere that Tojo and his colleagues dreamed of has become a twenty-first-century reality. The difference is that it is run out of Beijing and Shanghai, not out of Tokyo.

China, not the United States or Japan, is the political and economic colossus that overshadows the entire Association of Southeast Asian Nations (ASEAN). That region includes half a billion people and their vast natural resources.

China doesn't have to militarily conquer any of the ASEAN nations to control their resources; all it has to do is pay for them. Beijing is willing and able to do just that. Its successful protectionist policies against the United States have given it all the financial resources it needs.

China also controls the terms of trade between itself and the nations of Southeast Asia, just as the Japanese did during the brief period from early 1942 to August 1945 when they actually controlled their own Co-Prosperity Sphere.

In fact, China has already advanced far beyond the strategic ambitions of the 1930s–1940s Japanese militarists with their relatively modest needs for raw materials. As we have seen, Beijing's Co-Prosperity Sphere has already gone global: The Chinese have already created entrenched economic zones of interest. They are the dominant customers in many countries across sub-Saharan Africa and Latin America and even in Australia.

As the US dollar has consistently fallen in value against most global currencies since the financial crisis of September 2008 exploded on the world, Beijing has kept the renminbi weak as well.

This is now a stinging political reality. America and Europe both have to dance to Beijing's tune. So do the currencies of China's Asian neighbors. Watch the Malaysian ringgit, the South Korean won, the Singapore dollar, the Thai baht, and the Indonesian rupiah. They all have to dance to Shanghai's tune.

The territories of the current independent nations of South Korea, Malaysia, and Indonesia were all within the short-lived Japanese Co-Prosperity Sphere. South Korea had been an integral part of the Japanese Empire since before World War I, Indonesia was seized in full from the Dutch Empire in 1942, and the territories of Malaysia were all conquered from the British Empire in that same year.

China's strategy has kept the renminbi weak relative to the dollar to ensure continued structural trade imbalances in Beijing's favor. This isn't a flat-world policy of mutual free trade and rising prosperity on both sides, the way David Ricardo 190 years ago and complacent Thomas Friedman today imagined it was. It is a zero-sum, binary-math Tilted World where wealth and power either flow one way, or they flow another. And the leaders of China have tilted that playing field steeply in their favor.

The Asian nations whose currencies have been rising against the renminbi have been forced to buy large quantities of dollars. They did this to prevent their own currencies and exchange rates from rising to high levels. These Asian governments were determined to keep their own exports competitive. They paid no attention to David Ricardo or Thomas Friedman. They lived in the real world and they knew it was round.

That's how China controls its terms of trade with neighboring and Southeast Asian nations. It is now so important to these nations that they are already being forced to follow the same financial policies as Beijing.

This behavior is not new and it is certainly not unique to China. Through the first half of the twentieth century the dominions and subject nations of the British Empire echoed the line from London in their own economic policies. Britain had a sterling zone; its finances and economic policies were set by the City of London.

China now has a vast renminbi zone across the ASEAN. In that zone nations from South Korea to Thailand have to dance to the strings of Beijing and Shanghai.

China's foreign currency reserves in US dollars soared by the end of September 2009 to $2.27 trillion. Taiwan, Thailand, and South Korea, still the most important, healthy, and confident of the Asian economic tigers, increased their combined holdings of dollars in September alone by $20.9 billion (Thailand by $5.3 billion, Taiwan by $6.8 billion, and South Korea by $8.8 billion), to a total of $720 billion.

The Chinese, in other words, have already achieved the strategic and economic goals that Japan fought World War II in vain to win: adequate and guaranteed access to the oil and other raw materials of Southeast Asia. And unlike Japan, Beijing hasn't had to run the risk of fighting a world war to achieve its aim.

Southeast Asia also is the nexus region between India's maritime sphere of influence in the Indian Ocean and China's in the East China and South China Seas. Both India and China have been vigorously expanding their naval capabilities to ensure the security of their vital maritime import routes.

The fact remains that China is still a vastly more important player than India in the ASEAN region and in Africa. China has reached a far greater degree of industrialization than India and has far greater financial reserves. China needs even more oil, foodstuffs, and raw minerals than India. But China can afford to pay for them. (Keep this in mind as Friedman, or anyone else, tells you it's better to write software than make hardware. If we could have China's economy or India's, we'd be far better off with China's.)

The very different nations of ASEAN argue about almost everything. But they all recognize that they need to "balance" China while staying on good terms with it. No serious leader in Asia dreams that China can or should in any way be "contained." You can only find that kind of dangerous nonsense in the think tanks of Washington or the in the op-ed columns of supposedly "serious" American newspapers.

China is already by far the biggest customer for the raw resources and raw materials of the ASEAN nations. In power projection terms, China vastly outclasses Japan.

As US financial power gets weaker, China's gets stronger.

This is sobering news for Vietnam and Indonesia in particular. China can be counted upon to protect multinational Singapore, with its Chinese elite, from any future pressure or threats from neighboring Muslim Indonesia. The Vietnamese have feared their huge neighbor to the north for more than a thousand years.

The current US leadership is unwilling to take a high diplomatic or military profile in Southeast Asia. The ASEAN nations are divided and suspicious among themselves on strategic and diplomatic issues. That leaves China ideally placed to fill the vacuum.

Is this the picture of a world where state power no longer counts for anything? Of course it isn't. It is the picture of the real twenty-first-century world. It is a world of seven billion people. It is a world where powerful, responsible states compete with each other tooth and claw to lock up the resources to ensure prosperity and security for their own people.

China's amazing drive to guarantee to it so much of the hydrocarbon energy riches of the world over the past decade should teach us a lot more lessons.

First, whatever Thomas Friedman says, the Chinese are not betting on solar power or biomass or fusion. They are admirable realists: they recognize that the world is going to have to depend on hydrocarbon energy for a long time to come.

Second, the Chinese have been able to pull off all these deals because they have money to burn. They can *afford* to make all these deals. How did they get the money in the first place? From the ordinary American consumer and working Joe, and with the help, above all else, of Walmart.

The annual US balance of payments or balance of trade deficit with China is the largest run by any major nation to another in the recorded history of the world. In 2010 it was $273.065 billion — more than a quarter of a trillion dollars. To update the famous punch line attributed apocryphally to the late senator Everett Dirksen, a quarter of a trillion here and a quarter of a trillion there, and pretty soon we'll be talking about real money.

This disastrous one-sided trade deficit with China took off under President Ronald Reagan. But it reached the point of no return under presidents Bill Clinton and George W. Bush. All three men were committed free traders.

Respected economist Peter Morici of the University of Maryland is a rare and valued voice in the wilderness. He warns about the disastrous results of this colossal annual deficit on the people of the United States. In his August 5, 2011, online column titled "Jobs Report: Better but Not Good Enough" and published in thestreet.com he wrote:

> Jobs creation remains weak, because temporary tax cuts, stimulus spending and large federal deficits do not address structural problems holding back dynamic growth and jobs creation — the huge trade deficit and dysfunctional energy policies.
>
> Oil and trade with China account for nearly the entire $600 billion trade deficit. This deficit is a tax on domestic demand that erases the benefits of tax cuts and stimulus spending.
>
> Simply, dollars sent aboard to purchase oil and consumer goods from China, that do not return to purchase U.S. exports, are lost purchasing power. Consequently, the U.S. economy is expanding at less than 1 percent a year instead of the 5 percent pace that is possible after emerging from a deep recession and with such high unemployment.
>
> Without prompt efforts to produce more domestic oil and redress the trade imbalance with China, the U.S. economy cannot grow and create enough jobs.

Morici is right.

By contrast, liberal, Reagan–Bush II conservatives and libertarian free traders from the *Wall Street Journal* to the Cato Institute repeatedly proclaim that these deficits make the Chinese more dependent on us than we are on them.

This glib talk is simply nonsense. It flies in the face of the clear record of modern economic history. When major nations fall into gigantic debt to other countries, they become far weaker and dependent on those countries.

The Bible puts it perfectly. The borrower is servant to the lender, never the other way around. As it is for individuals, so it is for nations.

Americans don't realize this because thanks to a century of protectionist policies from Abraham Lincoln to Dwight D. Eisenhower, they were the ones who piled up the trade surpluses with other countries and pulled the strings of other countries instead.

Many British policymakers and historians, for example, remain bitter over the way the United States from the 1940s through the 1960s leveraged Britain's economic and security dependence. US leaders stripped Britain of first its empire and then of its most advanced industries. British aerospace was gutted in the 1960s to prevent them from becoming significant competitors to us.

Now, thanks to the feckless administrations of the past fifty years since free-trade policies were fully embraced, the United States is in a similar position of humiliating dependence on China and, to a somewhat lesser extent, on Japan and other nations.

Where did the Chinese learn to pull off this amazing reversal of fortune over the past fifty years? They learned it from the people who had previously created and run the greatest economy in history—us. They learned the lessons of Americans' success just when Americans themselves were throwing the same lessons out the window.

THREE

Oil and Why We'll Always Need It

Myths and Realities of the Energy Economy

America is a living contradiction when it comes to energy and its dependence on oil. It all comes down to apathetic ignorance of basic chemistry by 310 million Americans: this ignorance starts with the nation's leaders and goes all the way down through the vastly overrated college system to the appalling high schools.

The liberal, idealistic "green" half of the country imagines that some new, magical renewable-resource "clean" fuel is either with us already or just around the corner. All the country needs to do, according to these dreamers, is just go on investing another $10 billion or $20 billion a year in biomass, solar energy, and hydroelectric sources and all our problems would be magically solved.

Interestingly, I've never seen a single one of them volunteer to do what the Chinese people have industriously and successfully done for thousands of years: keep their own feces instead of flushing it down the toilet and recycle it as nutritional "night soil" to grow crops in their own backyards.

The Chinese way of keeping and recycling sounds obscene and disgusting to fastidious, ignorant Americans, but it actually works. The lesson here is that Chinese will make use of anything and everything to succeed, even what Americans would toss or ignore.

Thomas Friedman devotes an entire section of *Hot, Flat, and Crowded* to holding up the Chinese as another kind of example to the American people when it comes to energy policy. China is investing big in solar power, Friedman argues; therefore we must, too. That familiar refrain is repeated in *That Used to Be Us* as well.

Friedman is enthusiastic about the future of China's "green" energy-generating industries. He cites dozens of pages of apparently impressive statistics to show that China has imposed much stricter rules than the United States to cut down on energy pollution and in investing in a wide range of clean energies.

But Friedman simply neglects to inform his readers of the far greater reality: All of China's genuine investment in alternative energy, especially solar panels, is just a sideline: the overwhelming mass of Chinese investment in its future energy growth goes into the same old trinity of energy sources that the United States relies on to this day: oil, coal, and nuclear. Why do we never hear Friedman admit this simple truth?

In chapter 2 I document the extraordinary scale and success of China's government-backed drive to lock up the oil resources it is going to need in the twenty-first-century real, round world. China's leaders don't believe in free trade and they don't believe in green energy. They prove it every day by where they put their money.

China is the main energy investor in central Asia. It has become the biggest customer for the natural gas of Turkmenistan and is locking up Kazakhstan's natural gas reserves in lucrative deals too. It is displacing the United States as a prime customer for Iraqi oil even while fifty thousand US troops still sit marooned at vast expense in that benighted country. That process is going to accelerate after the total US military pullout.

One shouldn't single out President Barack Obama for creating this ridiculous state for affairs for, as I document in chapter 2, China's first big energy deals with Iraq were done under the noses of President George W. Bush and Vice President Dick Cheney while they were still in office.

America's greens include crunchy conservatives as well as passionate liberals. They regard coal as a greater threat to the world than nuclear power. They have bought into the delusion that nuclear energy is "clean" and leaves vastly less pollution than coal-burning plants.

This is quite simply absurd. The element plutonium, a by-product of uranium 238 used to generate electricity in nuclear power plants, is so toxic that it cannot be found anywhere in nature. It has to be stored safely for thousands of years. The radiation it emits eventually cracks and crumbles any concrete containment structures it is stored in. Terrorists of every kind would always try to steal it to make nuclear and other radiological weapons.

You won't read a word of this anywhere in Thomas Friedman's books, but China has already embarked on the biggest program of building both coal-fired and nuclear-fueled power stations in human history.

China currently plans to build and operate 198 civilian nuclear power plants over the next twenty years. The United States, currently the largest operator of nuclear power in the world, operates only 104 of them. We haven't built a new one in more than thirty years, since before the Three Mile Island emergency in Pennsylvania in 1979.

The US nuclear power industry, with the unlikely support of a large army of green activists, was just warming up to get President Obama's approval to build a new generation of civilian nuclear reactors in the United States as well when the Fukushima Dai-ichi nuclear disaster struck Japan in March 2011. Four of the six nuclear reactors at Fukushima were smashed by an unprecedented tsunami that killed an estimated 20,000 people. But far larger numbers will eventually die from the waves of radioactivity released in the consequent meltdowns of the Fukushima reactors. Doubtful? Let's look into it further.

Thomas Friedman and Michael Mandelbaum acknowledge the existence of the Fukushima disaster in their new book *That Used to Be Us*. But they also focus on American popular reaction about the nuclear accident at Three Mile Island, and they make a big issue of how no one was seriously injured there. Their conclusion, of course, is that Three Mile Island really proved how safe nuclear power really is.

Yet nowhere in their book preaching the virtues of what they imagine is "clean" nuclear energy do Friedman and Mandelbaum mention the Chernobyl nuclear accident in the Soviet Union in April 1986. Yet Chernobyl resulted in a casualty toll considerably in excess of the zero casualties at Three Mile Island.

How many people died as a result of Chernobyl? A 2005 report for the United Nations prepared by the International Atomic Energy Agency (IAEA) claimed that the total toll was only about 4,000. However, my old friend Dr. Helen Caldicott, founder of the Nobel Peace Prize–winning organization International Physicians for the Prevention of Nuclear War, claimed in her book *Nuclear Power Is Not the Answer* that this figure was simply absurd. Caldicott wrote, "Out of the 650,000 people called 'liquidators' involved in the immediate clean-up 5,000 to 10,000 of them are known to have died prematurely."

In April 2006, a new Greenpeace report, based on Belarus national cancer statistics, concluded that some 270,000 cancers and 93,000 fatal cancer cases had been caused by the Chernobyl disaster in the small former Soviet republic of Belarus alone. The report, using demographic data, also documented that during the fifteen years from 1991 to 2006, 60,000 people died in Russia from diseases, mainly cancers, directly caused by radioactive contamination and fallout from Chernobyl. Greenpeace also concluded that the total death toll for Ukraine and Belarus could reach another 140,000. That would amount to a combined ultimate death toll of nearly 300,000.

And in 2010, in a book called *Chernobyl: Consequences of the Catastrophe for People and the Environment* by Alexey V. Yablokov of the Center for Russian Environmental Policy in Moscow and Vassily B. Nesterenko and Alexey V. Nesterenko of the Institute of Radiation Safety in Minsk, Belarus concluded that no less than one million people had already died as a result of the fallout from the disaster. Caldicott has publicly supported this assessment.

Now, one does not have to accept Yablokov and the Nesterenkos' conclusions uncritically to suggest that (a) they deserve a fair hearing and (b) the potential for such massive death tolls as they claim to document is far from inconceivable. For even at its safest, nuclear power is an exceptionally demanding and potentially unforgiving technology.

How strange it is that Friedman and Mandelbaum are so remorselessly hostile to the risks of fracking yet don't take the time to sort through the dangers associated with every other kind of fuel source.

Ironically, and with a perfection of timing Yablokov and the Nestorenkos could not have dreamed of, their book was published in the United States only a month after the Fukushima Dai-ichi nuclear disaster in Japan. (The late Arthur Koestler described such apparent coincidences that hinted at a purposeful fate being on the job as "synchronicities.")

Fukushima may have stopped the US nuclear renaissance in its tracks, but it didn't cause even a hiccup in the Chinese program. China plans to operate a colossal 500 nuclear civilian power reactors by 2050. In 2010, in a huge deal that Thomas Friedman never noticed (nor did the rest of the pundit class), China bought a total of 55,000 metric tons of high-grade uranium oxide from Kazakhstan. That uranium oxide will be used to fuel the next generation of China's nuclear reactors. Not much faith in the future of solar energy panels there.

The new design of the Chinese reactors will make them vastly safer than either the Fukushima or the Chernobyl reactors. But at the end of the day, nuclear power is still nuclear power: and plutonium and uranium-235 are extremely dangerous things to work with, even in the best of times.

China's drive to increase its reliance on coal-fired power stations is even more striking. The Chinese leaders and their scientific and technological community simply do not share Al Gore and Thomas Friedman's phobias about carbon emissions causing global warming. China is opening on average a new coal-generated power station every month. India is opening new coal-fired power stations almost as fast.

Why are China and India ignoring Thomas Friedman's "wisdom"? Aren't they afraid that pumping so much carbon emissions from burning coal into the atmosphere will burn the planet to a frizzle? Apparently not.

Global climate change and overall warming are certainly real; I've seen them. When you helicopter over huge areas of Siberia in late fall, as I've done, and see golden brown leaves still on trees with temperatures in the comfortable sixties Fahrenheit, where more than twenty years ago, conditions at the same time of year were a lot colder, you don't have to be convinced that global climate change and overall warming are real.

However, it doesn't matter if you don't believe our climate is changing, or that humans are causing it, or even if there's no point in doing anything about these things. I don't want to slide down that slippery slope. The key point is that the leaders of China and India, directing the destinies of more than 35 percent of the human race, don't care if they're causing climate change.

The scale of construction of coal-fired power stations by China alone will swamp anything the United States can possibly do to curb our own carbon emissions. In other words, the United States could completely deindustrialize tomorrow, living in yurts and eating a raw food diet, but it's not going to solve anything. China would still be pumping out far more new carbon emissions than the United States was saving. (In fact, if we gave up oil, prices would fall, and they'd buy a whole lot more of it to burn.) And they are going to go on doing it.

Isn't it interesting that Thomas Friedman is so eager for the United States to follow China's example when it comes to investing in solar power and clean energy? But he never suggests once that we should also follow "wise" China's example in investing big in old-fashioned oil, coal, and natural gas?

According to Thomas Friedman, this is all good news for the United States!

He actually writes in *Hot, Flat, and Crowded*, "The longer China focuses on getting its share from a world that no longer exists—a world in which people could use dirty fuels with impunity—and the longer it postpones imposing the policies, prices and regulations on itself that will stimulate a clean power industry at scale, the happier I am as an American.

"America wins! America wins! America wins!"

These timeless words of peerless prose (and they handed out three Pulitzer Prizes to this guy?) were really and truly published in 2008, the last full year of President George W. Bush's second administration.

Yet Bush spent those eight years investing $13 billion in the development of alternative, sustainable, and clean energy technologies. He was especially big on corn ethanol and biomass. Billions went into wind and solar, too, just the way Thomas Friedman wanted.

Well, it turns out that Thomas Friedman was just as ignorant of engineering and the laws of chemistry as George W. Bush was.

Understand this: the technology to store solar energy on a gigawatt (billion watts of power) scale does not yet exist. If you want it to, invent it. But to imagine that it does exist is to indulge in science fiction.

The energy output of a single medium-size coal mine in West Virginia or Kentucky, Robert Bryce writes, is greater than the entire solar and wind energy output of the United States.

This is not because some mythical evil oil and nuclear corporation executives have plotted to sabotage virtuous "clean" and renewable wind and solar power. It is because wind and solar power do not work. Wind power never will. Solar power may, fifty or a hundred years from now. But right now, to bet on wind and solar power to run the US economy is ludicrous. It is science fiction.

And to dream that hydroelectric power, biomass, or thermal power can make the American people energy-independent is worse than science fiction; it is a fairy tale for babies.

Hydrogen-powered cars are another absurdity that George W. Bush, a true Jonah among modern American presidents, madly embraced. Could our forty-third Chief Executive get nothing right?

Hydrogen is enormously flammable. Just click onto YouTube and watch the still-amazing footage of the German airship *Hindenburg* burn and crash when it was preparing to land at Lakehurst, New Jersey, on May 6, 1937. How many Americans do you think would want to risk that for their families every time they pulled into a gas station?

A credible, safe, cost-effective technology to use hydrogen for millions of cars at a time simply doesn't exist. I don't rule out the extreme possibility of one being developed, but to do so, and then to build the infrastructure to support it, would take decades. And we haven't even got the technology yet.

Corn ethanol has probably reached and passed its own Hubbert's Peak of possible maximum production. The prominent role of the Iowa caucuses in our long, drawn-out four-year presidential election ritual made them a third rail of American politics for decades. But in terms of simply chemistry and those magic figures of horsepower and watts, the units of measuring energy and power densities, corn ethanol was always simply absurd. It just doesn't have the power density and the energy density to do the job. The iron laws of chemistry reject it.

At its peak, thanks to the benighted policies of George W. Bush — eagerly backed by just as many Democrats as Republicans — 140 million tons of corn per year in the United States was turned into ethanol. This was far more expensive than using oil or coal. And now the Fracking Revolution has made it just absurd. But it had other dire consequences, too.

The corn ethanol boondoggle drove corn prices in the United States and around the world through the roof as well.

Experts say that as of 2010, the global economy fell short of its cereal/grain production needs by 50 million tons. That meant the United States was turning into expensive, unnecessary corn ethanol almost three times as much corn as the global shortfall. Scores of millions of people were suffering around the world because of the ethanol boondoggle.

Wind energy is never going to be more than a marginal energy source. That is because, quite simply, it depends on the wind. Electrical generating stations need to have regular, sustainable sources of energy their machinery can constantly rely upon. Storage batteries and technology to store wind energy do not exist. Hopefully, one day soon they will. But we simply cannot count on it.

Also, as Robert Bryce, the managing editor of *Energy Tribune*, has pointed out, the most effective wind turbines require major quantities of the extremely rare minerals or rare earths lithium and lanthanides. "That means mining," Bryce writes in his book *Power Hungry*. "And China controls nearly all of the world's existing mines that produce lanthanides."

In other words, when Thomas Friedman is telling us to embrace a wind energy future, he is not making us less energy-dependent on the Middle East, he is making us far more energy-dependent on China.

Even in Germany, wind-generated electricity fell in both gross terms and as a percentage of total national energy consumption between 2008 and 2010. And this happened even though the Germans had invested big in this "good" and green technology and boosted their electrical generating capacity by 25 percent.

The figures were: 40,574 gigawatt-hours of electricity produced by wind-turbines in 2008, making 6.6 percent of total national power consumption; 38,639 gigawatt-hours produced in 2009, making 6.7 percent of national power consumption; and only 36,500 gigawatt-hours produced in 2010, making 6 percent of total power consumption.

Yet the installed capacity to produce wind power rose during the same time, from 23,836 megawatts in 2008 to 25,716 megawatts in 2009 to 36,500 megawatts in 2010. That represented a rise in wind-power-generating capacity of almost 33 percent, or a third in only three years.

Yet because of the uncertainty of the winds, more turbines actually generated less power. And that unpredictability is a headache for grid controllers. Usually gas power plants that never run at peak efficiency have to be built to supplement wind turbines on calm (or, ironically, incredibly windy) days. Indeed, Germany's steel and aluminum industries are now in serious decline precisely because of the problems in turning to wind from old-fashioned, more reliable power sources in the past half decade.

Of course, the Chinese government and many of its major institutions fund programs to improve energy efficiency and reduce pollution. Any sane government would. Of course they would like to get as much energy from solar panels for their people as they possibly can. The energy hunger of 1.3 million Chinese is so great that they will increase their output any which way they can.

But solar panels and even huge enterprises such as the Three Gorges Dam on the Yangtze River can provide only a tiny fraction of China's vast and rapidly growing energy hunger every year.

That hunger can only be satisfied by four energy-dense sources: nuclear, coal, oil, and gas power.

I have never met Robert Bryce, but he will be one of our guides through this subject. In *Power Hungry* he slaughters more sacred cows than an abattoir on a binge.

Why is China investing on such a colossal scale in coal and uranium? And why is it going all out to lock up as much of the recoverable oil reserves in the world as it possibly can? The reason ought to be obvious.

It all comes back to the magic figure in chapter 1: seven billion. There are now seven billion human beings living on this planet at the same time. If we want to avoid catastrophe we should pray for humane and dramatic falls in global reproduction rates that would bring us down to three billion in a century without war, famines, or pandemic diseases and mass die-offs. Unless that happens, those four Horsemen of the Apocalypse are certainly going to come. That is another dark probability, if not already an inevitability of our seven-billion-strong round world.

But as long as there such enormous, unprecedented numbers of people in our world, they are going to need far more energy than they ever did before. And the only realistic sources they can get that from are oil, natural gas, coal, and uranium.

Do you want to see your family die hideously before your eyes, slaughtered by war, plague, famine, or death—the Four Horsemen of the Apocalypse? Then you have to recognize the only four Energy Superheroes who can save you: those Fantastic Four are oil, gas, coal, and uranium.

Anything else is science fiction. It doesn't exist.

I am all in favor of unlimited research and development to harness cosmic electricity, the ambient power of the Sun—you name it, whatever powers your lightbulb, baby. But those technologies still have to be invented, or at least perfected. (And to be sure, if Exxon thought they were far enough along and cheap enough to replace oil, you'd already know all about it.)

The leaders of China, India, Japan, France, Germany, Russia, and many other countries recognize all this very clearly. They are energy-literate. They don't take Thomas Friedman seriously. Only Americans are fool enough to do that.

So when Thomas Friedman pretends to jump up and down shouting "America wins! America wins! America wins!" like Tom Cruise on a TV talk show sofa, take a deep breath and repeat to yourself—very often, "America loses! America loses! America loses!"

Because that's what happens when the government of China very sensibly focuses on oil, natural gas, nuclear, and coal. It isn't abandoning the future to America in a flat world. It is seizing control of the future for itself and its own people in the real round world we all live in.

The United States ought to be sitting pretty for its energy future. America is more favorably endowed with natural resources than any other major industrial nation in the world.

The United States every year is still the second- or third-largest producer of oil in the world. Only Russia regularly produces more. In 2010, we even produced more oil than Saudi Arabia.

However, our use of that oil is wasteful and stupid. Republicans are in deep denial about this, but Democrats are pathetically ignorant about what to do about it as well.

Understand this: there is *no* alternative to using oil to power aircraft. There just isn't. No alternative technology to fly airliners and cargo aircraft exists.

But there are alternatives to greatly reducing oil use in cars in urban areas, which is where most Americans live anyway.

That alternative is the gasoline-electric hybrid engine. The Chevy Volt is not quite to the early twenty-first century what the Ford Model T was to the twentieth century a hundred years ago. But it shows us the way.

There are alternatives to flying huge numbers of people and millions of tons of cargo around the country by air. And there are alternatives to trucking them around the country on eight-lane highways.

The best and most practical alternative is simply a quick, vast, low-tech expansion of CSX, the national cargo rail network.

When the Democrats ran both houses of Congress as well as the White House, they couldn't even get that right. They poured multiple billions of dollars into superfast bullet train technology, studies, and projects. As Senate Majority Leader, Harry Reid of Nevada even insisted on funding such a route from his home state to Los Angeles.

First-class high-speed train (HST) systems already exist all across Europe and are being developed in China. But they aren't essential. They aren't what the United States desperately needs. And we frankly lack the technology to build them quickly and cheaply anyway. Anyone who has ever felt like throwing up on Amtrak's pathetic Acela tilt trains going up and down the East Coast knows what I mean.

The federal and state governments also need to invest much bigger and more boldly than they have in electric or hybrid-powered bus services in major cities and, eventually, when we can afford it again, in more and bigger mass-transit rail systems.

We don't need to rely on oil to generate electrical energy either. In the United States we don't even need to rely on nuclear power to do that. The United States still sits on some of the biggest and most easily accessible reservoirs of coal and natural gas on the planet. As recently as a decade ago, we didn't dream how much natural gas we were sitting on and or how cost-effectively we would be able to access it.

But America's oil, coal mining, and general energy extraction industry is still by far the best in the world, Thank God. If you want energy extraction expertise, go to Houston. No one in green Massachusetts, Oregon, Hollywood, or Manhattan seems to know this. But every energy industry executive in Moscow and Riyadh knows it by heart.

You would never know it from Friedman's latest book, but America's energy renaissance has already begun. It is already far advanced. But Friedman, and President Barack Obama, who worshipfully follows his every recommendation, both want to bury it.

In the past decade, America's energy extraction engineers have developed an entirely new industry—horizontal underground mining using liquid hydraulic chemical "cocktails" to cost-effectively access methane gas in clay shale formations. The technology is called fracking. (Not to be confused with words we do not use in serious books for a family audience.)

The gas that fracking produces is not only abundant, but also natural gas burns cleaner than coal and oil and is remarkably cheap. Global gas prices in recent years have stayed stable and even declined when oil prices soared.

Fracking has transformed the prospects for America's self-reliance on energy, certainly for many decades, even generations to come. And this miracle is taking place in conservative-leaning, so-called red states. Cheap energy for all Americans will not take away our need to use energy far more sensibly. But it is already pulling the rug out from our reliance on Saudi Arabia and the Middle East that Thomas Friedman weeps over with crocodile tears.

The discovery of new abundant sources of energy within the United States already has resulted in great flows of investment and even population into the areas where the oil and gas are found. You won't find a single acknowledgment of this in Friedman's new book or in any of his old ones. It upsets his fantasy of a world powered only by his sacred greens. But it is real. It is already happening.

North Dakota shows the shape of things to come. Its unemployment rate is the lowest in the nation—down to 3.5 percent. Its economy is growing by leaps and bounds every year. Skilled workers and their families are pouring in so fast that there is actually a housing shortage in the state. While most of the United States reels from the past three years of Obama economics, North Dakota's state income is soaring from oil and gas mining revenues so dramatically that its legislature is considering abolishing all property and income taxes in the state.

Harold Hamm, founder and CEO of Continental Resources, was a key pioneer of fracking technology. In an interview published on October 1, 2011, he told the *Wall Street Journal* that the gigantic Bakken oil and gas field below North Dakota and Montana alone may prove to have 24 billion barrels of extractable oil. A few years ago, the US Geological Survey put the estimated reserves there at only 4 billion to 5 billion barrels.

If Hamm is right (and the rapid discovery of new oil reserves across the Bakken area suggests that he probably is), then the field would double the total of proven oil reserves in the entire United States.

It also would mean that all the dire prophecies about how America is running out of oil will be proven false.

However, Hamm warned in his *Wall Street Journal* interview that the Obama administration was looking its gift horse in the mouth. The White House wants to push through a new plan to end the credits that go to all domestic manufacturers for oil and gas corporations. If that happens, Hamm warned, the current boom in oil and natural gas extraction would be stopped in its tracks overnight. Back in the late 1970s, President Jimmy Carter crippled the domestic US oil industry at the very time we needed it most to cut oil imports from the Middle East. Carter imposed a windfall profits tax. Hamm told the *Journal* that that single move caused the number of working rigs in America's oil fields to implode from forty-five hundred to fifty-five in just a few months.

Thomas Friedman will certainly support the president's benighted, even bizarre, idea: his latest book bemoans the alleged—and utterly false—political clout that he wrongly claims major oil and gas corporations currently have in Washington.

But stop and think for a moment. Thomas Friedman endlessly bemoans America's rising dependence on Middle East oil in general, and on the oil production of Saudi Arabia in particular.

Yet when the very first realistic prospect appears to break that dependency decisively, Friedman sneers at it and belittles it. He wants to shelve it.

President Obama has swallowed Friedman's snake oil, too. Hamm told the *Wall Street Journal* that the president showed no enthusiasm whatsoever for raising America's domestic oil production. In a recent conversation with the president, Hamm told the newspaper, "He turned to me and said, 'Oil and gas will be important for the next few years. But we need to go on to green and alternative energy. [Energy] Secretary [Steven] Chu has assured me that within five years, we can have [a] battery developed that will make a car with the equivalent of 130 miles per gallon."

Stop and think for a moment about the frightening energy ignorance that the president's reported remarks reveal. And even if such a miracle car battery could be developed within the next five years, it won't affect the need for gasoline to fuel every airliner and cargo aircraft in America.

Will the same little battery be powerful enough to work for eighteen-wheel trucks and eliminate their need for oil as well?

It won't do anything for the need to produce all that nitrate fertilizer to grow the huge, cheap, abundant crops and fruits and vegetables we've all taken for granted for so long.

It won't bring down the price of oil for pharmaceuticals.

It won't bring down the price of oil to make plastics.

President Obama simply doesn't understand that oil will remain essential for all these things.

Neither does Thomas Friedman.

And, of course, all we have is Obama and Chu's blind faith that this miracle battery will be developed within five years and that it will deliver the results Chu so carelessly predicted for it.

Also, will the new battery need rare earths or other scarce and expensive metals, minerals, or elements? These are usually found in China, Kazakhstan, or other nations of central Asia within the Russian-Chinese sphere of influence. In other words, the world's main source of rare earths for most of the high-tech wonder gadgets Friedman worships so passionately is in the hands of powerful nations that do not bother to disguise their profound opposition to the United States.

The cold, clear truth is that our need for oil isn't going to go away. Not for decades, probably not for generations: possibly not ever.

That is because we desperately need oil to produce the organic chemicals we need to make many pharmaceuticals. You want to live in a world without oil? Then get ready for a world without ibuprofen as well. Oil is essential to make things such as plastics and medical supplies.

There are now more trees in the United States than there were in the time of Theodore Roosevelt a century ago. That is because we no longer cut down trees to provide our fuel, make our furniture, or build most of our apartment buildings and houses. (Sounds like a crazy, antienvironmental talking point, right? Nope. It's actually a common conservationist talking point, something they count as a rare victory for everyone.)

If you want to live in an oil-free world, be prepared to give up all your plastics. And prepare yourself to see the axing of half the forests in North America.

And oil is essential to grow food.

Today seven billion human beings, especially the 2.5 billion in China and India alone, eat better than the only two billion human beings on the entire planet did eighty years ago.

Sure, tractors and refrigeratored train cars and high-tech food processing make their contributions to that achievement, but the biggest reason for that transformation is probably the use of nitrate fertilizer. That fertilizer is made from nitrogen "fixed," or extracted, from the atmosphere in enormous industrial plants.

So if you want cheap food around the world, and in your local American supermarket, forget about buying green and using paper bags. You're going to need cheap oil as well.

And the people in India, China, and around the developing world are going to need that oil for food even more than you are.

That is because Norman Borlaug's famous "miracle" rice and wheat strains that created the global Green Revolution need far greater supplies of nitrate fertilizer than ordinary crops do. More than two billion people in the world today are directly dependent on those miracle strains of wheat and rice to live. And that means they are directly dependent on the oil that makes the fertilizer without which those crops would not grow at all.

But neither oil nor food is going to stay cheap because there are now seven billion people around the world demanding record quantities of both of them. And that population pressure is the ultimate driving force in the race to control finite, ultimately limited resources.

The government of China recognizes that better than anyone. They are at least fifty years ahead of giant India in the professional and meticulously organized scale of their global drive to lock up food and energy resources. They may now be centuries ahead of the United States. We continue to stumble around, blind and mad, crazed by the infantile dreams of the American left and the American right.

The left dreams of a corn-ethanol, biomass, wind-powered, solar-paneled world that never was and will never be. (Solar power in particular can help a bit—but no more than a bit.)

The right dreams of an unregulated free-market world of unlimited growth. Just keep investing more in broadband, keep investing in sustainable green technologies. Keep your faith in the magical entrepreneurial power of the American people. Bill Gates, Mark Zuckerberg, and the *Wall Street Journal* will ride to your rescue.

Yeah, right.

I think there's more hope in singing "Kumbaya" myself.

Get ready for $4 per gallon gasoline and maybe $5 per gallon or even higher sometime soon.

The reasons for this are very simple: global oil reserves are still ample, and more are being discovered all the time. But there are now seven billion people in the world, more than there have ever been in human history. In 1930 the world population was only two billion. Today China and India alone have nearly 2.6 billion people between them, and both countries are industrializing and expanding their appetite for oil at breakneck speed.

As for the United States, we are not out of oil—quite the contrary. US annual oil production is the third-largest in the world after Russia and Saudi Arabia. We even outproduced Saudi Arabia in 2010.

The problem is not the lack of domestic US reserves. The problem is that our appetite for oil is larger than that of any other major economy in the world. We still have to import twice as much oil as we produce every year. In other words, even though we are always one of the top three oil producers per year, we still only produce a third of the oil we need. We desperately have to break that habit of dependence.

The worst way to do that would be to pour more multiple billions of dollars into wind, solar, biomass, corn ethanol, or any other magic bullet solution that's far from making practical economic sense. After all the decades of investment and at least $13 billion that have already been put into those projects, their combined annual energy output for the US economy is less than a single reasonably sized coal mine in West Virginia or Kentucky. The best way would be to construct as many coal-fired and natural gas–fired power stations as possible. (Of course, increasing money-saving energy efficiency in our homes and factories can help, too, as long as we don't end up buying all the upgrades from China. But that will only tinker with the problem. It won't come close to solving it.) In 2010 the United States outstripped Russia as the greatest producer of natural gas in the world. The Fracking Revolution in extracting methane gas from clay shale formations has transformed America's energy prospects.

The enormous Marcellus Shale formation alone contains at least enough extractable natural gas to meet the electrical energy–generating needs of the entire East Coast for the next fifty years.

And we haven't even begun to document the enormous coal reserves of the United States, which are the largest in the world, more than 150 percent the size of Russia's.

If we buckled down to developing our real alternative energy resources—coal, fracking-extracted oil, and natural gas—we could dramatically reduce annual oil imports. Just what Thomas Friedman claims he wants to see. And it makes sense to invest big in established, low-tech, greatly expanded rail transportation, especially for cargoes as well. Hybrid electric-gasoline cars hold great promise, too.

But don't expect oil prices to fall in the near future—or to fall at all in the medium term. They might, but only if the global and US economies both spiral back into crisis, and no sane person wants that.

Just remember this: in November 2010, the Institute for Energy Analysis in Paris flatly warned that within a few years, $100 per barrel oil is going to be the baseline routine norm, not the exceptional spike, in energy prices.

Expensive oil doesn't mean the end of the world.

In fact, oil production has increased under Obama, a fact he ought to be celebrating. Instead, he wants to destroy the great American oil and gas industry. His administration is ceaselessly harassing domestic energy producers. With President Obama's support, the Securities and Exchange Commission is cracking down hard on domestic energy producing companies. They are killing the goose that lays the golden eggs.

You *never* see the government of China harassing CNOOC or any other of its major energy mining companies that way. You never see the government in Beijing harassing its energy companies at all. They have more sense.

But make no mistake: if President Obama and his administration are allowed to go on demonizing and harassing the US energy industry demonizing the oil industry, and freaking out about hydraulic fracking in gas shale formations or the expansion of coal mining, our standard of living will collapse and our 310 million people will be plunged into a destitution and misery that will last for generations.

I am a strong optimist about a lot of things. But I am very clear about that.

US environmentalists can go on saying what they like. But China and India will both go on opening a new coal-fired power station at least once a month on average every year.

The leaders of China and India understand a stark reality: civilized life is impossible without enough abundant, cheap, easily available energy on tap.

I can do no better on this than to quote Robert Bryce:

> Americans must reject the notion that energy should be scarce and expensive. . . .
>
> Cheap energy will allow the production of more potable water. As the world's demand for fresh water continues to grow, the need for desalination and other water-treatment technologies becomes more acute. In the coming decades, the energy-water nexus will be ever more important as the need for safe drinking water, water distribution and wastewater treatment grows. . . .
>
> Cheap energy also means better mobility. . . . Cheap energy will allow for greater increases in productivity. . . .
>
> More energy means more power. And we are all of us, power hungry.

Amen to all that.

FOUR

America the Abundant

Why We Have All the Coal and Natural Gas We Need and Why You Don't Know about It

I f there are three facts you need to remember from this book, here they
are:

1. There is no need for the lights to ever go out in America.
2. The United States has infinitely greater coal, oil, and natural gas
   reserves than China.
3. Natural gas is the true clean energy of the future.

We are not running out of oil (yet) or coal (for centuries). We produce
more oil every year than any other country in the world except Russia and
Saudi Arabia. We even outproduced Saudi Arabia in 2010. And that's even
with all the environmental restraints against unlimited exploration and production. Think about that: the United States already produces every year
more oil than Venezuela, Nigeria, Kuwait, Iraq, Iran, or Indonesia. We have
more coal reserves than China—more than 150 percent the size of China's
coal reserves. Since China has four times America's population, that means
the United States has six times the amount of coal per capita than China
does. There is enough coal in the Rocky Mountains Northwest alone to fuel
the baseline generating needs of America for hundreds of years.

Is the world running out of coal? Of course not. The amazing fact is that the world may run out of uranium long before it runs out of oil and long, long, long before it runs out of coal.

That is because uranium U-238, the (left to itself) harmless version of the element uranium that we find in nature, is one of the rarest elements in nature, at least on our planet. And as a species we've been seeking it out and mining it with frenzy since 1945. The Organization for Economic Cooperation and Development (OECD) in 2010 published an up-to-date survey of uranium mining and reserves around the world with the snappy title *Uranium 2009: Resources, Production and Demand.* Understandably it didn't make the top ten best-seller lists. That report said total global uranium resources stood at the end of 2008 at 5,404,000 metric tons. That sounds like a lot. But it also said that in the sixty-three years since the first three nuclear bombs were detonated in 1945 (one in the New Mexico desert and the other two over the Japanese cities of Hiroshima and Nagasaki), 2,409,591 metric tons of the stuff had been used up for either nuclear weapons or to power civilian electricity-generating reactors.

Think about the implications of those two figures for a minute. They really merit your attention.

No one used uranium-238 for anything before World War II. Therefore in only sixty-three years we have used up a third of all the known supplies of U-238 in the world.

That means that at the current rate of consumption, there'll hardly be any of it left in 125 years.

In fact, we'll run out a lot sooner than that in a hundred years, because China alone plans to build more than three times the number of reactors over the next forty years that the United States, Germany, and Japan combined operate now.

By contrast, there are enough coal resources in the world to last for at least another 147 years at current rates of consumption.

So we're going to run out of the fuel of the future far sooner than we're going to run out of the fuel of the past.

Does this sound like an open, flat world of unlimited energy and future resources to you? It sounds like a shrinking, closed system round world of very finite, limited energy resources to me. And since there are seven billion people in this shrinking, round world, the competition for the fuels that actually work is going to get more intense than ever.

Now, since some readers are bound to have gotten the wrong idea, let me make very clear here that I'm not opposed to research and development to introduce other sources of energy in the future. I'd be all in favor of tesla coils if they work.

But there's the rub, as Shakespeare had Hamlet say: the new alternative energy sources have to be real, cost-effective, and large enough to really solve our long-term problems, or at least buy us another century or two of more time.

Right now, in the real round world in which we still live, it is suicidal to throw more good money after bad on wind, biomass, or corn ethanol.

Why is there so much more coal in the world? That's just been a fact of life—and geology—since the Carboniferous Period 300 million years ago or so. The World Energy Council concluded in its *Survey of World Energy Resources* in 2010 that there were 909,064 million tons of *proven* coal reserves worldwide, or 147 years of reserves to production.

The Marcellus Shale formation in the Appalachian Mountains alone has enough extractable natural gas to meet all the baseline generating needs of the entire East Coast for the next fifty years.

Nick Hodge, editor of *Energy and Capital*, cites the US Geological Survey as saying that through the use of fracking, the Marcellus shale "produced 200 million cubic feet [of natural gas] a day in July 2008. Two years later, 1.4 billion cubic feet a day were being pumped out."

Sensible energy experts on both the left and right divide of American politics have welcomed the Fracking Revolution.

Hodge cites former Halliburton CTO Vikram Rao, who has praised fracking gas extraction as "the most important energy event in the U.S. since the discovery of Alaskan oil."

And a traditional dean of environmentalism, Sierra Club president Carl Pope believes fracking and shale gas mean the United States can "run the railroads on natural gas, not diesel . . . (and) run fleet vehicles on natural gas," and "replace peakers with fuel cells."

Listen to what energy analyst Jack Barnes wrote in his February 10, 2011, column, "Gas Shale Revolution Is Changing the Politics of Energy" for Business Insider at oilprice.com: "Shale gas is quite simply changing the whole energy paradigm in real time. The unlocking of source rock, has altered the future history of mankind. *The world has discovered and unlocked its newest true world changing source of stored energy.*" (italics added)

Well, Mr. Barnes, tell us what you really think.

I added the italics to the last sentence of that quote. The American people have been crying out for a new clean wonder fuel for nearly forty years to rescue them from the tyranny of imported oil. Now it's actually arrived, and most of the American people still don't even realize that it's there.

Thomas Friedman and Michael Mandelbaum certainly don't in their new book, *That Used to Be Us*. One of the four focuses of the book, they claim, is how the United States needs to solve its energy problems. In fact there is not a single idea about energy there other than the stale, old, factually absurd clichés that Friedman has recycled so often before.

Fracking technology does not rate a single index reference in *That Used to Be Us*. There is no discussion whatsoever of America's rapidly expanding proven reserves of natural gas.

In Friedman and Mandelbaum's much-trumpeted new book, there are only three references to natural-gas companies—and every one of those references is unremittingly hostile. There is no discussion anywhere of the merits of using natural gas as a major energy source even though it is cheap, abundant, and has an exceptionally small carbon footprint.

Clearly, Friedman and Mandelbaum belong among the tribe of green-romantic defeatists who look on the inevitable engineering and ecological challenges raised by fracking not as problems that can and will be solved but as excuses for refusing to move ahead with the whole exercise.

The truth is the exact opposite of their technophobic, scientifically illiterate meanderings: in reality, natural gas is about to become the kind of once-in-a-century paradigm-transforming dominant fuel that pronuclear fantasists have been promising us in vain for the last sixty years.

Jack Barnes deserves being quoted at more length on this. He certainly takes the long view in his February 10, 2011, column:

> In the 1700s, the world used wood for its energy source. The great mansions were heated with wood.
>
> In the 1800s, coal provided the go-to source of transportable fuel. It allowed railroads to rapidly move people at a pace faster than a horse. Coal powered the Industrial Revolution.
>
> In the 1900s, crude oil became the primary fuel. It was refined into fuel for aircraft, for ships at sea, and into gasoline and diesel. Crude oil provided the necessary cheap energy to fuel the rapid expansion of civilization to the rest of the world.

The 2000s arrived with the onset of peak light sweet crude oil. The US had peaked in overall oil production decades before, and as the new century started its reserves in both oil and conventional natural gas were shrinking.

Barnes also explains how fracking mining works:

A natural gas or oil well is engineered to have an extremely long horizontal leg. The idea is to provide as large of a circular surface as possible in the productive zone. They are drilling these legs a mile long or more now. The long horizontal leg is stimulated with extremely high pressured water, sand, and proprietary particles into the zone around the pipe.

This process opens up crevices in the rock, opening up cavities with larger surface areas than you would get normally around the pipe. This allows the hydrocarbons to be pulled into the well at higher than normal flow rates for the type of rock. The combining of long legs with extremely high pressure multi-stage fracturing unlocked the hydrocarbons bound in the rock itself.

According to a 2011 report in the respected British news magazine the *Economist*, America's proven natural gas reserves as well as its natural gas production are soaring by the year as fracking technology is introduced across the country.

"At the end of 2009 the United States had estimated reserves of 283.9 trillion cubic feet (8 trillion cubic metres) of natural gas, up 11% from the year before. In 2010 the country produced 22.6 trillion cubic feet of natural gas, up from 18.9 trillion cubic feet in 2005. The price at the wellhead has dropped from $7.33 per thousand cubic feet to $4.16 during the same period."

The *Economist* acknowledged that "natural gas is cheap and plentiful." Wind and solar power are neither of those things. The *Economist* describes them both as "relatively expensive and erratic."

The magazine also acknowledged that "plants powered by gas emit far less carbon dioxide than those powered by dirty coal."

Some 49 percent of America's electricity is still produced by coal-fueled power stations, and they also account for 40 percent of US carbon-dioxide emissions. The more natural gas replaces coal in the short term, the lower carbon emissions will fall. And they're already falling fast. In 2009, US greenhouse-gas emissions were at their lowest level since 1995, the

Economist reported. The implications of this single fact are enormous. They mean that greenhouse US emissions can be lowered without further deindustrializing America.

In any case, China and India are rising fast to become the main polluters and emitters of greenhouse gases on the planet. Environmental-romantic Americans have beaten up on their own country long enough as the alleged archpolluter of the planet. It fits their narcissistic, egocentric obsession that they should be at the heart of the universe and that they should be uniquely charged with saving the Earth from the evil of their own country.

But the harsh, true fact is that as a result of free-trade policies over the past half century, the United States is going to be increasingly marginalized in the current century as other economies, led by China, ruthlessly expand using all the coal, natural gas, nuclear power, and oil they can without any of the environmental anguish and opposition these fuels face in America.

The only way to reverse that trend is to embrace the technology of fracking to extract cost-effective natural gas and to use it to fuel an industrial revival within our own borders. It's already clear that fracking technology alone can slash America's annual balance of payments trading deficit and a lot more as well. Here is energy analyst Christopher Swann, writing in the *New York Times* on January 16, 2011: "As gas reserves have ballooned, so has the potential to help solve decades-old policy conundrums, starting with an addiction to foreign oil. Last year, the tab for the 12 million barrels of oil [that] the nation imports daily came to around $260 billion, accounting for roughly half the total [US] trade deficit."

Swann also notes that natural gas is a far more technologically realistic alternative to ethanol- or hydrogen-powered cars: "Gas can be used directly in vehicles and to generate electricity. So it offers great hope of kicking the habit. By shifting America's gasoline-guzzling heavy vehicle fleet and buses to natural gas the United States could cancel orders for up to three million barrels of oil a day. This could shave $100 billion off the annual trade deficit at current oil prices."

And he adds: "It would also represent a giant step toward energy independence, reducing reliance on unstable foreign powers. Three million barrels a day is equivalent to more than half of imports from OPEC [the Organization of Petroleum-Exporting Countries]; Saudi Arabia, Venezuela and Libya combined sell around two million barrels daily to America. Even greater import savings could accrue if such a move gives way to the next generation of domestically manufactured electric cars."

• • •

The Fracking Revolution is an extraordinarily new and rapid development; if you blinked, you missed it.

The first breakthrough came as recently as 2007, when a team of those big, bad petroleum engineers used fracking to tackle the Bakken shale formation under North Dakota and Montana. During 2010, gas production from that formation alone rose by 50 percent, to 458,000 barrels per day.

As happens with so many world-changing breakthroughs in technology and human possibility, the great architects of the new era didn't dream at first of the gigantic scale of what they'd done. They thought they'd just solved the difficult drilling and extraction problems of a single formation that was uniquely difficult.

Within a few months of starting, however, they found that the same techniques worked equally well—and equally cheaply—on another shale formation, in South Texas, called Eagle Ford. Results there were even more dramatic. The scale of gas extraction there soared 1,100 percent, or by eleven times, in a single year.

At the beginning of 2011, the Associated Press reported that the same fracking techniques are expected to be used successfully on the gigantic geological Niobrara clay shale formation, which goes all the way from Wyoming through Colorado and Nebraska to Kansas; on the Leonard clay shale under New Mexico and Texas; and on the Monterey, which (as its name indicates) is in California; and, of course, on the enormous Marcellus Shale formation under the length of the entire Appalachians.

According to the AP, the Bakken and the Eagle Ford fields are also oil bonanzas, each holding about 4 billion barrels of oil. If those estimates are confirmed, they will prove to be the fifth- and sixth-biggest oil fields ever prospected in the United States. The biggest four are Prudhoe Bay in Alaska, Spraberry Trend in West Texas, the East Texas Oilfield, and the Kuparuk Field in Alaska.

The AP noted another significant development. International oil giants are already pouring billions of dollars of investment into these clay shale formations rich in natural gas. These big global players already include Royal Dutch Shell of the Netherlands, BP of Britain, and Statoil of Norway. The smaller, far more innovative US companies that developed the new techniques, such as Chesapeake, EOG Resources, and Occidental Petroleum, are also still very much in the game. And our old friends the Chinese are there, too. At the beginning of 2011, China's state-owned oil giant CNOOC closed a deal with Chesapeake for $570 million to buy a one-third stake in a drilling project in the Niobrara. Back in October 2010, CNOOC and Chesapeake closed an even bigger, $1 billion, deal to work together on the Eagle Ford oil field.

An expert for Credit Suisse told the AP that by 2020, US oil imports could tumble by up to 60 percent. What does that mean in current dollar terms for the American people?

The ever-helpful AP did the necessary arithmetic: if oil prices remain at about $90 per barrel (and they could go much higher, even double that), a 60 percent fall in oil imports would save this country $175 billion per year. The AP noted that in 2010 global oil prices ran on average at about $78 per barrel. That cost the United States $260 billion in all. And as economist Peter Morici of the University of Maryland likes to point out, that accounts for more than half of America's $500 billion trade deficit.

Anne-Sophie Corbeau of the Institute for Energy Analysis in Paris told the British Broadcasting Corporation that before fracking technology was applied to natural methane gases locked in clay shale formations, global total supplies of natural gas were believed sufficient until only sixty years from now, with experts holding their breath and hoping that they might eventually find another sixty years' worth at current production and use rates. Thanks to fracking they have found a lot more than that. Corbeau now says experts believe the new reserves that can be accessed will last for 250 years at current rates of global use. "The resources are really huge," she told the BBC. "We probably have 920 trillion cubic meters—that is more than 300 times the current annual demand for gas."

No sane person should oppose reasonable regulation of fracking operations by state and federal authorities (or better enforcement of current regulations). Although fracking operations are carried out at 5,000 to 6,000 feet below surface level, there is enough evidence to suggest that they can certainly have an environmental impact on the water table. But to consider a federal ban on fracking would be in our current condition equivalent to national economic suicide.

The Natural Gas Subcommittee of the Department of Energy issued a report in August 2011 that struck a sensible middle ground on the regulation issue. To their credit, President Obama and his energy secretary, Steven

Chu, have supported the extended use of fracking subject to reasonable environmental regulations.

Think about the amazing ironies of the fracking breakthrough: for nearly forty years since the 1973–1974 oil shocks, environmentalist greens and endless politicians have been filling the atmosphere with worthless hot air with all their witless, meaningless, lazy ideas about how to achieve energy independence. *None* of them has worked, not a single one. The United States is far more dependent on imported energy today than it was thirty-five or forty years ago.

Republicans refuse to act like grown-ups and face the painful fact that Americans have to scrap their gas-guzzling habits, especially when they drive, and opposition to safety regulations.

Democrats refuse to act like grown-ups and face the painful fact that America's energy future may include solar and wind, but it's going to include even more coal, gas, and oil than we use now, too.

All their solutions have turned out to be worthless boondoggles. Add to that the money President George W. Bush threw away on farcical schemes such as biomass and corn ethanol.

Thomas Friedman never dreamed that the fracking gas-mining break-through was coming. Like a modern demented version of the Pied Piper, instead he played his seducing song and led all his willing dupes up the garden path of solar, wind, and green romanticism. If any of the tough old Texas-based mining engineers who developed fracking had listened to him, they would have abandoned their historic work and wasted their years chasing his energy culs-de-sac instead.

Friedman doesn't predict anything like the fracking breakthrough in his books: some futurist. Instead, he is filled with defeatism about the future of the United States. Yet the fracking breakthrough ensures that if the American people reclaim control of their government, keep their government strong, and protect their own natural resources from foreign control, *their future is brighter than ever.*

Not a single green expected or predicted this solution. The Clinton, Bush II, and Obama administrations didn't have a clue it was going to happen. That is one of the biggest reasons it has taken off so well. Fracking doesn't require any really new technology. It is just an expansion of an old technique that has been around in a far more modest way for sixty years. And that is just as well, too. The fracking answer to OPEC and energy dependence didn't come with the support of a single *Washington Post* or *New York Times* pundit. The *New York Times* in fact has devoted its resources and prestige to trying to block fracking technology. Oil and energy companies didn't try to block it. They have jumped on its bandwagon to try to make money from it.

As for oil, the world isn't running out of it per se, although a lot of countries, most of all the United States, are going to be forced to radically restructure broad sectors of their domestic economies. The real issue isn't lack of supplies of oil; it is the vast increase in global demand ultimately posed by the energy, food, medical, and chemical requirements of seven billion people in the world, a figure 350 percent higher than the two million total global population of eighty years ago. Saudi Arabia's oil wells are certainly not running dry. It is one of the few major oil-producing nations in the world (Kazakhstan is another) with the potential to greatly expand its production if it had to. Michael Lynch, former director of Asian energy and security at the Center for International Studies of the Massachusetts Institute of Technology, has documented that Saudi Arabia has at least seventy major oil fields it has never started to access because the Saudis don't want to collapse global oil prices.

For that matter, US domestic oil production, despite President Obama's ban on offshore drilling and his refusal to allow drilling in national parks, was higher in 2010 than in any year since 2003. In 2010 the United States produced more oil than Saudi Arabia. It is regularly among the three largest oil producers in the world. And in 2010 a total of 11,000 new wells were drilled in the United States. (There's no better sign of our broken political system than the fact that neither party wants the public to be aware of this fact.)

The real problem for the United States is not lack of production; it is America's prodigious appetite for oil. The United States every year imports three times as much oil as it produces. It imports vastly more oil than any other major industrialized nation. Even a street-level drug dealer knows you don't smoke up all the product. The United States produces 5 million barrels of oil a day, or more than 1.8 billion barrels a year. As I've previously noted, that is a higher level of oil production than any other nation in the world except for Saudi Arabia and Russia. The first problem, though, is that the United States actually uses 20 million barrels of oil per day, or 7.3 billion barrels per year. So currently we have to import 5.5 billion barrels per year to make up the difference. Replacing oil with natural gas and coal wherever possible really is the only way to go.

As for what's left in the ground, the situation with oil is the opposite of coal and natural gas. There is, as we've seen, vastly more coal and natural gas still not extracted within our borders than almost anyone outside the mining industry dreams. But there also is far less oil left there.

There should be no surprise that Saudi Arabia's oil only started to be extracted in really significant quantities after World War II, and there is some speculation already that Saudi production may be peaking. (It should also be noted that this doesn't mean it is running out. It means the Saudis cannot increase their production with the infrastructure they have right now.)

Iran's oil fields are certainly "mature." That is a tactful way of saying they are close to exhaustion. This is no secret. The Iranians have sensibly invested enormous effort into pumping natural gas into many of their remaining oil fields to boost the pressure in them. That is the only way they can still pump out the remaining oil. They need to do this because Iranian oil has been extracted in significant quantities since before World War I. The far-seeing, visionary British statesman who recognized the importance of seizing control of Iranian oil supplies went on to bigger and better things. He was Winston Churchill. From 1911 to 1915 Churchill was first lord of the Admiralty, the civilian head of Britain's Royal Navy. Churchill in 1911–1912 didn't believe the world was flat. He was sure it was round. Churchill was convinced that his country had to seize control of the main sources of Middle Eastern oil. He succeeded in Iran then. And he succeeded in keeping control of Iraq and its oil for Britain after World War I. He failed only in Saudi Arabia. King Abdulaziz ibn Saud drove the Hashemite dynasty, Churchill's puppets, out of the Arabian Peninsula in the 1920s. I document this story, almost unknown to the current generation of history-ignorant Americans, in my 2008 book *The Politically Incorrect Guide to the Middle East.*

Churchill was a liberal free-trade romantic in his domestic policies. But he left his free-market principles at the door whenever issues of national security and survival were at stake.

It shouldn't surprise us that China's leaders today are acting exactly the way Winston Churchill acted for the British Empire a century ago. They are ignoring the principles of free trade and locking up the oil resources around the world that their country desperately needs, just the way Churchill did.

The second lesson we need to take from Churchill's actions on seizing Iranian oil a hundred years ago is why we shouldn't expect to find much more oil within the United States. We certainly shouldn't expect enough to make any real difference to our long-term energy prospects.

Iranian oil is running dry now because it's been pumped out for a hundred years, since 1911–1912. But America's own oil has now been pumped out for more than 150 years. Edwin Drake built and operated the first modern oil well to strike black gold in Pennsylvania back in 1859, even before the start of the Civil War. That oil was as valuable then as it is today. Ford's Model T didn't put millions of Americans behind the wheel of their own cars for another fifty years. But during all that time, oil was already essential for efficient heating, cooking, and light in America's homes. It was distilled into kerosene and sold for those purposes in metal cans. That was how John D. Rockefeller Sr. became the richest man in the world building up his Standard Oil Trust. Rockefeller didn't just sell his kerosene more cheaply than anyone else; he also sold safer kerosene than anyone else. Kerosene is highly volatile and flammable. Poorly refined kerosene exploded when ignited. Such flash fires killed thousands of Americans every year in the mid-nineteenth century. They killed the young and the old, the rich and the poor. They killed impartially.

Even President Franklin Roosevelt as a boy witnessed a beloved young aunt incinerated alive by one such fire. It left him with a lifelong fear of fire.

In those days being burned alive by unstable kerosene was far more common, and far more feared, than dying from lung cancer.

But Rockefeller banished that terrible plague. Because he ran the biggest, most modern and efficient oil refineries in the world, he could produce far more uniform, guaranteed, stable kerosene than any of his far smaller rivals. Scores of millions of Americans bought his kerosene — in the familiar, jaunty bright blue Standard Oil containers — not just because it was cheap but also because it was safe.

Rockefeller's triumph underlines another inconvenient truth (to adapt Al Gore's favorite cliché): the energy business is expensive, and we desperately need big, efficiently run corporations to develop it for us. And if we don't protect and support our own energy corporations, we'll have to rely on those of China, Russia, and the Middle East. As Herman Cain likes to say, "How's that workin' out for ya?"

Rockefeller made his fortune in an America whose domestic market was protected by high industrial tariffs. But his Standard Oil, even in its heyday, couldn't lock up the global energy market. Its chief global rival for generations was Royal Dutch Shell, which started out developing the oil in what is today the nation of Azerbaijan (in the 1870s Azerbaijan was part of the vast czarist Russian Empire). Still America remained self-sufficient in oil for more than a century, from Edwin Drake's epochal discovery in Pennsylvania in 1859 through 1967, when Saudi Arabia supplanted the declining wells of Texas to become the world's dominant oil producer.

America hit its Hubbert's Peak—the crucial moment when its own domestic oil production peaked and began to go into a slow but steady long-term decline—in that crucial 1967–1970 period.

I've noted above that the United States still is one of the world's top two or three oil-producing nations every year. But let's be clear: that can't last forever at current rates of consumption.

Today, experts agree that the United States has only about 21 billion barrels of oil left. That could mean we will use up all our remaining available reserves in a few years. Given the intensity of prospecting, most experts believe we won't run dry of domestic oil. And as I've explained above, the fracking breakthrough has revolutionized the amount of oil we can cost-effectively extract from clay shale formations. But ultimately our oil reserves remain finite, and some day they will eventually run out. So it makes sense to use them for essentials and not in areas where we can easily substitute other fuels for them.

And if necessary, the technology exists to extract vast quantities of oil from the coal deposits we sit on, the largest in the world. The technology to do that is mature and reliable. But it certainly isn't cheap. However, the cold fact remains that we still sit on enormous oceans of natural gas and coal, but despite our current abundance of oil, we can't take it on tap forever.

Admittedly, some incorrigible optimists believe that there might be three and a half times that amount still lying around waiting to be found. The odds on finding it are definitely better than finding a live Bigfoot, but not by much. And for the same reason, if there were any more bigger and better oil fields lying around, we would have found them a long time ago. When there's money to be made from it, Americans are at their most efficient and inventive best. The optimists are still out there, but the smart ones such as George Mitchell, the legendary developer of fracking techniques, have turned their main focus to natural gas and to maximizing output from the very impressive oil fields we still have.

Yet the United States has many realistic and major options to dramatically reduce its need for oil to fuel its endless fleets of automobiles and trucks and its array of power stations.

The new mining technology of hydraulic fracking has made the methane gas locked in colossal clay shale geological formations across the United

States cost-effective to extract for the first time ever. Natural gas, coal, and nuclear energy can substitute for oil for all electrical generating power, and hybrid cars are now a cost-effective industrial reality at last. The best way would be to construct as many coal-fired and natural gas–fired power stations as possible. Coal will be our future if for no other reason than we have so much of it. That doesn't mean clean coal is any closer to reality than switchgrass biomass or any other green daydream. But clean or dirty, there will be coal. Coal and natural gas development is also going to be essential to cushion the inevitable rise in oil prices over the next decade.

Oil, as I've said, can relatively easily be substituted for baseline electrical generation and even for long-distance trucking fleets by reviving a serious continental-scale cargo rail network. But it *cannot* be substituted for aircraft fuel, the production of plastics, the production of pharmaceuticals, and— most important of all— the production of nitrate fertilizers to maintain the bumper global crop levels the human race has come to depend on over the past century.

Expensive oil therefore is going to come. It is going to generate enormous economic, social, and political problems. It is going to force dramatic changes in the sacred American lifestyle. It doesn't matter how many talk show hosts rant and rave that this isn't going to happen; it is.

But much more expensive oil is not going to mean the end of the world. And it doesn't mean that the world is running out of oil, either.

It is certainly true that the United States has still failed to come up with any kind of realistic energy strategy to deal with the unavoidable reality of rising basic oil prices for generations to come.

Republican conservatives remain in willfully ignorant deep denial about this reality. Liberal-green Democrats continue to dream that power from wind, sun, fusion, biomass, and many other proven fiascoes will somehow come to their rescue. Even Friedman and Mandelbaum seem to recognize that this just isn't going to happen.

But there is an energy knight on a white horse riding to our rescue through this new century. As I've documented in this chapter and the preceding one, there is already one very strong blinding ray of hope to light a way out of this darkness: that hope is the Fracking Revolution, unleashing the miracle of cheap, abundant natural gas. And Americans simply can't afford to ignore their enormous untapped reserves of coal, either. Yet Friedman and Mandelbaum would have Americans throw away and contemptuously reject the only realistic energy alternative that can possibly save them.

This reminds me of the old joke about the pious believer who was convinced God was going to save him when the Great Flood came. The flood came, the waters rose, but the old believer piously refused to accept the offers of rescue from six boats and a helicopter that were offered to him. He told them all, "God's going to save me."

The waters just kept rising, and the old believer drowned.

When he went to Heaven and was admitted through the Pearly Gates, the old believer was filled with anger at God. "You never saved me though I prayed and served you loyally all my life," he lectured the Almighty. "Stop talking nonsense," God replied. "I sent you six boats and a helicopter, didn't I?"

Fracking technology and abundant coal are the rescue boats and helicopter that God, the universe, and fate have sent the American people at the beginning of the twenty-first century. But Friedman and Mandelbaum are piously telling everyone to reject the rescue, stay piously on their rooftops in energy purity, and quickly drown.

Of course, without the new, available sources of cheap energy, millions more Americans will lose their homes anyway before they can drown or otherwise die in them. But as long as Friedman and Mandelbaum imagine that they can save the world, that mundane consideration is never going to bother them.

Meanwhile, our so-called national energy debate remains depressingly stuck in all its far-too-familiar clichés.

The time for a broad, adult public dialogue on energy is long overdue. But it must start with the realization that all the virtuous "green" fuels we're always told about won't begin to solve our problems.

At the end of the day I remain extremely optimistic that the potential exists to solve America's energy problems. This country has led the world in the cost-effective development of energy resources for more than two hundred years. George Mitchell's fracking breakthrough shows that there are still holdout remnants of the old miracle-working, can-do, practical Industrial America left in this country. They can be found in hard-hat, industrial, and truly free-market buccaneering enclaves of American society that haven't lost their touch. The more we listen to leaders, engineers, and technologists from those regions, the better off we will be.

The more we listen to energy executives and engineers who have worked firsthand at the problems of extracting the coal, oil, and natural gas we need, the better off we will be. The more we painstakingly relearn the fundamental facts of chemistry, as Robert Bryce says, the better off we will be. The United States does *not* have to fall to Third World levels of per capita energy consumption. Its vast middle class and respectable, prosperous working class do not have to be driven into destitution. America does not have to remain a helpless, passive victim of global forces it cannot master or insulate itself against. That is the false gospel of Thomas Friedman and his collaborators.

In fact, it is not really a gospel message at all; gospel literally means "good news," but Friedman's "prophetic" message is all bad news. The price his admirers pay for basking in the glowing, reflected light of his supposed "genius" is the ruin of their country.

It is time to reject that intellectually lazy, defeatist, and just plain flat wrong easy pessimism. America can still regain its future. The transcendent vision of the great Founding Fathers is not dead, but it has certainly been pushed into eclipse.

But the American people must finally wake up first. They must start to reject the endless waves of arrogant, loud, ill-informed, scientifically ignorant, empty rhetoric of both right and left about their energy dilemma and the real ways to solve it. Environmental liberals and know-nothing conservatives have been allowed to control the debate for too long. Both sides have had plenty of turns at bat in the nearly four decades since the 1973–1974 Arab oil embargo and the OPEC price rise burst upon us during the catastrophic presidency of Richard Nixon.

Above all else, the American people have to start relearning the basics of geography they have been brainwashed to reject for so long.

If the American people won't develop their own real energy resources, other, wiser, and more determined nations will seize control of them for their own use.

If the American people won't retake control of their government from the special interests and the ignorant, deeply established prejudices of left and right, they will became the laughingstock and deserve the contempt of the world.

If the American people don't commit to maintaining a strong central government that can protect them from external challenges in a dangerous world, they will be helpless prey to powerful predator nations and movements that already roam the global jungle of a world filled with seven billion people.

These are the stakes of the current great debate on America's energy future. They couldn't be higher.

The false gospel of Thomas Friedman and his flat worlders has brought this country to the brink of ruin. It's time to reject that false gospel and learn different, better ways.

FIVE

False Prophets

Thomas Friedman, Milton Friedman, and the Theories of the University of Chicago

Thomas Friedman devotes 566 pages in his book *The World Is Flat* to making the case for a flat and converging world. This is a very easy case to make. All you have to do is to ignore all the evidence to the contrary. And that's just what Friedman does.

Of course, in literal, real physical terms, Friedman's image of a flat world is childish and obviously false. The world is round—more or less (it is by no means a perfect sphere). Christopher Columbus successfully argued this to the court of King Ferdinand and Queen Isabella of Spain in 1492. It was another thirty years before the survivors of Ferdinand Magellan's crew proved it by sailing around the world from east to west.

This is much more than a debating point. Economics, prosperity, power, and weakness and security and strength in the world are dictated by factors of geography. The state of human societies and economies around the world remains dependent on the degree to which they can master the challenges of their geographical locations and best use their raw resources—or the lack of them. That was true of Columbus's world at the beginning of the sixteenth century; it is true half a millennium later today. Columbus opened up the New World and connected it to the Old World. He was the first of the globalizers. But this was not good news for the indigenous peoples of the Western Hemisphere. Their world did not suddenly become flat when Columbus used the cutting-edge communications, financial, and trading technologies of his day to connect them to the economies of his native Europe. The opposite happened: the first thing Columbus did when he discovered the native peoples of the Caribbean islands was to enslave them. Today they are all virtually extinct. Columbus did not flatten the world when he connected the Old World to the New World. He tilted it. Wealth, power, economic opportunity, and population growth all flowed to Europe and away from the Americas.

The same thing happened in the nineteenth century: the imperial and colonizing powers of Europe used their new industrial technology to gain direct control of most of the world. It happened in reverse in the twentieth century: the nations of Europe smashed themselves into a bloodstained shambles in two world wars, from 1914 to 1945. During this modern "Thirty Years' War," as Winston Churchill called it, wealth, power, knowledge, confidence, and leadership flowed from east to west — in the opposite direction from the time of Columbus. The United States of America rose. It became the wealthiest, most dominant power and society the world has ever known.

Friedman's fantasy that the world is flat wasn't original to him. It was revived in its current late-twentieth- and twenty-first-century form by Francis Fukuyama in his best-selling 1994 book *The End of History*. Unlike Friedman, Fukuyama is a serious intellectual thinker. He took the tools of analyzing history and trying to discover its patterns from Georg Friedrich Hegel, who died in 1830.

Hegel was a German philosopher. He argued that the human race advanced by developing ideas, and furious opposition to those ideas, and that these ideas clashed. Eventually, out of the war of different ideas, a combination, or synthesis of them, emerged. This guided the world to its next level until the whole process started again.

Hegel's idea was vague enough to be fitted to virtually every different kind of political society you can imagine. The Nazis, the Communists, and even the supporters of the last czars of Russia all claimed that he proved their case. They were all wrong. All their societies were based on despotism and the enslavement of people. The Nazis and the Communists were the greatest mass murderers the human race had seen since the days of Genghis

Khan. All of them collapsed or were destroyed. They all left legacies of horror, contempt, and shame.

For this very reason, the moderate pragmatists and tolerant democrats of Britain and America always despised and distrusted Hegel. He has been out of fashion across Western Europe since Nazism fell. But writing only three years after the Collapse of Communism in the Soviet Union and Eastern Europe in 1991, Fukuyama dusted off the old German pedant and gave him a topical twist.

Fukuyama claimed that the final, lasting, perfect form of human government to complete Hegel's historical process had finally emerged: it was Western capitalism and democracy. Margaret Thatcher loved this idea. So did the "Third Way" capitalists who followed Bill Clinton in the United States and Tony Blair in Britain. And so did the American neoconservatives. For twenty years after the Collapse of Communism, they demanded that the US Air Force rain down bombs on every country controlled by a government they disapproved of. Fukuyama's idea fed the boundless vanity of all these people. Who needed a messiah, a mahdi, or the End of Days anymore when History, as Fukuyama taught, had already Ended?

According to Fukuyama, the collapse of communism had finally ended the Hegeliam process of historical development. The End of History had come. The liberal, democratic, free-market, minimum-government state was the most perfect form of rule that humanity had ever seen; it would last forever. Sure, there would be a few wars to come: but they would just be minor, mopping-up processes. Nothing on the scale of World War I, World War II, or the Russian and Chinese Revolutions would ever happen again. History was Over.

No serious Christian, Muslim, Jew, or Buddhist could believe such arrogant nonsense for a second. It flew in the face of all recorded history, human experience, and common sense. The Classical Greeks would have called this idea hubris—a dangerous idea of such towering arrogance that it was bound to call down the retribution and judgment of the gods and which they called nemesis.

But Thatcher never had any trouble telling God, the Universe, and History how they should behave. I saw her make the classic "End of History" case to an applauding audience at the National Press Club in Washington, DC.

Other eminent figures were wiser than Thatcher. When Fukuyama's book was published, I phoned Zbigniew Brzezinski, the former national security adviser of the United States and one of the most eminent American policymakers and historians of the past century. I wanted to get a quote from him about the Fukuyama thesis for an article I was writing for the *Washington Times*. There was a portentous silence at the other end of the phone line after I asked the question. Then "Zbig" replied with his usual laconic, dry wit, "Martin, after the End of History comes—More History." That, I thought then (and still do), summed it all up.

You don't have to take Hegel seriously to reject the simplistic nonsense that History has Ended, as Fukuyama claimed in 1994. But it helps. Because what Fukuyama did—and what Friedman, following Fukuyama trustingly and blindly, also did—was to switch off Hegel's machine.

The historical process discovered by Hegel, Fukuyama claimed, worked smoothly for thousands of years. But as soon as the Berlin Wall came down in 1989 and the Soviet Union disintegrated at the end of 1991, it was switched off.

If that was the case, it would be natural to swallow Thomas Friedman's argument that the world really had become "flat." All the societies of the world were becoming the same. The processes of free trade and of unlimited emigration, immigration, and travel were leveling all differences. War was going to be a thing of the past.

But Hegel's engine wasn't turned off in 1989 or 1991. It just kept on running. A new force started rising in the world. It was implacably opposed to liberal democracy and unregulated free-market consumerism. It was a revival of Islamist fundamentalism.

The Islamists showed their teeth on September 11, 2001. They killed about three thousand people, almost all of them Americans. They hijacked airliners and flew them into the Twin Towers of the World Trade Center in New York City and into the Pentagon, the symbol since 1943 of America's global military might.

In the world of ideas, new, counterideas also quickly emerged to oppose and contradict Fukuyama, just as Hegel had predicted. In America, the most cogent was in a book titled *The Clash of Civilizations* by Samuel Huntington, one of America's most eminent historians.

Huntington studied the world and concluded that it was not flat at all; Huntington's world was mountainous, conflicted, divided, and full of raging contrasts that were growing more extreme, not less. Nor did Huntington agree with Fukuyama and Friedman that the world was converging into one nice, blended, tolerant cocktail or milk shake that would treat and reward everyone the same way.

Huntington identified a list of radically different civilizations rising in the world at the same time: Hindu India, Confucian China, the Muslim Middle East, post-Christian Europe, and Roman Catholic Latin America.

The real world history of the past decade proves that Huntington was right. Fukuyama and Thomas Friedman were wrong.

Fukuyama back in 1994 argued that the ongoing processes of history had reached perfection in his own theory. But history didn't stop moving because Fukuyama told it to. Every action creates an equal and opposite reaction. After the swing toward capitalism comes the inevitable reaction against it. The principle of equal and opposite reaction is enshrined in physics in Sir Isaac Newton's Second Law of Motion. That seems to be where Hegel got the idea from. But Friedman was obviously ignorant of Newton, too.

We see that reaction in the wars that the United States is still fighting in Iraq and Afghanistan. One should expect democracy in Iraq to rapidly collapse and the extreme Islamists to take over in Iraq after the US armed forces leave that country.

If Fukuyama and Friedman were correct, Iraq should have quickly and enthusiastically turned into a Western-style democratic state after the US invasion of March–April 2003. It was no coincidence that Friedman enthusiastically supported that invasion to topple President Saddam Hussein.

Thousands of brave American soldiers died in vain in the ridiculous efforts of George W. Bush's administration to turn Iraq into a Western-style democracy overnight. If Fukuyama and Friedman were right, the Iraqi people should have recognized that the world was flat. Powdered Instant Democracy—just add hot water and stir—should have solved all their problems overnight.

Donald Rumsfeld, arguably the worst secretary of defense in US history, flatly refused to bring in hundreds of thousands of American soldiers (or policemen and sheriffs, which would have been even better) to Iraq. They were vital to maintain law and order during the transition period to a new government. But Rumsfeld never understood that. He and his neoconservative intellectual "geniuses" in the Pentagon, led by Paul Wolfowitz and Douglas Feith, insisted on a complicated, Rube Goldberg–style system of constitutional democracy. They imposed it on the Iraq people by American decree.

It took years to produce the rudiments of parliamentary government in Baghdad. By then Iraq had collapsed into a bloody sectarian civil war between many different feuding Sunni Muslim and Shiite Muslim militias. By 2005 and 2006 more Iraqis were dying per day and per year than had died during the worst of Saddam's domestic repressions.

It took the return of thousands more American soldiers in the "surge" strategy of General David Petraeus, successfully implemented under Robert Gates, Rumsfeld's vastly superior successor as secretary of defense, to stabilize the situation. But that does not mean that the invasion of Iraq and the policy of turning Iraq into an instant democracy were justified or that they will be successful.

I have no hesitation in predicting that it will not be. Petraeus and the surge strategy bought us a little time. But only as long as scores of thousands of US troops waged ceaseless war to suppress the Islamist militias. As soon as we pull out, Iraq will collapse again.

Friedman's vision of a converging world is also based on the free-trade fantasies of an earlier Friedman—no relation. That was Milton Friedman, the often infuriating, often lovable, but irrepressibly self-confident bald little gnome who shaped half a century of economic theory in the United States.

Milton Friedman was lucky. He lived at the right time to ride the waves of Ronald Reagan's free-market revolution in the 1980s. And he died before the absurdities of his theories started exploding on the American people. President Ronald Reagan in the United States and Prime Minister Margaret Thatcher in Britain both revered him. The British and American economies recovered and then surged for almost two decades in the 1980s and 1990s. While they boomed, Milton Friedman toppled John Maynard Keynes from his pedestal as the guiding economist of the Western world.

Milton Friedman, like Keynes, was a genuinely brilliant man. But Keynes had a breadth and a tolerance that Milton Friedman always lacked. Liberals for generations—including Republican president Richard Nixon—revered Keynes. Free-market conservatives of the Reagan-Thatcher era continue to worship blindly at the feet of Milton Friedman.

To this day, liberals still embrace Keynes's brilliant but simplistic and often misleading analyses of the causes of the Great Depression and the reasons why it finally ended. They have always refused to recognize that the economic woes afflicting Europe and the United States in the 1970s required policy solutions that could not be found in Keynesian theory.

Milton Friedman provided some of those new and needed policy tools. He was entirely right that economies performed far better, grew far faster, and generated far more jobs when they had stable currencies, when the tax burdens on them were greatly reduced, and when their currencies were sound.

Keynes in fact recognized the importance of economic confidence and sound currencies. Most of his self-appointed successors did not. Milton Friedman, to his great credit, did. The rapid economic growth of the West and China in the last two decades of the twentieth century was built on his teachings. But Milton Friedman wasn't Moses, didn't hand down iron laws directly from God, and didn't say the last word on economic policy. No single human being ever has or ever can. Therefore changing circumstances demand different solutions.

Thomas Jefferson understood that. Thomas Friedman never did. He bought into the Kool-Aid of Milton Friedman's teachings at the very time the great failings and flaws in those teachings were already revealed. Despite all the good that Milton Friedman and his successors did in stabilizing the American economy and restoring business confidence in the 1980s and 1990s, the damage they did was far greater. They destroyed America's industrial leadership of the world, a dominance that had lasted for 120 years, to 1980.

Thus, the Economics Department of the University of Chicago, where Milton Friedman and his ideas held sway, in the end did something the Communists never could: they sacrificed our future on the altar of a misbegotten economic ideology.

How did this happen? Unlimited free trade was the core of the Milton Friedman gospel. This was a policy—as I shall show in later chapters— that was rejected by the entire Republican Party and by every Republican president from Abraham Lincoln to Dwight D. Eisenhower. But Richard Nixon (a man who thought the study of business and economics beneath his intellect), rejected them. Then Ronald Reagan made free trade, which had always been the most cherished doctrine of liberals and loathed by traditional conservatives, a new orthodoxy for the GOP.

The Democratic Party always had a romantic free-trade wing. Its main champion was Cordell Hull, arguably the worst and even most infamous secretary of state in US history. (Before and during World War II, Hull blithely allowed outright anti-Semitic officials to prevent Jews, Slavs, and other refugees fleeing Hitler's genocides from finding refuge in the United States.)

But the unionized labor wing of the Democratic Party distrusted free trade because it threatened the jobs of American industrial workers. Their last real champion was Speaker of the House of Representatives Tip O'Neill in the 1980s. But the genial, glad-handing O'Neill lost every political battle he had with President Reagan, a communicator of genius.

In the 1990s, Bill Clinton made unrestricted free trade as central a pillar of neo-Democratic Party orthodoxy as it already was to the post-Reagan neo-Republicans. Clinton cooperated enthusiastically with Newt Gingrich, the first Republican House Speaker in forty years, to push through the North American Free Trade Agreement (NAFTA) in 1994.

NAFTA was sold to the American people with the argument that it would bring a new generation of well-paying jobs and secure prosperity to the United States. It was supposed to bring prosperity, security, and peace to the US border with Mexico. In this free-trade golden age, illegal immigration would shrink to insignificance across the US-Mexico land border. Americans in living in the southwestern border states would never have to worry about floods of illegal immigration, soaring crime rates, or a breakdown of law and order.

Well, we're back to Herman Cain's (and Dr. Phil's) "How'd that work out for ya?"

Today's citizens of New Mexico, Texas, Colorado, California, and Arizona know the answer to that question only too well: NAFTA delivered none of the wonderful benefits that were promised from it. Unfortunately, it only had two outspoken and trenchant critics at the time.

By far the more successful and constructive was the Texan self-made billionaire H. Ross Perot. Perot ran as an independent third-party candidate for the presidency in 1992 and 1996. He was by far the most popular and successful third-party candidate for eighty years, since Theodore Roosevelt had run on the Progressive Party ticket in 1912. And unlike TR, Perot did not enjoy the advantage of having been a previously elected president.

But the only other major critic of free trade in general and NAFTA in particular in the 1990s was columnist Patrick Buchanan. He reveled in being abusive, outrageous, and downright repulsive in public controversies.

Therefore his impassioned support for protectionism guaranteed its unanimous rejection by all sides.

Buchanan was a racist. He delighted in taunting Jewish people in his columns. Even archconservative William Buckley accused him publicly of anti-Semitism. Unlike the tolerant and constructive Perot, Buchanan crashed and burned whenever he tried to run as a presidential candidate. For Buchanan to embrace any policy was to guarantee that it would be tainted by association with his ugly prejudices.

The 1990s therefore saw free trade raised to revered iconic status by both the Republican and Democratic parties. Their phalanxes of think tanks and identikit columnists and pundits always nodded thoughtfully and with dignity on the appropriate talk shows while they mindlessly, ceaselessly brainwashed the American people with the free-trade gospel.

The 1990s and even the troubled first decade of the twenty-first century were thus a tranquil era of consensus on real economic policy between conservative Republicans and liberal Democrats. Both parties happily jousted mindlessly with each other in their endless, pointless "culture wars." Only the American people paid the price for the cowardice and complacency of their political and chattering classes.

American industrial jobs had been hemorrhaging to Japan and South Korea since the days of Nixon. In the 1990s, China had the greatest impact of them all. Steelworks shut their doors forever in Pittsburgh. But George Will wrote numerous columns claiming that the loss of scores of thousands of well-paying industrial jobs was really a good thing. He thought it was just making the US steel industry more competitive. New steel-making plants opened across China's booming southeasten coastal provinces instead. The Big Three US automakers—General Motors, Ford, and Chrysler—stumbled deeper into crisis. But the endless op-ed columnists who couldn't build a toy car among them put all the blame on the carmakers and their unionized work-forces.

The US steel and auto factories were swamped by floods of imports from northeastern Asia. But the Asian companies producing the cars that were destroying Detroit remained closed to any possibility of serious competition from their American competitors. In the first decade of the twenty-first century, US IT jobs started flowing away to India as well.

Even Thomas Friedman recognized this reality. Indeed, the dominant theme of his three books *The World Is Flat*; *Hot, Flat, and Crowded*; and *That Used to Be Us* is to lecture the American people as to why it's really all their fault why this process is continuing. At the same time, Friedman argues, contradicting his other arguments, that this process is an inevitable and welcome one.

But there has been nothing inevitable about the hemorrhaging of US high-paying industrial jobs to China and Japan. It was the direct consequence of presidents from Ronald Reagan to George W. Bush embracing free trade and unregulated domestic economy policies.

Thomas Friedman loves to lecture Americans as to why their ancient system of tolerant, pluralistic, and democratic government is vastly inferior to China's authoritarian regime. But nowhere does he mention the fundamental reason for China's success and for that of Japan, South Korea, and Taiwan as well.

All four of those Asian nations have heavily protected industrial economies. American companies have never been allowed to export to them more than a fraction of the goods that those four nations pour into the United States every year.

In other words, there is no free trade between the United States and the eastern Asian rival nations that have supplanted it for global industrial supremacy. And there never has been.

This is the core of Thomas Friedman's world-is-flat fallacy. In none of the combined 1,334 pages of his three books does the author anywhere seriously address the case of tariffs (taxes on imported goods to protect domestic US manufactures) and government intervention to protect the major industries of the United States—or of any other country—from unfair foreign competition.

Yet the superiority and inevitable triumph of protected free-market industrial economies over naively open, unregulated free-trade ones is a universal law of history that has been unerringly proved in every case since the Industrial Revolution began in England a quarter of a millennium ago.

Most of the lessons proving the superiority of protected trading and productive industrial societies at the expense of open, unprotected ones can be learned from history. Indeed, they go back five hundred years, *before* the beginning of the Industrial Revolution. The success of these policies goes back at least eight hundred years, to the rise of the Hanseatic League in northern Europe and of Venice in the Mediterranean.

Could Thomas Friedman possibly be ignorant of all this? Nowhere in his books does he cite any of the abundant evidence confirming the universal success of protectionist policies. But they always favor industry and create tremendous prosperity in any of the countries where they have been applied.

Could it really be true that Friedman is totally ignorant of any history he didn't live through (or hear about in Aspen)? In this he is very typical of his own benighted generation of American intellectuals. None of them knows about the universal success of protectionist policies in European nations over the past eight hundred years. They are even totally ignorant of the critical role that protectionist policies played in creating the industrialized, prosperous, and secure America they have ceaselessly undermined. The intellectual argument for free trade has been taught for three generations now across the American higher educational system. It is supposed to be as self-evident and factually established as the law of gravity. But the case for free trade is false. It is nothing more than an intellectual fantasy.

Universal free trade in theory assumes that it exists in fact. But it does not exist in fact. It never has and it never will.

All countries protect their most prosperous militarily or financially important industries from foreign competition. Many countries preach free trade, and many practice it when it is in their own interest. But the world is never really flat, and getting two countries to sign free-trade treaties between them does not make it so. Instead, the stronger, more competitive economy prospers; the less well developed, weaker economy stumbles. This isn't a world where everyone wins. This is a zero-sum world where one side always wins. And the other side always loses.

Sometimes this has catastrophic consequences. Once, it caused the French Revolution.

The Revolution of 1789 followed a three-year period of economic recession and growing hardship. It was caused by the disastrous 1785 Free-Trade Treaty that France signed with the smaller but much more advanced industrial economy of England. More advanced English industrial manufacturers destroyed thousands of companies in France. They threw hundreds of thousands of laborers out of work.

Three-quarters of a century later, England abandoned two centuries of highly successive full protectionist policies: Sir Robert Peel repealed the Corn Laws in 1846. Over the next quarter century, English agriculture crashed. Hardship and poverty then plagued the English countryside for more than forty years, until the start of World War I in 1914. The English were swamped by a tsunami of cheap agricultural food imports from the United States.

At first it looked in the 1870s that Germany's agriculture would collapse into ruin the way that Britain's had. But in the 1880s, German chancellor Otto von Bismarck, the finest political and economic mind of his generation, approved a new wave of industrial tariffs, or customs taxes. These tariffs made American imports uncompetitive against Germany's domestically produced grains and meat.

Bismarck was an old-fashioned European aristocrat. He had no emotional or intellectual attraction to free trade. He was able to judge that policy independently on its own merits, and he could see the havoc it was inflicting or Germany's landowners. It helped that Bismarck was a wealthy landowner himself.

But William Ewart Gladstone, Britain's prime minister from 1868 to 1874 and from 1880 to 1885, was the founder of Britain's Liberal Party. He shaped the ideology of modern liberal politics and economic theory for the United States as well as in Britain.

Gladstone, like Peel, revered free trade. The result was what Lord Correlli Barnett documented in his classic history *The Collapse of British Power* in 1970. Britain remained vulnerable and wide open to unfair competition from American agriculture and from German industry for more than thirty years, until the start of World War I. This was the beginning of Britain's great industrial decline. First, the British lost their industrial supremacy. Then they lost their leadership of the world. Finally, they lost the greatest empire the world had ever seen.

The negative experiences of France at the hands of England after 1785, and of England/Britain at the expense of the United States after 1870, contrast with the success of Bismarck's protectionist policies in Germany at the same time. All these examples expose the myth of free trade as a principle that benefits both sides automatically.

The truth is very different. Free trade creates a binary, or zero-sum world. Both partners can benefit if their economies are in roughly comparable stages of development. But if one partner has a stronger, more advanced economy than the other, it all boils down to one simple, commonsense argument: Would you strip down to your underpants if you were going to fight a knight in armor who was trying to kill you with a sharp sword? That is the simple reality of applying unrestricted-free-trade theory in a dog-eat-dog world.

That was the reason why free trade within a single, protected market benefited Britain from the 1650s to the 1840s and why it worked for more than a hundred years within the United States.

But when the protected English economy gained free, unrestricted access to the French domestic market after 1785, the result was the ruin of France. When American farmers and exporters gained free, unrestricted access to the English market after 1870, the result was the collapse of English agriculture. Then the United States opened its doors wide in the 1960s and 1970s to industrial imports from northeastern Asia, and in the 1990s to a massive wave of imports from mainland China. And the result was the collapse of American domestic manufacturing, the greatest and most successful wealth-creating complex the world had ever seen.

Liberals and conservatives, Democrats and Republicans in American politics will argue till they are blue in the face about everything else except this. They will argue for God and for atheism, for and against Christianity, Judaism, and Islam. They will defend higher taxes and fight till their last breath to try to abolish all taxes. They will make endless elegant intellectual arguments to prove how more regulation ruins the economy or how lots of new government intervention and pump-priming can stimulate the economy. They can be as relentless, closed-minded, and boring as medieval theologians in their arguments about how many angels can dance on the books written by Milton Friedman or John Maynard Keynes.

But they all remain woefully ignorant of the fundamental lesson of modern economic history repeatedly confirmed over hundreds of years. Tariffs, or customs import taxes, protect large internal domestic markets and their industries from unfair foreign competition. Free trade destroys those factories and companies that are the basis of long-lasting, general prosperity.

This reality modifies the economic principles of Adam Smith. It completely contradicts the economic theories of David Ricardo. Ricardo's theories are taught by free marketeers and libertarians in the United States and usually misattributed by them to Adam Smith. For all those who worship at the temples of Smith and Ricardo, any mention of tariffs and protection for home industries is an outrageous thought. It is far worse for them than any call to embrace communism, or to apply Sharia (Muslim religious law) or medieval Christian canon law.

But Adam Smith and David Ricardo were not gods. Like Milton Friedman and John Maynard Keynes, they were men. And therefore they were as perfectly fallible as you and I.

Thomas Friedman is open about his obsessive faith in the economic theory of Ricardo. At the beginning of chapter five in his revised version of *The World Is Flat*, he admits that while watching a flood of young, educated Indians flood into the Infosys center in the southern Indian city of Bangalore while he was filming a television documentary there, "My mind just kept telling me, 'Ricardo is right. Ricardo is right.'"

But what was Ricardo allegedly right about? Ricardo (1772–1823) was an English-Jewish theoretical economist who developed the free-trade theory of comparative advantage. He was a passionate advocate of universal free trade. He may therefore be said to be one of the masterminds behind the collapse of the British Empire, without even realizing it.

British prime minister Sir Robert Peel started applying Ricardo's basic principles of free trade to national policy less than a quarter century after his death by repealing the Corn Laws in 1846. As we have seen, the result was forty years of hardship and suffering for millions of English farmers, agricultural workers, and their families from the mid-1870s to 1914. Ricardo was writing in England, a nation that was the most prosperous per capita in the word, with the exception of the United States, at the time. The English of his era endlessly preached the virtues of free trade to other countries. The English wanted their trade partners to open up their domestic markets to more cheaply manufactured and better-quality English products. But England still applied for its own advantage the Navigation Acts, starting in 1651. These imposed impossible barriers to other countries that wanted to export their goods back into England, or to the whole United Kingdom of England, Scotland, Ireland, and Wales. Ricardo was therefore like Cordell Hull in the 1930s or Milton Friedman in the 1960s in the United States: he, like them, took for granted the secure industrial supremacy of the economy he lived in.

Like Hull and both Friedmans (Thomas and Milton), Ricardo had no idea how the principles he advocated so passionately would destroy the natural defenses of his country against unfair foreign competition. In practice, it sounds a lot like having a baseball team send a batting-practice pitcher to the mound and saying you'll make up the runs because your team has the better hitters. Or not bothering to send out defensive linemen in football because you'll make it up in touchdowns thrown by your team's great quarterback. Having a good offense doesn't mean you don't need a defense. Like most economic and general philosophers, Ricardo lived in a sheltered, dream world: messy facts that contradicted his beautiful, elegant theories were never allowed to intrude.

Ricardo also had no idea of the scale that global trade would reach. He never dreamed how rapidly global communications would develop. He died in 1823, twelve years before the American artist Samuel Morse and British inventor Sir Charles Wheatstone invented the electric telegraph. It was therefore Morse and Wheatstone, 150 years before Steve Jobs and Bill Gates, who invented the first Internet, the first worldwide web of universal, speed-of-light communications across oceans and continents.

Ricardo never even imagined the invention of railways. The first steam engines and railroads in his native England were only built in the decade immediately following his death. And he never dreamed about the creation of the internal-combustion engine or the automobile.

Nor did Ricardo dream of a world lit by carbonized filament electric lightbulbs. He had no conception of the power of electricity. He did not dream of the coming importance of oil for energy, transportation, and heating. In other words, Ricardo didn't have a clue about any of the industrial processes and scientific developments that have shaped the modern world.

During Ricardo's lifetime, doctors thought they were curing patients of every illness from pneumonia to cancer by draining blood out of their bodies. They didn't even know that elementary hygiene was necessary to dress and clean every kind of cut or injury. The Hungarian physician Ignaz Semmelweiss proposed the modern concept of medical hygiene, and of doctors and nurses washing their hands with chlorinated solutions, in 1847. Any doctor who tried to treat patients today the way Ricardo's contemporary Dr. Benjamin Rush "treated" his patients in eighteenth-century America, would immediately be arrested. He would be charged with manslaughter, convicted, and banned from practicing medicine for the rest of his life. Yet the free-market ideologists of both the Republican and the Democratic parties continue to blindly worship David Ricardo's inflexible theoretical teachings on free trade as if they ever actually worked in the real world; they don't.

• • •

Financial analyst Martin Hutchinson pointed out one of the crucial falla-
cies of Ricardo and his theory in his July 18, 2011, Prudent Bear column
titled "The Fading American Century" at prudentbear.com.

Hutchinson wrote, "David Ricardo's 1817 'comparative advantage' doctrine, that outsourcing low-skill operations to cheaper labor markets would
maximize welfare all round, fails to consider the possibility that the cheap
labor markets, by participating in the outsourced activity, could clamber up
the value chain and eat the outsourcer's breakfast."

Hutchinson then shrewdly observed, "That appears to have happened
in software with India, in solar panels with China and doubtless in other
sectors we will discover in the years ahead."

Hutchinson agreed with Friedman about the success of US IT services.
But unlike Friedman, he did not buy into the fantasy that Facebook and
Twitter could ever compensate for the annihilation of almost all American
manufacturing and heavy industry.

"Meanwhile, U.S. innovation is mostly confined to trivia like 'social
media,' in essence largely a mechanism for transferring consumers' personal
data into the hands of the Russian mafia," he wrote.

Elsewhere, Hutchinson has convincingly argued that minor tariffs and
adjustments in exchange rates would annul the wholly artificial advantage
that China and other countries have established over the United States
through the manipulation and undervaluing of their own currencies and
by their de facto protectionist policies. Hutchinson also points out that we
live in a world completely different in its nature and capability to rapidly
change from the static world that Ricardo—wrongly—took for granted in
his own time.

Ricardo's theorem of comparative advantage, Hutchinson noted, assumed
a static world. However, "In reality the world was not quite static in 1817
and it has been growing progressively less static ever since."

In Ricardo's time, Hutchinson continued, "It might have taken a Third
World manufacturer [many years] to acquire not only the manufacturing
techniques but also the design, control, and marketing know-how of its
Western counterparts."

Today, however, that response time has dramatically shortened. In the
twenty-first century, Hutchinson warned, "with modern business techniques, widespread travel, and ubiquitous communications that process can
be accomplished in well under a decade. Hence the calculus of comparative advantage changes quickly once outsourcing and technology transfer

are undertaken, generally substantially to the disadvantage of the wealthier country's workforce."

Translating Hutchinson's measured conclusion into language that even Thomas Friedman can understand: "Ricardo was wrong! Ricardo was wrong! Ricardo was wrong!"

And: "America loses! America loses! America loses!"

How could that happen? Simple: Ricardo assumes that comparative advantage never changes: he imagines that it is an absolute value and a mathematical constant. But Hutchinson recognizes that as technology and communications develop the rate of technology transfer changes all the time. In other words, insofar as comparative advantage exists, it is not a universal constant at all—it is a calculus, and its value and rate of change are never constant.

Friedman showed his hand in *The World Is Flat*. He was fond of looking down his nose at the admittedly ignorant, crass, and incompetent national leadership of President George W. Bush. But he was even more blindly adoring and worshipful of Ricardo's obsolescent, early-nineteenth-century English intellectual creed than Bush II ever was.

In intellectual terms, the most popular columnist of the *New York Times*, the newspaper of record of liberal, futuristic, intellectually cutting-edge, and snobbish New York City, therefore still lives in a world lit by candles. He hasn't even progressed to the age of kerosene lamps.

Friedman's theory of convergence in a flat world isn't new, either. It was a weird revival and reboiling of one of the most acclaimed, stupid, and just plain wrong prophets of the past century: the English do-gooder Sir Norman Angell.

If you think Barack Obama and Al Gore were the only high-minded disastrously naive fools short on actual accomplishments to win the Nobel Peace Prize, think again. Angell won it in 1933 for his lifetime of work arguing that war had become obsolete and a waste of time. He was given the award the same year Adolf Hitler took power in Nazi Germany. But Angell a quarter century earlier had already boldly prophesied that a new age of globalization and perfect peace had already begun. He claimed to have a sophisticated understanding of the global economy and the new technologies that were transforming the world. He insisted that major global wars had already become impossible. The world had become mutually interconnected and interdependent. Angell claimed that the leaders of big business in all nations held the "real power." (He was wrong.) He was sure Big Business would prevent any major war from ever breaking out. War was bad for business. No one could profit from it. Therefore it couldn't happen: simple.

Of course, four years after Angell published *The Great Illusion: A Study of the Relation of Military Power to National Advantage*, World War I broke out anyway.

We can do no better than quote from the Synopsis (what he calls his introduction) of this "classic" 1910 book, a text helpfully preserved in Angell's entry on Wikipedia (though you can find the whole thing free on Google books). There the great man claimed to prove

> that wealth in the economically civilized world is founded upon credit and commercial contract (these being the outgrowth of an economic interdependence due to the increasing division of labour and greatly developed communication). If credit and commercial contract are tampered with in an attempt at confiscation, then the credit-dependent wealth is undermined, and its collapse involves that of the conqueror; so that if conquest is not to be self-injurious it must respect the enemy's property, in which case it becomes economically futile.

Angell, with the know-it-all confidence and blithe ignorance so characteristic of Thomas Friedman, then claimed that "the wealth of conquered territory remains in the hands of the population of such territory."

This would be news to the victims of the Nazi German Wehrmacht in World War II. The Nazis seized the wealth of all the countries they conquered for their masters and the German people during that war. The Soviet and Chinese Communists acted in the same simple, barbaric, and genocidal way. I guess they never read Norman Angell either. Pity.

Obviously Hitler, with his obsession with achieving lebensraum, or "living space," for Nazi Germany hadn't read Angell's argument: "For a modern nation to add to its territory no more adds to the wealth of the people of such nation than it would add to the wealth of Londoners if the City of London were to annex the county of Hertford."

Angell's argument, with breathtaking ignorance and hypocrisy, also ignored the simple fact of his own British Empire. That empire and its ruling class, of which he was a member, controlled the resources of a quarter of the population of the world and a quarter of its territory when he wrote these memorable words.

But most of all, Angell never anywhere addresses the simple problem of what happens when any powerful nation is run by rulers who simply don't believe in his enlightened arguments, *regardless of whether they are true or not.*

In today's real world, the hard truth is that many countries still have armies, or even nuclear weapons. Real wars do break out. Many countries simply fall into chaos because their governments are no longer strong enough to guarantee law and order. That is certainly the case today in northern Mexico, where powerful drug cartels continue to defy the Mexican federal police and armed forces. It's starting to happen in London, too.

Rereading Angell's fatuous stupidities and clichés today is a thought-provoking experience. He isn't even an attractive writer; he is as pompous and full of inflated self-regard as a bullfrog. He cannot imagine any view other than his own. He always displays the particular arrogance of the supercilious do-gooder who knows he is not only infinitely more virtuous but also infinitely wiser than the rest of the poor, long-suffering human race. But what Angell does provide is a sense of déjà vu, the shock of recognition. Reading him for the first time, you realize you have read him before. You have read him endlessly for decades. He is the ghostwriter of all of Thomas Friedman's high-minded, content-free columns, lighter than helium gas, on the op-ed page of the *New York Times*.

Here are precisely the same assumptions, precisely the same empty, sweeping pronouncements and predictions delivered as if from the top of Mount Sinai with the confidence and calm of Moses (at least the way Charlton Heston played him).

History in any meaningful sense of war or even of economic rivalry or conflict is therefore over. Angell ghostwrote Francis Fukuyama's notorious book more than eighty years in advance. And he dictated from the grave all those endless, complacent Thomas Friedman columns.

Friedman's arguments about the inevitability of a united flat world because of all the high-tech communications and transportation developments he lists is the same argument that Angell made more than a century ago.

- The world is flat and the world is converging. The differences between and among nations, cultures, religions, and civilizations are disappearing fast. They are disappearing so fast that no further major conflict is conceivable anymore in the world.

- Free trade is good for all.
- Economic protectionist policies are not only wrong, they are also evil.
- War is unthinkable. And because we do not think about it, it won't happen.
- Defending your own country's borders is stupid, wrong, a waste of time, and anyway impossible to do.
- Investing in armed forces to protect your country or your continent is a waste of time and, of course, evil.
- The weapons manufacturers of your own country are evil and the masterminds behind world conflict.

History in any meaningful sense of war or even of economic rivalry or conflict is therefore over.

Thomas Friedman's ostensibly brilliant and original new insights of the first decade of the twenty-first century are therefore identical to those of the most celebrated pacifist thinker of the first decade of the twentieth century, exactly a hundred years earlier. President Harry Truman was right: there is nothing new in the world except for the history you don't already know.

But surely the world has changed for the better? Haven't we learned all the great lessons from World War I and World War II? Hasn't communism collapsed? Don't we now have the United Nations? Doesn't Barack Obama sit in the White House? Aren't we living in the Age of Globalization 3.0, as Thomas Friedman said? Don't we have the Internet?

Think about this: at least a hundred million people have been killed in wars across what we now call the developing world in the past sixty-five years. The great powers of the world failed to prevent the Rwanda genocide of eight hundred thousand people in 1994. In the past fifteen years at least ten million people have been killed in civil wars, anarchy, and massacres in the Congo (formerly known as Zaire) alone. At least thirty thousand people have been killed in the war between the Mexican government and the mighty Mexican drug cartels that feed US demand over the past five years. Probably several hundred thousand people have died in the violence in Darfur in western Sudan over the past eight years. I guess none of the people doing all that killing ever read Norman Angell. Perhaps we can drop millions of leaflets to them reprinting some of Thomas Friedman's most optimistic columns.

Remember what national security adviser Jesus said in his Olivet prophecy: "You shall hear of wars, and rumors of wars. But the End is not yet."

I guess Jesus never read Thomas Friedman either.

Will we have a better chance of enjoying security and safety within our borders if we have free-trade policies and no high-paying manufacturing or heavy industrial jobs? Or will we do better if we have prosperous industries that employ scores of millions of people?

Jesus also had a very simple litmus test to separate false prophets from true prophets. He said, "By their fruits shall you know them."

How do you like the fruits of unrestricted free trade for the United States and for your own family?

To apply Ronald Reagan's famous line from the 1984 presidential election, are you and your family better off now than you were thirty years ago?

Are the American people getting richer or poorer?

Are you optimistic or pessimistic about the future of your country?

Do you believe that the free-trade policies the United States has followed have brought prosperity or destitution to this country?

Do you expect your children to earn more money in better jobs than you ever did?

Or do you expect them to earn a lot less, in more degrading jobs?

Have Thomas Friedman's policy prescriptions helped you and your family in any way?

Or have they impoverished you?

The answers to those questions should be obvious to everyone.

SIX

True Leaders

How Abraham Lincoln Made America an Industrial Giant and the World's Greatest Nation — and How Franklin Roosevelt Kept It That Way

W ho was Abraham Lincoln — and what did he really do? Lincoln was the creator of modern America in a round world. He was the greatest leader of nineteenth-century America. He won America's greatest war. But to Thomas Friedman, Lincoln is a dinosaur, an extinct fossil. He does not have a single index reference to America's greatest leader in *The World Is Flat* or in *Hot, Flat, and Crowded*.

Lincoln rates a little better, finally, in *That Used to Be Us*. But one of Lincoln's three greatest achievements along with winning the Civil War and freeing the slaves is never mentioned once: the creation of the first two major industrial tariffs that protected American industry from unfair foreign competition for more than a century.

This is not a coincidence, for Lincoln, more than any other single man, was the architect of America's industrial might and prosperity. And Thomas Friedman is one of the most influential figures behind the policies that have ensured its destruction.

Abraham Lincoln held the Union together through its greatest trial. He freed the slaves. He won the Civil War. He became the inspirational prophet of democracy, strength, and freedom. His speeches and example have inspired and guided the American people for nearly 150 years since his death.

All these achievements were real. They actually happened. They are easily enough to earn Lincoln his uncontested place in the pantheon as one of the three greatest American presidents along with George Washington and Franklin Delano Roosevelt. Yet there was even more to Lincoln than all that.

For Abraham Lincoln also was the real architect of the unprecedented global colossus of Industrial America. He pushed through and shaped the laws that allowed industrial and financial corporations to organize on an unprecedented scale. He gave these corporations more security from interference or depredation from government than private enterprise had ever before enjoyed in human history.

Lincoln held America together through the unprecedented shedding of blood. And then he tied it together with literal bonds of steel. He pushed through financial incentives for private companies to build railroads that united the continent. This made continental-scale trade possible for the first time.

The financial and land grants Lincoln offered the new railroad corporations were unprecedented. Nothing comparable was offered by a European country. It took Russia nearly forty more years to build its first transcontinental railroad. Lincoln gave the United States a forty-year start on Russia.

Lincoln believed in industry over agriculture. He believed in the primacy of manufacturing over the mining, basic commodities, and agricultural sectors to ensure the wealth and future economic security of the American people. He was obsessed with technological innovation, invention, and the practical application of science to business and war. And he encouraged these processes in every way he possibly could.

In his four short years as president (we think of Lincoln as a twice-elected president, but he was assassinated at the very beginning of his second term), he transformed the Union from a huge agricultural "empire of liberty" half dependent on slave labor into the world's industrial giant.

We think of Lincoln as a saintly hero—a gentle, beloved male version of Mother Teresa in the White House. This vision of Lincoln is a relatively modern one. It owes a great idea to the portrait painted by Carl Sandburg.

But Sandburg was a terrible historian. He was a shameless hagiographer. He distorted the real life of a great American leader to produce a childish caricature of reality.

Sandburg came from Illinois. He was a pretentious, terrible poet. But he found his true calling as an exceptionally successful biographer of Lincoln. In fact, he was a terrible biographer. He painted Lincoln powerfully as a suffering saint of the prairie. Since Sandburg, it has been impossible for ordinary Americans to think of the Great Liberal Emancipator in any other way. Sandburg's achievement was extraordinary. After eighty years the image of Lincoln he painted with his maudlin words continues to define Lincoln for the American public. Sandburg's clichés still blot out the lessons to be learned from the continuing flood of genuinely first-class scholarship about Lincoln's life.

The real Lincoln therefore continues to hide in plain sight from the American people. This development would have given him wry satisfaction.

The real Lincoln was no Suffering Servant of Isaiah 53. He suffered, but not as a servant. He was no devout Christian. He wasn't a Christian at all.

Lincoln's skepticism was well known in his home community in Springfield, Illinois. In 1846, he turned up at one Sunday morning church meeting to campaign for support in his first election to Congress (and the only one he ever won). The clergyman holding the meeting was fulminating on the horrors of the fires of hell that awaited unbelievers. Seeing Lincoln, whose skepticism he knew well, the minister asked, "And where do you think you're going, Mr. Lincoln?" "I don't know where you're going, Reverend," Lincoln replied, "but I'm going to Congress."

Lincoln was passionate in his genuine abhorrence of chattel slavery, but he was no pacifist. He wasn't at all gentle in his conduct of the national affairs of the United States. And he wasn't into forgiveness at all to those who crossed him or failed him. He approved military executions of deserters from the Union Army, although he also issued many pardons. There was, as biographer Stephen Oates has documented, no disagreement between Lincoln and the Radical Republicans in Congress over the need to impose a harsh peace over the conquered South in 1865: his proposed peace behind his soft words was as harsh as theirs.

We all know *who* Abraham Lincoln was. But nobody knows *what* he was.

● ● ●

What was Abraham Lincoln? He was America's Bismarck. Otto von Bismarck, chancellor of Prussia, Lincoln's exact contemporary, won the respect and fear of the world because he fought and won three wars to create the new German Empire. He boasted that he would unify Germany and impose his will on it by Blood and Iron. And he did. Bismarck, of course, is even more unworthy of Thomas Friedman's attention than Lincoln.

Lincoln reunited America just as Bismarck did Germany. But Lincoln's achievement was on an incomparably greater, far more terrible scale. More than three times the number of soldiers were killed in the American Civil War than in the 1870–1871 Franco-Prussian War. Total fatalities on both sides of the war between Prussia and France were almost 185,000. Some 650,000 soldiers died on both sides of the Civil War. And Lincoln built up America as a far greater industrialized nation than Germany became in Europe.

Lincoln was willing to submit the American people to this frightful death toll because he had a vision of the better America that would emerge from the war. Had Lincoln lived, he would not have recoiled in horror from the rise of American industry. He would have rejoiced in it. If Lincoln had lived to retire from the presidency in 1869, he would have sat on the board of Union Pacific. If he were invited, he would certainly have sat on the boards of Standard Oil and Carnegie Steel.

To prove this, we only have to look at who Abraham Lincoln was and what he did for a living.

Abraham Lincoln was a lawyer. But he was no simple, poor champion of the "forgotten man," the way legendary movie director John Ford portrayed him in *Young Mr. Lincoln* in 1939. That movie, starring Henry Fonda as the young Abe, is still widely watched and hugely influential today. It embraced Carl Sandburg's rose-colored picture of Lincoln and gave it flesh and blood.

The real Abraham Lincoln, the real unknown Lincoln, was a very different kind of man: he was a railroad lawyer and a wealthy man. Harold Holzer, writing in the *Washington Post* in February 2011, put it clearly:

> [In] the 1850s he ably (and profitably) represented the Illinois Central Railroad and the Rock Island Bridge Co.—the company that built the first railroad bridge over the Mississippi River—and earned a solid reputation as one of his home state's top appeals lawyers.

Holzer continued, "Lincoln's legal papers testify to a diverse and profitable practice. Had he not been 'aroused,' as he put it, to speak out in 1854 against the pro-slavery Kansas-Nebraska Act before seeking a Senate seat, he likely would have remained a full-time lawyer and earned fame and fortune at the bar."

It was Lincoln who created the basic protectionist tariff walls for American industry. The five Gilded Age and six Progressive Era Republican presidents who followed him merely maintained them. Lincoln erected those protectionist measures in the two great wartime tariffs of 1862 and 1864. They endured for a century. Behind their walls, American manufacturing and construction industry fed on its vast national market and become the greatest productive force the world had ever seen.

Writing in 1934 in his book *The Robber Barons*, historian Matthew Josephson summarized the achievements of the first Lincoln administration. Josephson believed Lincoln was naive, not deliberate. But he recognized that in the four years of Lincoln's presidency, Honest Abe created a political-legal infrastructure for the new industrial world: "In a hurried partition, for nominal sums or by cession, this benevolent government handed over to its friends or to the astute first comers, the most daring undertakers, all those treasures of coal and oil, of copper and gold and iron, the land grants, the terminal sites, the perpetual rights of way—an act of largesse which is still one of the wonders of history. To the new railroad enterprises in addition, great money subsidies totaling many hundreds of millions were given. The Tariff Act of 1864 was in itself a sheltering wall of subsidies; and to aid further the new heavy industries and manufactures, an Immigration Act allowing contract labor to be imported freely was quickly enacted; a national banking system was perfected." Josephson's one mistake was to assume that Lincoln did not know what he was doing.

Lincoln conscripted even the US Constitution and the abolition of slavery to the cause of building a vast capitalist-industrial state. The Fourteenth Amendment to the Constitution preserved the freeing of millions of African American slaves. But it also included a "process clause." For seven decades, that clause was upheld by the US Supreme Court to protect business corporations. It was repeatedly applied to defend the unregulated freedom of great concentrations of property and wealth.

America's Gilded Age Industrial Revolution did not begin after the Civil War. It was launched during the Civil War with Lincoln's full approval and active encouragement. In Philadelphia alone, 180 new industrial factories were built from 1862 to 1864. This rate of growth and expansion dwarfed anything seen on the far smaller scale of Britain's Industrial Revolution during the previous seventy-five years.

Enormous land grants were made to the Union Pacific Railroad during the Lincoln administration. Lincoln set the precedent for the next forty years of full-scale federal government financial and legal support to giant corporations in developing the West. The federal government gave the corporations hugely advantageous terms to deal with local communities.

It is false to assume that Lincoln was blind to or unaware of the implications of these initiatives. He handcrafted or approved all of them. He agreed with the energetic, young new Republican majorities in Congress over all of them.

When it came to extending the power of railroads and northeasten finance, Lincoln knew what he was doing. He had earned his living before becoming president as one of the most successful railroad attorneys in the central United States.

In the 1850s, Lincoln fought to prevent a syndicate of northeastern business interests from controlling new railroad programs in his home state of Illinois. But he did not oppose the concentration of capital and industrial power on principle. He represented a rival Illinois-based syndicate that wanted control of the project itself.

Lincoln lived well and was unapologetic about doing so. As Stephen Oates wrote, "Lincoln was proud of the way he made his money." Revealingly, he sent his son Robert—the only one of his four children to survive into adulthood—to Harvard University. Lincoln was born a son of the frontier. But unlike Andrew Jackson, he never wanted to stay there. Jackson had unleashed the populist energies of the Scotch-Irish pioneer people. Lincoln's war crushed them.

The flood of legislation that made Industrial America's amazing growth possible all came under Lincoln. It was all enacted in only four years and one presidential term, from 1861 to 1865.

The Homestead Act, the Immigration Act, the two Tariff Acts, and the crucial land grants to the Union Pacific were all enacted during Lincoln's first term. He also fostered the organizing of the new "money power" in New York City. It financed the war and industrial expansion on a continental scale.

Morison, Commager, and Leuchtenburg in their classic *Growth of the American Republic* observed, "The fortunes of the Armour (meat packing),

Havemeyer (sugar), Weyerhaeuser (lumber). Huntingdon (merchandise and railroads), Remington (guns), Rockefeller (oil), Carnegie (iron and steel), Borden (milk) and Marshall Field (merchandise) fortunes were laid during the war."

All this was immediately clear to the young Henry Adams, who returned from his father's wartime diplomatic duties in England to an America that had become alien to both of them. "Had they been Tyrian traders of the year 1000 B.C., landing from a galley fresh from Gibraltar," Adams wrote, "they could hardly have been stranger on the shore of a world so changed from what it had been ten years before."

For Lincoln, industrialization and the concentration of capital were not betrayals of the cause the war was fought for. They were fulfillments of it.

Writer Robert Kaplan understood this crucial point in his book *An Empire Wilderness*: "Since a weak, divided American continent would have been easily dominated by the European powers, Lincoln knew that war was necessary: that an expanding, industrialized economy of scale required a landscape of scale."

Learning the truth about Abraham Lincoln in the nineteenth century is essential to restoring America's prosperity and national greatness in the twenty-first century.

American conservatives certainly don't get it, either.

Lincoln was the first Republican president, and the real architect of modern American unity and strength. So he ought to be their hero and their role model. If he was, they would eagerly embrace his policy of industrial tariffs. But they are totally ignorant of it. And they wouldn't want to know about it anyway. It flies in the face of their worship of free trade. And as we've seen, free trade is actually a romantic nineteenth-century liberal faith. It was only grafted into so-called conservative thought in the United States by Ronald Reagan and his followers in the 1980s.

Yet Lincoln's understanding of the way that the world is round remains crucial for our survival and success in the twenty-first century.

Nothing is more important for America's future than that its business and political leaders throw the false prophet Thomas Friedman off the ship of state (along with his many followers). America's leaders need to sit down instead to learn the basic ABCs of a protected and secure, continental-scale, market economy. Their first and best teacher is Abraham Lincoln.

The rate of technological change was far faster—and far more unprecedented—in the 1850s than it is in the twenty-first century. Lincoln was a member of the first generation that had to come to terms with an interconnected country. The electric telegraph was invented by Samuel Morse in 1835 and perfected by Charles Wheatstone a few years later. By 1860, its "grapevine" of long, looping cables slung between trees and carrying basic information at the speed of light was already crisscrossing America. When our Internet took off in the 1990s, we had already been used to a literally wired world for 150 years. No one before Lincoln's generation had even imagined that such a thing was possible.

Like Benjamin Franklin and Thomas Jefferson, Lincoln loved the promise and potential of advancing technology. If Lincoln lived today, he would be communicating on his tablet and listening to his iPod 24/7. He would be e-mailing, tweeting, and blogging with the best of them. He would probably have been more of a *Drudge Report* than a *Huffington Post* blogger, but he would have been arguing his causes ceaselessly on both of them.

We know this for a fact. Jefferson Davis, the president of the Confederate States of America, never showed any serious understanding of the new scale and nature of industrial war. He never had a clue about the new opportunities in communications that the electric telegraph gave him.

Lincoln understood them perfectly; probably too perfectly. As his biographer Stephen Oates relates, Lincoln spent long hours every day in the US telegraph office across the road from the White House eager to be the first to read the reports coming in from his armies spread across the American continent.

Lincoln's armies were fed in the field by meat transported from the cattle herds of the expanding western frontier. Their food was transported in refrigerated railroad cars. These technological marvels were already operating across America as early as the 1840s. Only a decade after Lincoln's death, the new railroads and steamships allowed American wheat to be exported to Europe on a huge scale. It was a new Age of Globalization—part of what Thomas Friedman calls Globalization 2.0. But the principles that decided which nations should rise and which should fall were exactly the same ones that apply today in the twenty-first-century world that Friedman calls Globalization 3.0.

In fact, the transformation of the 1870s was far greater than the transformation of the 1990s and the first decade of the twenty-first century. The volume of goods that could be physically exported around the world did not change in orders of magnitude from 1990 to 2010. Neither did the basic speed of communication.

Information could travel as fast as the speed of light. But that had been true since the electric telegraph came into general use in the 1840s. The transformations from 1990 to 2010 were merely changes in *scale*; the changes of the 1840s to the 1870s were transformations in *kind*. Lincoln in America, even more than Bismarck in Germany, was the first world leader who truly understood them. *David Ricardo never dreamed they were coming.*

Lincoln believed in science and technological progress. But he also believed that these things needed to be protected for the good of the American people. The United States and its growing industries had to be protected by tariff taxes on industrial imports from other countries. Otherwise Britain could have done to America in the 1860s and 1870s what it had already done to France in the 1780s: Britain would have flooded America with cheap manufactured goods and undermined America's young new industries by unfair competition. Bigger, far better financed British companies would have choked the new industries of America at birth. Instead, Lincoln's round world protected by industrial tariffs prevented that from ever happening.

Our leaders in this age may claim that they love Lincoln, but they are dismissive of Lincoln's wisdom. In the 1990–2010 flat world, America's domestic markets were left open and defenseless. So any hope of a manufacturing and industrial revival within the United States was smothered at birth by the huge wave of imports from China. It was channeled by Walmart into the heart of the American continent. Thanks to Thomas Friedman, Sam Walton, and their political dupes, China succeeded in destroying America's industry where the British Empire, Nazi Germany, Imperial Japan, and the Soviet Union all failed.

Thanks to Lincoln's new tariffs, that never happened to Industrial America.

Lincoln was even a generation ahead of Bismarck, who only agreed to impose import tariffs to protect German agriculture in the 1880s. But he had inherited from the old German Customs Union, or Zollverein, industrial tariffs that created the industrial colossus of German industry in the first half of the nineteenth century.

The Zollverein made Germany the industrial giant of Europe. It still has that role today. We'll see in the next chapter how important the Zollverein was and still is, and how it also proves that the world is round and not flat.

Lincoln's America made the rich far richer. At first it created a hell for industrial workers. But that didn't stop more than thirty million immigrants from flooding into the United States in the seventy years from the start of the Civil War to the start of the Great Depression. They came to America seeking a better life. Most of them didn't find it at first. But their children and grandchildren did.

Within the United States, significant movements to improve life for ordinary industrial workers didn't start until Lincoln had been dead for nearly forty years. That began in the Progressive era before World War I. It continued in the underrated but very generous and prosperous era of the 1920s under Republican presidents Warren G. Harding and Calvin Coolidge. But the basic pathologies of urban poverty, misery, terrible industrial working conditions, and the destitution of the elderly were not tackled until the reforms of President Franklin D. Roosevelt's New Deal in the 1930s.

Today American conservatives and liberals alike revere Abraham Lincoln—or at least they pretend they do. But as we have seen, Lincoln's crucial role as the architect of industrial America is never recognized by either group.

Liberals continue to revere Franklin Roosevelt. Conservatives usually are distrustful of him. Like Lincoln, Franklin Roosevelt deserves his towering stature as one of America's greatest presidents. But the details of his achievements and failures are widely confused by both his admirers and critics.

FDR's record in fighting the Great Depression was impressive, but it was also seriously flawed. His economic record in the 1930s was very haphazard. Sustained recovery began only in 1939, after FDR suffered his first and greatest national political defeat. He and his liberal supporters lost control of Congress in the midterm elections of 1938. Business confidence then began to permanently recover for the first time in nine years, since before the Wall Street Crash of October 1929.

FDR was a far greater war leader and military strategist than he was given credit for. His record in this field towers above those of dictator Josef Stalin in the Soviet Union, or even of the revered Winston Churchill in Britain.

Franklin Roosevelt wanted a world freed of the old colonial empires. Had he lived to complete his fourth presidential term there can be no doubt that the United States would never have gotten sucked into the Vietnam War. For FDR was completely opposed to the French remaining in Vietnam and Indochina to the day he died. He would have prevented them trying to reassert control over Vietnam and the rest of Indochina in the 1940s. So the political process that led to American military involvement in Vietnam twenty years later would never have happened.

But Franklin Roosevelt also was an unabashed American economic nationalist. He confronted the greatest economic crisis in American history. He had to act in his first ten days in office to save the entire banking and financial system of the United States from collapsing. During the twelve years he was president, FDR presided over the industrial recovery of America.

When he took office, more Americans were physically miserable, destitute, and starving than at any other time in the nation's history, before or since. By the time he died, the American people were more prosperous and secure than they had ever been. And they were about to win the greatest war in human history under his leadership. They emerged from it as the most militarily and economically powerful nation the world had ever seen.

It was America's vast industrial strength that made this victory possible. FDR preserved and revived that industrial colossus. And one of the most important ways he did this was through the policy of protectionism and economic nationalism.

Franklin Roosevelt did not fight the New Deal by joining the World Trade Organization (so to speak; of course the WTO in its current form didn't yet exist in his day). He didn't do it by reducing industrial tariffs. In the 1930s, he made no effort to revive world trade.

Instead, Franklin Roosevelt, from his earliest days in the White House, did the very opposite. In June 1933, only two months after taking office, he shocked the world by unilaterally pulling the United States out of the World Economic Recovery Conference in London.

You should be able to imagine what Thomas Friedman would have made of that: He would have written that FDR was a cowardly little man. He would have sighed that FDR lacked "vision." He would have claimed that FDR didn't understand the brave new world of peace, interdependence, and international cooperation that was sweeping all nations.

In fact, reducing international tariffs in the 1930s might have helped the United States then, just as it is destroying us now. The United States in the 1930s was what China has become eighty years later—it was the largest producer of manufactured goods from the largest concentration of industrial resources in the world. Increased trade then might well have revived US industry a lot sooner than happened when the first flood of war orders came from Britain and France in fall 1939 after the start of World War II.

But FDR still did the right thing for different reasons. He recognized that the continent-wide United States, with a population of 130 million (less than half its population today) had a huge domestic market. Above all, business confidence had to be revived. Purchasing power had to be pumped back to the vast majority of Americans at the bottom of the wealth scale. Then America had a large enough market to absorb the goods and services its industries could produce.

FDR also correctly understood that other countries and their leaders wouldn't put America's interests first—they would put their own interests first. That's human nature. It was true then and it's true now. It hasn't changed in the past seventy-five years.

This basic principle of common sense flies in the face of Thomas Friedman's repeated theorizing that the world is flat. It flies in the face of the simplistic fictions and crazed secular theology of the University of Chicago's economic theorists. But as Franklin Roosevelt clearly recognized in 1933, it just happens to be true.

Newsweek columnist Jonathan Alter is a typical march-in-lockstep member of the post–Bill Clinton liberal wing of the Free Trade Is Good Brigade. He is an unabashed admirer of President Barack Obama. His book on Obama is as ludicrous and simplistic an exercise in starry-eyed hagiography as Carl Sandburg's simpering purple prose about the innocent purity of Ol' Abe Lincoln.

But when it comes to writing about FDR, Alter (perhaps because he is only talking about the past) is a lot more accurate and a lot clearer.

In his book *The Defining Moment*, Alter writes that FDR "finally decided after consultation with [his financial adviser and future treasury secretary Henry] Morgenthau that [the World Economic Conference in] London was a potentially dangerous distraction from domestic recovery. So sitting in the captain's cabin of the USS *Indianapolis* on July 3, the president wrote a brusque and undiplomatic public message. He said the London Conference was headed towards 'a catastrophe amounting to a world tragedy'. . . . The so-called bombshell cable worked as planned and effectively blew up the conference."

Alter accurately describes the World Economic Conference as "a much ballyhooed event that was expected to cure the global depression and bring peace on earth in one sweet package."

The conference's two biggest enthusiasts were Herbert Hoover, the same "genius" who nearly destroyed America by his economic bungling as president throughout the Great Depression, and British chancellor of the exchequer (finance minister) and future prime minister Neville Chamberlain, the same "genius" who later boasted of bringing "peace in our time" at Munich in 1938.

Now, if the world were flat and free trade were the magical solution to all economic problems, Franklin Roosevelt deserves to go down as one of the worst presidents in our history. He destroyed the World Economic Conference of 1933. You can imagine how our twenty-first-century self-styled geniuses would huff and puff today. The parade of Sunday morning talk shows, the conventional- wisdom manufacturers, would solemnly agree with Thomas Friedman that FDR was cowardly. They would say he was a small man. They would try to bury the president in a swamp of sickly-sweet, fake-dignified, bogus, and empty rhetoric.

In reality, of course, Franklin Roosevelt was showing common sense, wisdom, and courage. He was putting his own country's needs first. Unlike a Barack Obama, a Bill Clinton, or a George W. Bush today, he didn't hesitate to infuriate fraudulent media pundits at home or hypocritical leaders abroad. He took the actions that he knew the American people desperately needed.

Jonathan Alter also acknowledges that as early as his second Fireside Chat, on May 7, 1933, Franklin Roosevelt told the American people in a radio address "why tariffs were necessary to help the American economy revive, an indication of the nationalist thrust of his early foreign policy."

FDR as president also was a lot more "conservative" than either Barack Obama or George W. Bush when it came to balancing the budget. Unlike Obama, FDR was determined, as Alter acknowledges, to balance the budget. Unlike Obama, FDR was determined to make sure the US government retained its top-level international credit ratings.

•••

This leads us to a crucial point that Thomas Friedman has never realized. International investment has always been vital for America's prosperity and growth. *But international investment does not flow into an open, unprotected economy. It flows most of all into a successful, industrialized, and protected industrial economy.*

International investors are usually rational and farseeing. They want to invest in a country and an economy that will grow in the long term. In the short term they will invest more cautiously and then pull out fast.

The America of sky-high industrial tariffs under Abraham Lincoln and his successors from 1865 to 1928 never lacked foreign direct investment (FDI). During all that time it was the greatest magnet in the world for such investment.

In 2011 it is China, with the most heavily protected industry and the largest industrial economy in the world in terms of manufacturing output, that attracts more FDI per year than even the United States. And the worse the credit rating of the US government gets, the more FDI into the United States will dry up. I make that prediction not at all happily but with full grim confidence that it is going to happen.

Franklin Roosevelt was certainly ready to raise taxes in ways that would make Tea Party–backed Republicans drop dead on the spot. But he also was willing to slash government spending in ways that no modern, twenty-first-century Democrat would dare to imagine.

The personally liberal Alter correctly records, "For all the liberal reveries of later years, the first thrust of the Hundred Days was fiscal prudence. . . . Deficit spending offended [Franklin Roosevelt's] Dutch thrift. To the end of his life, FDR balanced his own checkbook (bolstered by subsidies from his mother) down to the penny."

Within a month of taking the Oath of Office in March 1933, President Roosevelt had pushed an Economy Bill through Congress and signed it. He had promised during his election to campaign to cut government spending by 25 percent if elected. He did far better than that. Once passed, Alter records, the Economy Bill "slashed federal outlays by an astonishing 31 percent, by far the largest reduction in government spending before or since."

While the act itself was poorly timed—it went into effect at the worst possible time to shrink government demand and was quickly overwhelmed by new spending—it was still FDR's idea. It's impossible to imagine President Obama having the governing change of heart or political courage to run for reelection on a 25 percent cut in federal spending.

Only British prime minister David Cameron among today's world leaders comes close to equaling FDR's record in slashing bloated government expenditures. He pushed through cuts of 20 percent in most British government departments during his first year in office.

By contrast, President Ronald Reagan quadrupled the annual budget deficit he inherited from his immediate predecessor, Jimmy Carter. George W. Bush turned the annual budget surplus, the best in forty years that he inherited from Bill Clinton, into a then-record annual deficit.

FDR's record was consistently one of implacable opposition to free trade. He always practiced economic nationalism to protect America's domestic industries. But this was obscured by his retaining Cordell Hull as secretary of state for almost three full terms, from 1933 to November 1944.

Hull was handsome and superficially charming, but he was not very bright and had a grossly hypocritical personality. Beneath his trademark clichéd charm as a "courtly Southern gentleman," he protected his close friend Breckenridge Long. Long was a vicious anti-Semite who systematically closed the doors of the United States to hundreds of thousands who could have escaped being slaughtered by Hitler in the Holocaust if America had accepted them. So monstrous were Hull's policies that in 1944, officials of the US Treasury Department produced for Secretary of the Treasury Henry Morgenthau an astonishing report titled "Report to the Secretary on the Acquiescence of This Government in the Murder of the Jews." Ironically, Hull's wife was Jewish.

Franklin Roosevelt retained Hull as secretary of state far longer than any other person has served in that office in US history. Yet he never trusted or respected him. FDR preferred to bypass Hull and deal directly with Hull's deputies. But the wily old Hull outlasted them all.

Hull was an admirer of President Woodrow Wilson and the early mentor of Senator Albert Gore Sr., the father of former vice president Al Gore. They all came from Tennessee and all three men were romantic free-trade internationalists. FDR described Hull as "the father of the United Nations."

Hull was a free-trade fanatic. He believed—completely falsely—that trade rivalries between and among the great powers had caused World War I and played a major role in causing World War II. Hull led the US delegation to the World Economic Conference in London from May to June 1933. But FDR already didn't trust him and sent one of his own most influential early advisers, Assistant Secretary of State Raymond Moley, along as well. Jonathan Alter admits that "Roosevelt had dispatched [Moley] to London as his personal envoy when he feared that Hull's free trade internationalism would lead to the Americans getting suckered."

We don't have an FDR in office today, and no Ray Moley is sent with President Barack Obama, or Secretary of State Hillary Clinton, or along with President George W. Bush and his secretary of state Condoleezza Rice to prevent US business, industrial, and manufacturing from getting suckered by Chinese negotiators in Beijing.

Hull was one of the most useless secretaries of state in US history. He had zero impact on the rise of Hitler and the slide toward World War II in the 1930s. He established diplomatic relations with the Soviet Union and did not raise a whisper as Josef Stalin slaughtered innocent millions of people in the famines and mass purges of the 1930s. He was too stupid to realize it was even happening. Jewish Americans and Ukrainian Americans in particular should remember him only with scathing contempt.

Hull played almost no role whatsoever in FDR's exceptionally successful diplomacy during World War II. His passion went into creating the United Nations. He was convinced it would lead to the end of war. (How'd that work out for ya?)

Hull's free-trade ideology had zero impact on US policy during all his years in office. But it heavily influenced future generations of US diplomats who shaped the State Department and the US Foreign Service long after. Hull died full of years and ill-deserved honors in 1955 at age eighty-four.

Since the 1950s, the State Department has been dominated and almost totally staffed by economic illiterates who know no economic history whatsoever. They are all convinced that universal free trade is a good thing despite all the evidence to the contrary. None of them raised a whisper as first Japan and South Korea and then China and India sucked millions of industrial and high-tech jobs from American workers through unfair terms of trade. For them, as for their political masters, free trade is an end in itself. It doesn't matter how much American businessmen and workers suffer from it. Like their hero Thomas Friedman, none of them has ever suffered from applying Hull's simplistic, childish, and plain wrong economic panaceas. They never imagine that their own jobs will ever be outsourced to China and India. (Every well-paid inside-the-Beltway lawyer, congressional hack, and think-tank drone I have ever met shares the same arrogant contempt for the rest of the American people.)

It's easy to forget or belittle the importance of Lincoln's and Franklin Roosevelt's trade policies. Lincoln was the real founding father of the Republican Party. The GOP dominated national politics for seventy-two years after Lincoln won the presidency in 1860. And it's been the dominant party again in the forty-four years since the election of Richard Nixon in 1968. Lincoln has been deified. He remains the most revered of American icons.

Yet no one pays any attention to Lincoln's economic principles and policies. They are never taught at American colleges. They are never discussed on radio and TV talk shows. There is almost no discussion of them on the Internet.

Franklin Roosevelt remains the most revered of Democratic presidents. He is routinely, and rightly, placed with Lincoln and George Washington in the pantheon of greatest and most important presidents. Over the past three years, liberal historians and columnists, including Jonathan Alter, have jumped through hoops to compare Barack Obama to Franklin Roosevelt. None of them has dared to face up to the simple, clear reality that Barack Obama is no Franklin Roosevelt.

FDR boldly charted a course of economic nationalism for the United States from the very start of the New Deal. Obama will not blow his nose without clearing it with the World Trade Organization first. FDR maintained the crucial tariff protections for American industry. Obama did not raise a finger to try to restore them.

The greatest of all Republican presidents invented the tariff system to protect American industry. The greatest of all Democratic presidents defied the world to maintain that system. And he kept tariffs high, too. Both of them believed in the free-enterprise system. Both of them believed that government and industry needed to work together to ensure prosperity for the American people.

Today's Republicans and Democrats pay lip service to both these great and heroic leaders. But none of them dreams of actually following their examples.

The American people have lost their way. Their current "leaders" haven't a clue what to do about it. Sitting at the feet of Abraham Lincoln and Franklin Roosevelt would be a good place for them to start.

SEVEN

The Hidden Hand in Global History

How Eight Hundred Years of Tariff Protection Policies Shaped the Rise and Fall of Nations

Americans are ignorant of the lessons of history, and that's why their country is going down the tubes.

The lesson of economic history is clear: there is no flat playing field in the world, and there never has been one. There are rich nations and poor nations. There are winners and losers. Nations are always rising or falling. The best way to rise is to avoid wars whenever possible and to be strong enough to win them when you have to fight them. The world is not flat and it certainly is not yet peaceful: acting as if it is will ensure the destruction of your country.

In the economic sphere, as I've said before, protecting domestic industries for any large-size country is like wearing a suit of armor. It protects you from being shot or stabbed by anyone else. It turns you into Iron Man. Anyone who voluntarily takes off his suit of armor in a world where everyone else is wearing theirs is going to get cut to pieces. That has been the fate of the US domestic economy for the past fifty years.

This is an old wisdom. This chapter will trace how old it is. I originally expected the pattern of the unseen hand in economic and global history to go back 250 years, to the start of the Industrial Revolution in eighteenth-century England. It doesn't; it goes back at least 800 years, to the rise of the Hanseatic League cities across northern Europe and of the great trading cities of Italy—Florence, Venice, Genoa, and Pisa—in the early Middle Ages. If we had enough data, we would find the same principle applied 2,000 years ago to ancient Tyre and Phoenicia, ancient Athens, Carthage, and the Roman Empire as well.

Americans today are stupid enough to think that even the history of twenty years ago, or earlier than yesterday's viral video on YouTube, is irrelevant and ancient. (And I'm not talking about kids here; I'm talking about everyone.) So, we'll start with the modern world and work backward. The United States was not alone in rising and falling according to the degree that it protected its real engines of prosperity, its value-added manufactures, from outside competition. The story of who did this and who didn't, who could and who couldn't, is the key to the rise and fall of power in the modern world.

The secret of Britain's rise to world power lies with Oliver Cromwell, Lord Protector of England in the 1650s after he executed King Charles I at the end of the English Civil War.

Cromwell was England's version of George Washington, sort of. He led the armies of Parliament in defending the traditional rights and laws of the English people against the king. Charles I claimed that as sovereign he could rule without the consent of Parliament and the people. The king paid the full price for his arrogance and stupidity. He quite literally lost his head.

Cromwell was a passionate patriot, and in 1651 he passed the first Navigation Act. Even when King Charles II of the old House of Stuart was restored to the throne, he wisely renewed the Navigation Act in 1660 and 1663. It remained, with some amendments, the law of the land for nearly two hundred years. It was a fundamental reason for the success of Britain's Industrial Revolution and for the rise of the British Empire, the largest and wealthiest empire the world has ever known.

Under the Navigation Act, trade to and out of Britain had to be carried in English ships. Cromwell didn't believe the world was flat. Neither did the canny oligarchs, the merchant traders, bankers, and local landowning squires who dominated British political life for hundreds of years after his death. They all enforced the Navigation Acts. So Britain built the largest trading, or merchant navy, the world had ever seen.

Because of the profits the British made from this trade, they were able to finance their own far-reaching Agricultural and Industrial Revolutions. They were then able to sell their own manufactured goods first around Europe and then around the world and make vast profits. With these vast profits, they could afford to build the largest navy the world had ever known and become lords of the seas.

In other words, Britain did then exactly what China is doing today.

There had been previous trading empires before Britain's. They all rose the same way that Britain's did. They all delivered peace, prosperity, and security for their countries for hundreds of years. These empires included Venice, Carthage, Athens, Tyre, the Mykaenian Greeks of the Heroic Age, ancient Phoenicia, and the Minoan Empire of Bronze Age Crete. But the British Empire was the greatest of them all.

At the height of its power and prestige, the British Empire controlled directly one quarter of the population and one quarter of the land territories of the entire Earth. No other nation, not the United States, the Soviet Union, Han or Qing (Manchu) China, not the Mongol Empire of Genghis Khan and his heirs, nor the Roman Empire, ever came close.

Britain was the most advanced country in the world in terms of its engineering, technology, and science from the sixteenth century on. The Navigation Acts made it almost impossible for other countries to make inroads into the British domestic market. But Britain was free to export its own manufactures to the whole world.

This was bad news for France. In the 1660s, its rise as the strongest power in Europe was assured by Jean-Baptiste Colbert, minister of finance from 1665 until his death in 1683.

The United States could use a Colbert running its affairs for eighteen years today (but not Stephen, heaven forbid). We can do no better than quote that universal authority Wikipedia in its entry on him: "He achieved a reputation for his work of improving the state of French manufacturing and bringing the economy back from the brink of bankruptcy. . . . Colbert worked to create a favourable balance of trade and increase France's colonial holdings."

Colbert believed in quality control. He issued regulations and sent inspectors to make sure the cloth France produced was of the best quality in Europe. (Lesson: regulations, fairly and universally applied, can actually be a good thing.) Today's managers would have sneered at him not just for the government intervention but also because he didn't just read the bottom line. He cared about more than cutting costs and firing workers.

First Ford, then General Motors, rose to become the largest, most profitable, and most successful automakers the world has ever seen: they did so by maintaining enormously high volumes of production with outstanding quality at cost-effective prices. Toyota and Honda in Japan rose to global dominance by applying exactly the same principles.

Strip the self-serving rhetoric and bogus statistics of the business school MBAs and Wall Street moneymen and you find a simple, clear reality.

They do not know what they are doing. Today's CEOs believe that the main goal of a small company's management is to keep expanding and hiring workers until they become an attractive takeover target, and the main goal of a big company is to keep cutting workers until they have enough cash on hand to buy smaller companies. They fire industrial workforces who actually make their products. Then they blame the industrial workers for the failures of their own management strategies. They fire only their victims. They never take responsibility and fire themselves.

Thomas Friedman is the perfect false prophet and guru for such people.

The dominant ideology of American business is that a workforce is expendable and so is quality: only cutting costs is sacred. Thomas Friedman enthusiastically approves the destruction of millions of lives in his worship of this ideology. This is like telling a man with a serious illness that if he jumps off a tall building he will feel better for a few seconds if he doesn't care about getting squashed to a bug as soon as he hits the hard, real, unforgiving ground below.

My family used to drive a Chrysler Dodge Grand Caravan because we wanted to drive American. But it was a nightmare. Things went wrong all the time. Quality control and maintenance were jokes. Finally we switched to a Toyota Sienna. The difference was like night and day.

The Sienna's quality control was excellent. That was because, as David Halberstam documented in his book *The Reckoning* a quarter century ago, Toyota is still run by a management culture that takes pride in what it produces. Toyota still has a large workforce that is primarily educated not with PhDs but with mechanical, technical, and practical engineering experience on the production line and the factory floor.

The central fallacy of American business orthodoxy over the past forty years is that you can continue to slash costs and better-paid workers, and the loss of quality will never matter. Or that, if quality matters at all, you can get it at a fraction of the cost from far more cheaply paid workers in China, elsewhere in East Asia, or India than you can at home in America.

But when the quality of your product is lousy, no one will buy it.

Your managerial structure, engineering design, and production expertise and efficiency of production have to be good. Only then will you be able to have large volumes of production and quality to sell a large volume of your product at competitive prices. Then people will buy your goods because they are both cheap and good at the same time.

Honda, Toyota, and BMW all understand this basic principle and profit by it. For many decades, so did Marks & Spencer, one of the most profitable and successful clothing retailers in Britain.

All these examples teach the same lesson: quality matters. And quality can be delivered at cost-effective prices in enormous volume. That is true for the oil tankers and container cargo carriers built in the shipyards of Japan and South Korea today. It was true for the steel of Andrew Carnegie and the cheap, safe kerosene sold by John D. Rockefeller's Standard Oil a century ago.

Minister of Finance Jean-Baptiste Colbert understood these same principles in France 350 years ago. Colbert had the enormous advantage that he had never read Adam Smith, David Ricardo, or Thomas Friedman, so he had no doubt that the world was round. He carried out what today we would call industrial espionage. He spent a fortune to buy the secrets of Venetian glassmaking. Once French experts had learned them, he fired the Venetian experts he had paid to bring them. He believed in using the state to make sure goods were kept to a high standard of quality control.

The *Wall Street Journal* editorial page would certainly have sneered at Colbert because he used the power of government to strengthen domestic companies. So would William Ewart Gladstone and his economic liberals in 1880s Britain. But Colbert didn't allow Wall Street–style predators to raid or take over prosperous companies and pay for them by leveraged debts. He protected French industries from outside competitors. China, Germany, South Korea, Japan, and Taiwan do the same thing today. It works for them. It used to work for us.

Today, of course, Colbert would be Chinese. Half a century ago, Taiichi Ohno would have hired him in a second at Toyota.

Colbert was one of the greatest finance ministers in history. He made France more prosperous than it had ever been for a century after his death. But then in the 1780s, King Louis XVI made a fatal mistake. He started believing in free trade. It cost him his life. Louis XVI lost his head to the guillotine in the French Revolution, just as King Charles I of England had more than 140 years before.

But where Charles I was a genuine would-be tyrant, Louis really meant well. He was very like Prince Charles in Britain today. He was always well-meaning, always wanting to do the right thing. But somehow it never worked out. Louis was the kind of king you would see played by the Monty Python gang, or by the Keystone Kops. He just couldn't help messing up everything.

Free trade was the fashionable idea in the 1780s, just as it's been in the twenty years since the collapse of communism. If Thomas Friedman were writing then, you can be sure Louis XVI would have avidly read and swallowed every word he ever wrote.

Friedman, for his part, would be liberally larding his books and columns with breathless, name-dropping anecdotes about the brilliant, forward-looking royal technocrat at Versailles who recognized that France had to scrap its tariff barriers to face the brave new world of the eighteenth century.

As it happens, Adam Smith had published *The Wealth of Nations* in 1776, and he was a free-trade enthusiast, too. Smith and his book were huge influences on William Pitt the Younger, Prime Minister of Britain for most of the twenty-three years from 1783 to his death in 1806. Prime Minister Pitt convinced the French to sign a fateful Free-Trade Treaty in 1785. So Adam Smith deserves a lot of the blame for the French Revolution and the conquest of Europe by Napoleon that stemmed from it. His free-trade dreams killed millions of people.

That treaty was the NAFTA of its time. It was supposed to bring enormous prosperity to both France and Britain. Britain had a much smaller population and resource base than France. But it was half a century ahead of France in its business organization and engineering technology.

Cheap British manufactures flooded into France and outsold French-produced products at far cheaper prices in their home markets. Tens of thousands of French companies collapsed. Hundreds of thousands of people were thrown out of work. There was no unemployment insurance in that world, and most people had no savings to live on. They just starved. Despair quickly led to revolution.

Within four years of the treaty being signed, the monarchy was swept away in the French Revolution. King Louis XVI and his wife, Queen Marie-Antoinette, were both executed. Free trade had destroyed the oldest, richest, most powerful monarchy in Europe in less than half a decade.

The French Revolution plunged France into a quarter century of wars with Britain. But this turned out to be good news for the British, too. Britain's Royal Navy was larger, better organized, and far better than the French Navy, so the British were able to seize France's empire around the world at will.

By 1800, the world was literally Britain's oyster. Railways hadn't been developed yet, so great land empires such as China, Russia, or the infant United States weren't able to organize and integrate their own territories yet. There was no alternative to controlling the sea-lanes: they were the great arteries of global commerce, and Britain's Royal Navy controlled them all. The French emperor, Napoleon Bonaparte, conquered all of Europe between 1798 and 1812. But when Britain put the squeeze on his Continental System of trade, all of Europe trembled. The British, however, controlled access to the wealth of the rest of the world. So they didn't break a sweat.

This wasn't Globalization 1.0 or 2.0, as Thomas Friedman superficially and fatuously claims. The world is round now and it was round then. The global trading world was as fully unified and integrated in 1800 as it is in 2012—and the British ran it in 1800.

That moment of unipolar power couldn't last forever; it never does. It was inevitable after the end of the Napoleonic Wars in 1815 that other powers would eventually adapt the new technology and rise to rival Britain in power and wealth.

(In the same way, it was inevitable and basically a good thing that Western Europe was rebuilt by the US Marshall Plan after 1947 and that the United States poured even more wealth into building up Japan, Taiwan, and South Korea as well. The rise of China since the 1970s thanks to the new directions it was given by Paramount Leader Deng Xiaoping also was inevitable and should have been a good thing, too. The rise of China did *not* mean that the United States had to fall. American stupidity and greed were responsible for that. But since 1966 the United States has repeated the great mistake the British Empire made 120 years earlier. Both great nations abandoned protectionism and embraced the gospel of free trade. The false prophet David Ricardo, Thomas Friedman's simplistic hero, inspired both of them.)

In 1846, British prime minister Sir Robert Peel abolished the Corn Laws. This turned out to be a death knell for British agriculture over the next seventy years. It opened the way for American wheat exports to flood into Britain at far cheaper rates thanks to economies of scale after 1870. In the short term, Peel's policy also proved to be the literal death knell for at least two million Irish men, women, and children who starved to death in the Great Famine of 1845 to 1848.

Ireland was producing more than enough corn to feed its own people after the potato crop failed several years in succession. But Peel, like any neocon or libertarian today, was a doctrinaire believer in taking a good idea (free internal trade) to an absurd extreme. He rivaled US president Herbert Hoover during the Great Depression in his arrogance, stupidity, and indifference to real human suffering.

In the long run, Peel also doomed the British Empire. The corn was exported overseas, while the people of Ireland starved. Two million Irish people fled to the United States to start a new life. They were so weakened by famine, typhus, and other diseases that half a million of them died making the crossing, mainly in the year 1847. Since then, it's been known in Ireland as Black '47.

After 1815, the scores of small, weak, and usually feuding German states had had enough of being on the economic and political apron strings of France, as they had been for hundreds of years. They forced the creation of a new Zollverein, or Customs Union. It created a new unified internal market across Germany just at the time that the Industrial Revolution was moving to Central Europe.

Here's how American historian William Manchester described the creation of the Zollverein: "In effect, this was a common market, a first surge towards a reunited Reich, and on January 1, 1834, its architects reached an agreement with thirty-six Teutonic states. All intra-union tariffs were abolished. Economically, the pact created a single nation of thirty million Germans."

The Zollverein transformed Germany. Before the Zollverein, Germany was known throughout the world as a land of lovable professors and fairy tale castles with tiny, ridiculous little states ruled by princes, counts, and dukes. The French invaded it, stole its crops, and raped its women whenever they liked. After the Zollverein, Germany was the most powerful nation in Europe, and everybody knew it: it was payback time.

Coal mines were developed, and iron- and steelworks opened. Demand soared for iron and steel to build the new railways that had been invented in the 1820s in England. Germany's economy grew rapidly. So did its industries.

Prussia, the most powerful of the German states, used the new technology and science to reequip its army, especially with heavy artillery. In the war of 1870–1871, the Prussian Army, backed by its neighboring states in the Zollverein, smashed France. For 240 years France had been the strongest military power on the mainland of Europe. Now France was dethroned. Germany was the new supreme power in Europe. It got there thanks to the principle of economic protectionism.

In the 1880s, as we've seen, German chancellor Otto von Bismarck, the man of Blood and Iron, extended the principle of protectionism from industry to agriculture as well. Bismarck was a Junker, a wealthy landowner. His friends were complaining that business was bad because cheap American exports were flooding their home markets and depriving them of income.

Unlike Gladstone, Britain's liberal prime minister at the time and Victorian England's version of Ronald Reagan, Bismarck didn't worship free trade as the supreme god and he didn't revere David Ricardo as its one and only prophet. He didn't hesitate to pass new tariff laws. They protected Germany's agriculture and industry from foreign competition. Germany went from strength to strength economically.

By contrast, Britain floundered thanks to the disastrous policies of Robert Peel and Gladstone. It lost the world leadership in industry it had proudly held for hundreds of years.

There were a handful of farseeing British leaders, led by Colonial Secretary Joseph Chamberlain and the great historian Sir John Seeley. They preached the need to protect British industry from foreign competition. They saw the need to rebuild tariff protection the way Germany had under Bismarck and the United States had thanks to Lincoln. But they remained voices in the wilderness.

The election of 1880 was the great turning point in Britain. It bears eerie parallels to what happened exactly a century later in the United States.

"It's Morning in America," President Ronald Reagan famously declared. However, thirty years after he won the presidential election decisively for the first time, in 1980, it is now clear that his victory instead launched the United States into a long period of industrial decline and growing indebtedness to the rest of the world.

Reagan's two terms of office were defined by the worst industrial and jobs loss recession, in 1981–1982, that the United States had experienced since the Roosevelt Recession of 1937. This was followed by the start of a boom period that raised living standards and general prosperity to unprecedented levels.

The boom was in new high-tech industries, but it came at the expense of millions of jobs in the old, traditional heavy industries and consumer durable sectors of the US economy. They fell victim to tsunamis of cheaper imports, first from Japan and South Korea and then from China. It was no coincidence that during those same three decades, America's annual balance of payments trading deficit grew to become the biggest in the history of any nation in modern times.

Reagan's epochal election also led to the progressive abandonment of federal government regulation over the banks and financial institutions of Wall Street. Real estate boomed. The 1933 firewall of the Glass-Steagall Act, which prevented regular consumer banks from also functioning as far riskier investment banks, was demolished in 1999 by the Gramm-Leach-Bliley Act. An age of reckless financial speculation followed; it dwarfed the notorious era of the Roaring Twenties, which led to the Great Depression. The reckoning for this era only started to come due with the Wall Street meltdown of September 2008.

From today's perspective, therefore, it is clear that the election of Reagan over incumbent president Jimmy Carter in 1980 marked a historic choice by the American people.

The new leader they had chosen staked America's future on unleashing unregulated financial speculation. Reagan and his followers blindly trusted the wealth and job-creating powers of high-tech development over the old industries of steelmaking, basic engineering, and manufacturing, on which America's unprecedented economic expansion and prosperity had been centered since the end of the Civil War in 1865.

Ironically, it was no coincidence either that Jimmy Carter, the incumbent president so overwhelmingly rejected in 1980, also was the last president America ever had to this day who had been trained as an engineer and who had a basic knowledge of science and technology. He had qualified as one of Admiral Hyman Rickover's engineering elite in the US nuclear navy. Carter was expelled from power. He was widely ridiculed for his July 1, 1979, televised address to the American people titled "Energy and the National Goals: A Crisis of Confidence." In the long Reagan era of public confidence and apparent prosperity that followed, Carter's concerns about America's economic future widely appeared ridiculous and defeatist. But in fact he did clearly recognize the dilemmas of the new era of increasing global industrialization, competition, and eventual rising energy prices that America would have to face. These problems were delayed and denied for nearly three decades, but now those chickens are coming home to roost.

Carter, it must be said, did not have any good answers to the questions he himself recognized. If he had, he would have tamed the dragons of stagnation and inflation (stagflation) that blew him out of office in November 1980. Carter was a terrible, disastrous leader, but at least he asked the right questions.

Carter's defeat ushered in a thirty-year era of complacency and denial. America's old industrial base was allowed to collapse and die, without any effort being made to renew it. The nation ultimately became totally dependent on a huge flow of manufactured imports from China instead.

Reagan, the master magician of American political rhetoric, also redefined the concepts of conservatism and the core principles of the Republican Party in ways often the opposite of what they had stood for over the previous 120 years.

The Republican Party had always been the party of industrial policy and protectionist tariffs, from Abraham Lincoln to Dwight D. Eisenhower. The policy of reducing tariffs and supporting free trade had always been a policy of liberal Democrats.

But Reagan transformed the Republicans into free-trade liberals worshipping at the shrine of eighteenth-century economic theorist Adam Smith. Those policies previously in both the United States and Britain had always been definitive liberal policies.

Ironically, exactly a century before Reagan's first national victory in 1980, Gladstone, the greatest of all Liberal Party leaders, won reelection as prime minister of Britain. And he then had made exactly the same fateful choice to abandon any serious engagement with industrial renewal that Reagan did a century later.

Like Reagan, Gladstone bet his country's future on a policy of unregulated financial speculation and overseas investment instead.

The results were exactly the same. For two hundred years, Britain had been the most advanced industrial nation in the world. The growth of its empire and its unparalleled surge in population, per capita prosperity, and global power were all based on that industrial supremacy.

But in the next thirty years, from 1880 to 1910, as Lord Correlli Barnett documented in his classic book *The Collapse of British Power*, British industry fell (fatefully and permanently) behind the United States and Germany and became deeply dependent on continued technology transfusions from both countries.

In the first half of the twentieth century, this process accelerated until Britain became in strategic terms what George Orwell satirically called in *1984* "Airstrip One"—a large airfield for "Oceania," Orwell's nightmare vision of a United States that had gone Communist. (Obviously, that fate never befell either the United States or Britain, but Britain's strategic dependence on the United States through the second half of the twentieth century proved as massive and irreversible as Airstrip One's role in *1984*. And it was Gladstone's policies that put it there.)

Like Reagan's policy of unregulated financial activity, Gladstone's lasted just about thirty years. The Reagan financial bubble finally popped in September 2008. Gladstone's dream dissolved with the onset of World War I in 1914. The British suddenly found that they lacked enough industrial capacity to meet the demands of war with Imperial Germany, so they had to sell off most of the vast swath of overseas investments they had accumulated since 1880.

Like Jimmy Carter in 1980, Britain's defeated prime minister in 1880, Benjamin Disraeli, recognized the scale of the problems facing his industrialized society. And like Carter, he didn't have any real answers for them. But at least, like Carter, he recognized the problem.

Gladstone, like Reagan, was an economic naïf and a prophetic Pangloss. Like Voltaire's creation from *Candide*, he imagined that everything was for the best in the best of all possible worlds.

Gladstone and Reagan simply refused to acknowledge the existence of any facts or trends that contradicted their simplistic, rosy vision of the way things ought to be. So did Margaret Thatcher, Reagan's ideological partner in Britain. Like Reagan, Gladstone was a charismatic political tribal leader whose policies, principles, and faith were worshipfully followed by his successors for decades.

After 1880, British wealth flowed out of the country for cheap profit and financial speculation rather than being invested in the modernization and revival of the home industrial base. But this proved unsustainable after thirty years. After 1980, America's new leaders followed the same path as Gladstone and his Liberal Party supporters. After thirty years, the bankruptcy of that policy is becoming apparent, too.

Unfortunately for the German people, their political leadership was as lousy at grand strategy and diplomacy as it was good at protecting the domestic economy. In 1914 Germany needlessly blundered into a world war with France, Russia, and Britain that Germany could easily have avoided. To make matters worse, first Italy and Japan and then the United States ended up joining the war on the Allies' side.

Germany was therefore fighting a coalition of all the other greatest nations in the world. Yet its army was so good and its economy was so strong that it held out for more than four years, with only a weak Austro-Hungarian Empire and a dying Ottoman Empire as its allies.

In the 1930s, under Adolf Hitler, Germany economically recovered. This time, through the military tactics of blitzkrieg, it was able to conquer all of Europe. The Nazi swastika flew as far to the east as the Caucasus Mountains, and from the North Cape inside the Arctic Circle in Norway to Crete and Libya at the eastern end of the Mediterranean. Once again, it took an alliance of almost all the other great powers in the world to finally push the Germans back. This time they were crushed in total defeat.

Germany's economy in the 1930s was the second most powerful industrial economy on earth. It was protected by tariffs. The United States had by far the largest industrial economy in the world. It was protected by tariffs, too.

The Soviet Union was a special—and exceptionally horrific—case: many millions of people were killed through the 1920s and 1930s in famines, both accidental and deliberately engineered by the Soviet government, and in psychotic mass purges. The only thing in dictator Josef Stalin's list of positive achievements—but it needlessly cost millions of lives—was the creation of a massive industrial base. However, that industrial base proved vital to the survival of the Russian and Ukrainian peoples. Had it not been built, Adolf Hitler would have conquered the Soviet Union and won the war against both the Soviets and the Western Allies. Then Hitler would have followed his diabolical genocide of the Jewish people in Europe by an even more colossal bloodbath to virtually annihilate the Russian, Ukrainian, and other Slavic peoples, too.

The Götterdämmerung, or "Twilight of the Gods," of 1945 annihilated German militarism and the scourge of Nazism in Western Europe forever.

But it was made possible only because Hitler's enemies had protected their own domestic industrial manufacturing bases from the inevitable threats that arise in a round world.

Britain had done the same thing. The story of the great debate between protectionism and free trade in Britain in the quarter century before 1914 was told in part forty years ago by one of Britain's greatest modern historians, Correlli Barnett, in his masterpiece volume *The Collapse of British Power*. British prime minister Margaret Thatcher thought so much of Barnett that she made him a lord.

Yet Thatcher never practiced what Barnett preached. She let old British industry wither and die, refusing to use her government's power to significantly revive it. She always remained a simplistic believer in the automatic virtues of unlimited free trade.

But here is what happened: British industry in 1914 had fallen a generation behind the rising industries of Germany and the United States in electrical engineering, chemistry, agriculture, steelmaking, automaking, machine tools, and ball bearings—just like the United States compared with Germany, China, Japan, Taiwan, and South Korea today.

"England by 1914 was well on the way to becoming a technological colony of the United States and Germany," Barnett wrote. "In 1910 Britain produced 7,613,000 metric tons of steel—barely half the German total. . . . In Britain [before 1914] steelworks equipped with modern plant laid out on scientific and economic principles were exceptional."

Barnett quoted from the official *History of the Ministry of Munitions*: "British manufacturers were behind other countries in research, plant and method. . . . [T]heir costs of production being so high that competition with the steelworks of the United States and Germany was becoming impossible."

Yet during the great crisis of World War I, British industry dramatically revived. It rose to the challenge of producing the weapons and modern machinery the country desperately needed. Britain's revived under the dynamic leadership of David Lloyd George as prime minister and Winston Churchill as minister of munitions. They set an example for how twenty-first-century American industry could still revive and restore its country's place as a global leader.

Barnett wrote of that industrial revival nearly a century ago, "The contrast between the industrial mobilization that now followed in Britain and the previous years of drift and decline was remarkable. It was as if a portly and elderly retired gentleman had suddenly leapt from his armchair and embarked on a new career. Gone was the smugness and lethargy. Struck off were the shackles and blinkers of Victorian habits and Victorian beliefs. Once more the British tackled their problems by open-minded search for the best expedients. In three years, 1915–18, the British did much to remedy the accumulated neglect of their industrial machine, and to make good the deficiencies revealed by the demands of war. This was more than just economic mobilization—this was an industrial revolution carried through at breakneck speed."

The United States desperately needs exactly that kind of industrial revolution today to prepare it for the challenges it is going to face in the very round world of the twenty-first century.

Notice how private enterprise and the central government worked together to revive Britain in World War I, just as they brilliantly did in America a quarter century later in World War II.

Barnett wrote, "The wartime industrial revolution was led by a partnership between the state and private enterprise. . . . Huge extensions were built to existing private plant with the aid of government money—a heresy to make Gladstone's [and Ronald Reagan's and George W. Bush's] collars quiver under his shroud. . . . [T]he cost of shells made in national factories was below those made by private industry. It was the national factories indeed that received the bulk of the modern machine tools bought in America, Switzerland and Sweden. . . . British electrical generating capacity doubled between 1914 and 1918 and the average output of generating stations rose from 522 kilowatts in 1914 to 7,000 in 1918.

"To supply chemicals of explosives, the foundations of a great British chemical industry were laid. . . . German patents were seized to provide a short cut to technical expertise." (One can easily imagine how libertarian virgins today would turn up their noses in disgusted horror at that.)

New industries were created at Churchill's command and by the work of the Ministry of Munitions on nonferrous metals, optical instruments, aircraft, and aeroengines. Ball-bearing production doubled. The production of electric bulbs quadrupled. The value of production of scientific and optical instruments soared by 2,000 percent, from a value of £250,000 in 1914 to £5 million in 1918.

For the very first time, Britain learned how to manufacture panoramic dial sights, periscopes, range finders for aircraft, and sound-ranging and travel-corrective apparatus. Britain produced almost no aircraft engines in

1914. By 1918 it produced more and better-quality aircraft engines than any other country in the world.

Looking back on these achievements in 1918, Britain's colonial secretary Walter Long said, "This war has produced a new birth for the British Empire. Our duty is to see that we take full advantage of our [vast economic] opportunities [and] that we make for the future . . . a better use of our Great Possessions than we have made in the past."

The British pulled off that economic transformation in only four years nearly a century ago. We can learn from their example and still revive and transform ourselves now.

Ironically, only a few short years later, Winston Churchill, who had presided over so much of this great transformation during World War I, nearly threw it all away in the years of peace that followed.

Churchill served as Britain's chancellor of the exchequer (finance minister) from 1924 to 1929 in the Conservative (Tory) government of Stanley Baldwin. But he was still a Liberal a heart. In 1904 Churchill had joined the Liberal Party. He was a passionate champion of Gladstone's principles of free trade (except in times of war). In 1905 Churchill helped the Liberals rout the efforts of Joseph Chamberlain to protect and revive Britain's domestic industries. Chamberlain argued for a policy of tariff protection. He modeled it on the highly successful US tariffs started by Lincoln and increased by his successors.

The British people in 1905, like the American people in the decades following Ronald Reagan, disastrously put their trust in the false prophets of free trade. The free-trade Liberals won the 1905 elections by a landslide. But little more than a decade later, Churchill applied classic protectionist policies as munitions minister to revive Britain's domestic industries during World War I. Churchill had learned that the world was round, not flat, after all.

But in the 1920s Churchill forgot that crucial lesson. He made the same mistake that successive Americans presidents have made since the 1960s. He restored the pound sterling, Britain's national currency, to the Gold Standard. This made British exports far more expensive compared to those of the United States, Germany, Japan, and other rivals.

Germany and the United States boomed through the 1920s. But British goods were too expensive to export. So Britain's great industries plunged into recession. Unemployment soared—just as it has in the United States in recent years.

Remember, Peter Morici, the former chief economist of the US International Trade Commission, has calculated that by simply correcting the dollar's unfavorable exchange rate to the renminbi, China's currency for international trade, the United States would quickly regenerate five million jobs in its industrial sector. That is more than ten times the number of new (poorer- paying) jobs the Obama administration is now creating every year despite the unprecedented annual government spending deficits it is running.

In 1931, however, British industry was saved and given a crucial breathing space to prepare for the challenge it was going to face in World War II. Joseph Chamberlain's son Neville Chamberlain became chancellor of the exchequer or finance minister. He served in that role for a record six years, until 1937.

Neville Chamberlain is deservedly infamous for his catastrophic appeasement policy toward Adolf Hitler as prime minister from 1938 to the outbreak of war in 1939. But he was a vastly better finance minister than Churchill ever was.

Chamberlain launched a policy called imperial preference. In practice this protected British industry and the vast British Empire (which, remember, still controlled a quarter of the people on Earth and a quarter of the world's land area and resources) from the ravages of competition. This was the same policy that China has followed for most of the past decade under President Hu Jintao, with equal success. China has used it to lock up as much of the world's energy and food resources as it can to feed its vast population of 1.3 billion people.

That policy is working for President Hu and the people of China now; it worked equally well for Neville Chamberlain and the British people eighty years ago.

In the 1930s, Britain still enjoyed the third-largest industrial economy in the world, after the United States and Germany. But Britain never became a monstrous dictatorship like Nazi Germany. In the 1930s, Britain had far lower rates of employment and far better conditions for business recovery than the United States. That was because Chamberlain kept taxes down. He slashed government spending and kept it under control.

Now, according to the prophet of the op-ed page of the *New Yark Times*, these policies, especially protectionism, should have led to sad misery and failure. The opposite happened. As financial analyst Martin Hutchinson has pointed out, from 1931 to 1937 the British economy grew at a faster rate than it had for 110 years, since the days of Lord Liverpool in the 1820s. British industry and science revived. They unleashed an unrivaled wave of creativity and achievement throughout the 1930s that stunned the world.

In the 1930s Britain's recovering industrial economy built the two largest and most successful ocean liners in history, the *Queen Elizabeth* and the *Queen Mary*. British high-speed cars driven by Sir Malcolm Campbell and John Cobb broke the 300-mile per hour barrier and won the world land speed record. British superpowered boats broke the world water speed record. British seaplanes won the Schneider Trophy three times in a row and repeatedly broke the world air speed record.

Frank Whittle designed the jet engine. British private industry designed and built the Hurricane and Spitfire monoplane fighter aircraft that preserved crucial air superiority and won the Battle of Britain. The Mallard train broke the world rail speed record. In 1936 Britain produced trial public television transmissions years before the United States did.

British chemists and doctors led by Sir Alexander Fleming and Ernest Chain discovered penicillin. They revolutionized the treatment of injuries and postoperative infections. Britain led the world in atomic research under Lord Ernest Rutherford and John Cockcroft. Radar was invented under the direction of Sir Robert Watson-Watt. The British chemical, electrical generating, and automobile industries enjoyed unprecedented growth and became world leaders in their fields.

According to Thomas Friedman, none of these things should have happened. (Of course, Friedman has never given the slightest indication that he even knows they ever did.) Once Britain turned to protectionism in the 1930s, it should have lost all that spirit of innovation. Its best scientists should have fled to more open, optimistic, free-market economies. But it's hard to imagine where these would have been: the other most successful economies in the world—the United States, Germany, and Japan—were all practicing protectionism, too.

Friedman probably would argue that this wasn't a twenty-first-century world. But of course the countries with the most successful economies, the lowest levels of unemployment, and the healthiest trade balances with the rest of the world in the twenty-first century are China and Germany, followed by Japan, South Korea, and Taiwan. And every one of those countries is based on old-fashioned heavy industries, automobile and consumer durable-goods production, and massive steel and shipmaking industries. They all rely on these old-fashioned industries employing hundreds of thousands of engineers and old-fashioned industrial workers whom Thomas Friedman despises. Isn't it funny that Friedman *never* cites those industries as examples in his fairy-tale flat world?

Clearly, there is an important general principle at work here. And it contradicts the theoretical economic models that generations of Americans have blindly swallowed in their college courses. Then they sleepwalk for the rest of their lives blindly in love with their beloved theories. They never see the messy real world staring them in the face. It never occurs to them that the real world runs by very different rules from the ones they were taught in college—especially in Harvard Business School.

There is an old French joke that the British Constitution works wonderfully well in practice but it just can't work in theory. The punch line, of course, is that the French always preferred written, precise, logical political constitutions that looked wonderful on paper but could never work in the real world, but they turned up their noses at the British, who had a messy unwritten constitution that gave them far more security, freedom, and stability in the real world.

The same argument applies to the conflicting economic policies of protectionism versus free trade.

Free trade works wonderfully well in theory: it is described as "beautiful" and "elegant" by intellectuals who loathe the dirty, messy complexity of real life. The only trouble is that it brings inevitable ruin to every nation whose leaders are stupid enough to practice it in reality.

By contrast, whenever any significantly sized industrial economy in the modern world has followed a policy of protecting its domestic industries from too much foreign competition, that country has rapidly risen to unprecedented prosperity and power. That prosperity hasn't just been concentrated in the hands of a few rulers. It has raised the standard of living of the entire population.

Americans are totally ignorant of this history—indeed, of almost all history. Chinese leaders and those of other countries recognize this extraordinary blindness. They rightly have nothing but contempt for it. In twenty-first-century Washington, MBAs and slick lawyers with degrees from Harvard and Yale and all the dirty tricks of the Karl Rove, James Carville, and Lee Atwater schools of political snakes are held in the highest regard. But no one pays any attention to the history of their own country, let alone that of other nations.

It used to be very different: Franklin D. Roosevelt, Harry S. Truman, Dwight D. Eisenhower, and John F. Kennedy used to astound their own staffs by the depth and breadth of their historical knowledge about the wider world.

The Zollverein and Otto von Bismarck built the walls of economic protection that made Germany the formidable power it was in challenging for world supremacy in World War I and World War II. The lesson is always the same: protectionist policies give a nation great power to use for either good or evil. But free-trade policies impoverish a country. They leave it weak and defenseless, at the mercy of other, more powerful players on the world scene who do not have its best interests at heart.

Abraham Lincoln, followed by a succession of Republican presidents, most of all the woefully underrated William McKinley, built up America's tremendous industrial power. It defeated Germany and protected global democracy and freedom in both world wars.

David Lloyd George and Winston Churchill revived British industry to meet the challenge of World War I. Then Churchill nearly wrecked the British economy as finance minister from 1924 to 1929. But Neville Chamberlain revived it by applying the best principles of free-market economics on a national scale and reviving the protective walls of tariffs during the 1930s.

After World War II, these same unerring principles applied to the rise and fall of nations. European nations encouraged by both the US administrations of Harry S. Truman and Dwight D. Eisenhower and by Churchill as Britain's prime minister created their new Iron and Steel Community in 1951. In 1957 this was expanded into the European Economic Community of Germany, France, Italy, Belgium, the Netherlands, and Luxembourg.

The EEC created a protected industrial zone of the core European countries. It has generated peace, prosperity, and industrial growth for the European nations to this day. Germany, France, Spain, and Italy have consistently and sensibly protected their own core industries within the growing European Community, today known as the European Union.

Germany in particular provides a positive and constructive example for the United States to learn from and copy. Germany today is a tolerant, stable democracy like the United States. It also has a flourishing free-market economy. It enjoys an enormous annual trade surplus with the rest of the world. But Germany's banks are much more conservative than their Wall Street counterparts.

There are members of America's foreign policy elite who do get it. And let's give them a round of applause.

On June 15, Harold Meyerson, writing in the *Washington Post*, noted, "For a growing number of economists, pundits and even the occasional CEO, Germany offers lessons in how an advanced economy can compete globally and actually raise, not lower, its living standards."

Meyerson cited a March 2011 paper published by the Council on Foreign Relations by Michael Spence, winner of the Nobel Prize for economics, and Sandile Hlatshwayo, a researcher at New York University. They said that Germany's success in creating and preserving a prosperous manufacturing economy owed a great deal to "a broad agreement among business, labor and government" to keep wages at competitive levels and to preserve high value production in their own country.

Meyerson added, "German manufacturers, particularly the midsize and small-scale ones that often dominate global markets in specialized products, don't seek funding from capital markets (there's a local banking sector that handles their needs) and don't answer to shareholders. *They make things, while we make deals, or trades, or swaps.*" (italics added)

These are all good points. We can and should learn a lot from them. But Meyerson, Spence, and Hlatshwayo and other admirers of the German system he quotes all miss the biggest reason of all for the survival and success of German industry: it is protected by European Union policies from unfair foreign competition.

Wall Street over the past forty years hasn't raised a finger to protect American industry. The contrast between the traders of Wall Street and the cautious old bankers of Frankfurt couldn't be stronger. In 1999, the Republican-controlled Congress in the United States repealed the 1933 Glass-Steagall Act, which kept deposit savings banks and investment banks separate from each other. This freed savings-deposit banks in the United States to gamble the savings deposited by their customers in the riskiest fields of financial speculation.

An enormous multitrillion-dollar global derivatives market sprang up. Huge speculative bubbles grew first in the new IT industry and then in the

US housing market. It was driven by President George W. Bush's obsession with keeping interest rates at ludicrously and unrealistically low levels to encourage short-term economic growth, regardless of their economic realities. The IT bubble burst in 2000 and the real-estate market bubble burst in 2008, setting off the great Wall Street meltdown.

Neither of these disasters could have happened if the Glass-Steagall safeguards had not been repealed in 1999, or if Germany's far more cautious model of banking to meet the needs of real industries and businesses had been followed in the United States. (Of course, some might object that German banks did get hit hard in the subprime crisis, but if you look into it, you'll find that their biggest fault was believing American bankers and ratings agencies who said that everything they were buying was safe.)

Wall Street bankers, like Beltway political hacks, don't live in that real world. They really don't give a fig about Detroit—or about Pittsburgh, St. Louis, Newark, Albany, Cleveland, or a lot of other places, either. But a lot of other countries have prospered from following Germany—and old industrial America. Starting in the 1950s, Japan, South Korea, and Taiwan on the Pacific Rim all began their long, steady rise to global prosperity and power. They all did so in exactly the same way: they had internal free markets with relatively low tax rates, and they encouraged the growth of their domestic industries. The governments of these countries also encouraged their main industries to export as much as possible, especially to the United States. After the Kennedy Round of tariff cuts in the 1960s, Lyndon Johnson, Richard Nixon, and their successors obligingly kept that market wide open to them.

All these countries, as US allies, enjoyed Most-Favored-Nation (MFN) trading status. But all of them maintained enormous protectionist barriers against comparable quantities of US manufactured goods entering their home markets. And all of them manipulated their currencies to keep their own exported goods far cheaper and more competitive against America's own domestic industries.

Starting in the 1980s, China followed their example and practiced the same policies on a far vaster and even more successful scale—and with even more success.

It was the same pattern as we have seen before in Britain and America. Rising industrial economies protected by the armor of protective tariffs grew at the expense of naive, vulnerable countries. The sucker countries left their manufacturing sectors wide open and vulnerable. Their leaders didn't care; they kept their blind faith in the false gospel of free trade.

● ● ●

The False Gospel of Globalization 3.0 as preached by Thomas Friedman and his conception of a flat world turns out to be nothing more than a Trojan horse. It has deluded America's leaders into opening the economic defenses of their country. America's industries were left wide open to be conquered and destroyed by wiser competitors.

But this was an old, old story. We find the same principles operating eight hundred years ago across Europe. Even then they were deciding the rise and fall of nations.

Ian Duncan Colvin is unknown today. He is forgotten in his native Britain and he was never known at all in the United States. Colvin was a nineteenth-century British romantic nationalist and patriot who reached the apogee of his influence during World War I.

Many of his political passions look ludicrous today: He was a fanatical supporter of the Unionists of Northern Ireland. He hated like poison the Republican patriots who fought for a free Irish Republic. He was viciously anti-German. He would have hated the modern European Union.

But in his own time Colvin was an important and influential figure in British journalism and policymaking. You might say he was the Thomas Friedman of his day. He was a writer for the respected *Morning Post* newspaper. For all the limitations and prejudices of his time and place, he was a wiser and more accurate guide to the real round world of the twentieth and twenty-first centuries than Friedman with his flat fantasies.

Colvin, who died in 1937 at age sixty-one, was an energetic and talented economic historian. He wrote two seminal and now totally forgotten books. They uncovered a medieval world of unending economic rivalry and conflict driven by the same principles that drive the Globalization 3.0 world we live in today.

In these books—*The Germans in England* and *The Unseen Hand in English History*—Colvin traced the three-hundred-year era from 1200 to 1500 when the English wool trade was controlled by the Hanseatic League.

Colvin painted the league as a monstrous international trade organization. Today he might well be writing fierce conspiracy theory attacks against the World Trade Organization or the European Union. In reality, the city-states of the Hanseatic League were a powerful force to create prosperity, tolerance, trade, and civilization throughout Northern Europe. They were the gardens that grew the culture of wealth-creating, free-market capitalism throughout Northern Europe.

But Colvin was also, allowing for his prejudices, a careful economic historian. He understood and documented an important basic principle: nations and cities that protected their manufacturing industries from unfair competition prospered and rose. They quickly became strong enough to defend themselves. Then they all imposed their will on others. More idealistic and naive or simplistic countries fell under the control of the stronger countries. And the stronger countries didn't allow the weaker countries to become independent of them as long as they could.

"The Germans were always interfering in English policy for their own ends," Colvin wrote. "We find them bribing a Chancellor, financing an invasion and raising or pulling down a dynasty. . . . We begin to see the hidden springs and inner motives of what was before a mere orgy of civil and foreign wars."

There are a lot of hypocrisy and double standards to what Colvin wrote, for he loved and served the British Empire. And how did Britain become the greatest empire the world had ever seen? By "bribing a Chancellor, financing an invasion and raising or pulling down a dynasty."

Writing in the introduction to *The Unseen Hand in English History*, Colvin sounds very much like America's Founding Fathers in his candid, coldly realistic assessment of what motivates people to act as they do. He understood very clearly how the rich can almost always use their wealth to buy the support or influence of the poor.

"It is constancy of pressure which gives strength and influence to organized interest. A few men on great occasion work for a cause: most men all the time work for their own ends. If we quarrel with this truth, we quarrel with human nature. After all, men and nations must first of all live, and livelihood must therefore remain the basis of human action," Colvin wrote.

Remember, today we live in a round world of seven billion human beings. They are going to exert more pressure than ever before in history to fight for the energy, land, resources, food, and manufactured goods they need to lead a comfortable, or just sustainable life.

Americans of all ages have had it so good for so long that they have come to take the enormous wealth, comforts, freedoms, and opportunities of their great country for granted. But modern Chinese, Japanese, Koreans, Taiwanese, Indians, and many others know the world a lot better than that.

Their leaders may pay pretend lip service to the idiocies of Thomas Friedman and the dream-world theories of David Ricardo, Milton Friedman, and the neoconservative and libertarian true believers. But in reality they all know better. They agree with Ian Duncan Colvin: "*Men and nations must first of all live, and livelihood must therefore remain the basis of human action.*"

Colvin then followed this statement with another basic truth: "*We are in danger if our statesmen look for motive higher than the interest of the nation, for the statesman is a trustee and has a crooked view of morality if he indulges at the public expense.*" (italics added)

I guarantee you that if President Obama ever read that sentence he wouldn't understand a word of it.

But the current, forty-fourth president wouldn't be alone. Over the past half century every president except Gerald Ford has presided over a declining US manufacturing and real power base and made it worse by their own actions.

Every one of them thought that by destroying the real wealth of their own country they were really doing good for their own people. The worse things got, the more their faith in free trade and a flat world increased.

Over the past twenty-five years, Thomas Friedman's solutions have repeatedly been exposed as useless and disastrous in the real world. But he's learned nothing from all his false prophecies and fiascoes. He just keeps pumping out more of them. The poisonous Kool-Aid just keeps getting stronger. And his dupes drink more of it than ever.

If a delusional lunatic jumps out of a skyscraper and screams that he can fly, he may think he's getting away with it for a few seconds. He won't learn he's wrong until he slams into the ground at an acceleration of thirty-two feet per second squared.

Thomas Friedman's false gospel of free trade and his claim that the world is flat have led America's leaders to throw their country out the windows of the highest skyscrapers on Wall Street. They don't care how many hundreds of millions of American lives are smashed. They think everything is fine as long as they're still flying. None of them dreams that the hard, unyielding concrete of the real world is waiting for them to smash into, too.

But it is.

EIGHT

Free Trade and the Downfall of America

How Fifty Years of Open Markets Destroyed America's Industrial Base

We have already seen how Abraham Lincoln created a tariff wall to protect American industry from unfair and cheaper foreign competition. We also have seen how Franklin Roosevelt at the very start of the New Deal deliberately chose a go-it-alone policy of economic nationalism. He turned his back on free trade to rescue his nation from the crisis of the Great Depression.

But what happened to America in the sixty-four years from the assassination of Lincoln to the Wall Street Crash of 1929 and during the entire century from the death of Lincoln to the start of the Vietnam War?

It was not the abstract theory of democracy or the philosophical superiority of freedom that attracted more than thirty million immigrants to the United States in the seventy years from 1860 to 1930; it was the prospect of a better, wealthier life. Democracy flourished in the United States throughout that century for the same reason that it failed in Germany in the early 1930s. It failed in Weimar Germany because the economy collapsed, not just once, but repeatedly. Weimar's disasters plunged scores of millions of previously decent people into destitution and desperation.

By contrast, the mighty industrial heart of America kept beating even through the Great Depression. It churned out food, automobiles, homes, refrigerators, and growing wealth for an ever-increasing circle of ordinary people. It was able to do this because the great tariff walls built by Abraham Lincoln were maintained in their strength through all that time.

The Republican Party of Abraham Lincoln and Dwight D. Eisenhower was not a party of free trade. Every one of the ten Republican presidents who succeeded Lincoln remained committed to his tariffs policy. They were Ulysses S. Grant, Rutherford B. Hayes, James Garfield, Chester A. Arthur, Benjamin Harrison, William McKinley, Theodore Roosevelt, William Howard Taft, Warren G. Harding, and Calvin Coolidge. Only the ineffable Herbert Hoover, the bungler who made the Great Depression vastly worse, wavered from the protectionist creed. He eagerly supported the World Economic Conference in London in June 1933. It was Hoover's immediate successor, Democrat Franklin Roosevelt, who pulled the plug on it.

But during all those decades, when the US oil, steel, meat producing and exporting, auto, railroad, mining, chemical, and electrical engineering industries became the greatest in the world, they were all protected by steep tariffs on imported goods.

But according to Thomas Friedman, that shouldn't have happened. According to him and the "Classical School" economists at the University of Chicago, tariffs should have made the US industrial economy inefficient, uncompetitive, and complacent. Did they?

Of course not; in that Golden Century from the Lincoln Tariffs to the Kennedy Round, the US industrial economy was the wonder of the world. It stimulated a greater surge of invention, innovation, and technological advance than any other society had ever seen in history—or than the world has seen in the past half century.

What did that selfish, complacent, insecure, tariff-protected US industrial economy invent and produce during that "dark" century when it was protected by tariffs from foreign competition?

Automobiles, the modern assembly line, manned flight, the eradication of polio through the Sabin and Salk vaccines, the eradication of smallpox within the United States, manned space flight, steelmaking, the largest, most efficient ship-building industry the world has ever seen, the largest air force in history, the largest navy in history, jet airliners, nuclear energy, the oil industry, the electric lightbulb, television, electrical power generating stations, alternating current for long-distance electrical power, transcontinental railroads, the refrigerator industry, the air-conditioning industry, and vacuum cleaners.

And compared to all that, what do we celebrate today? Would you believe, Facebook?

All of this amazing record of achievement flies in the face of the fanatical orthodoxy of the free-trade Gospel. Not only did tariffs work, there were plenty of times when high tariffs worked better.

William McKinley, a Republican leader in the House of Representatives, raised US industrial protective tariffs to record levels in 1890. This raised the prices of some essential goods and proved very unpopular with the American people. So McKinley's Republicans were defeated in the national elections of 1892. In 1894, the Democrats lowered tariffs.

Now, according to classic free-trade theory and all our genius and statesmanlike neocon, libertarian, and Bill Clinton third way friends, this should immediately have boosted business confidence and global prosperity. Did it?

Not at all. The First Great Depression, which started in 1893, only got worse. It was the worst economic crisis in US history to that point. Hundreds of thousands of human beings went hungry. Millions of people fell into desperation and destitution. President Grover Cleveland, a Democrat who championed reducing tariffs, hadn't a clue how to restore business confidence. He left office in ignominy. In 1896 the American people elected McKinley, the architect of the 1890 tariff, as their next president. The first thing he did was raise tariffs again, in 1897.

Now, according to Thomas Friedman, that action—which he certainly would regard as cowardly, tragic, and shortsighted—should really have destroyed recovery prospects. Did it?

Not at all; the opposite happened. The US industrial economy boomed in a more spectacular manner than ever before in its history. It boomed continuously for nearly a quarter century, even though it was now protected by record-high industrial tariffs. According to David Ricardo, Milton Friedman, and Thomas Friedman, that never should have happened. It should have been impossible. But it happened anyway.

Free-trade theologians never tire of quoting the genuinely disastrous Smoot-Hawley Tariff of 1930, which certainly made the Great Depression worse. But Smoot-Hawley didn't cause the Great Depression and it wasn't the main impediment to economic recovery. President Herbert Hoover imposed a freeze on wages and prices that blocked the free market's main recovery mechanismAnd he did a lot of other amazingly stupid things, too.

But free-trade theologians never mention the McKinley Tariff of 1897. How can they? For the US economy responded to that tariff law by breaking free of the worst economic depression in its history and a quarter century of far too heavy unemployment and hardship. After 1897, the economy expanded. It generated more new jobs than ever before in its history. According to free-trade theology, that never could have happened. But it did.

The Lincoln–McKinley era of high tariffs during the era of Industrial America also allowed the country to successfully absorb and integrate more new immigrants than any other nation in history had ever done before.

From 1860 to 1930, a total of thirty-two million immigrants entered the United States. The key to their successful absorption was the country's enormous and rapidly growing economy.

This historic achievement contains a lot of lessons for "postindustrial" societies today. The best way for the United States to absorb its million immigrants a year, mainly illegal, from Mexico and Latin America would be to revive its industrial sector and generate decently paying jobs for them. That is also the real solution for France, Britain, and other European countries with large, increasingly alienated immigrant populations, in their case mainly Muslims from North Africa, South Asia, and the Middle East.

Industrial America boomed under the McKinley Tariff. Tariffs were adjusted in later years, but they stayed high. Far from damaging business confidence, the tariffs boosted it. It was only in the aftermath of World War I, a generation later, that the US economy stumbled seriously again.

In 1920, as Woodrow Wilson lay ravaged by a stroke in the White House, the US economy plunged into a new depression. Wall Street stocks plunged farther and faster, and jobs were lost at a greater rate than at the comparable opening period of the Great Depression a decade later.

The American people then elected Warren Harding as their president, and Harding appointed Andrew Mellon as his secretary of the treasury. Mellon went on to hold that job for longer than any other person in history—too long, in fact. He couldn't prevent Herbert Hoover from messing everything up during the Great Depression and took a lot of the blame for Hoover's bungles. But 1921 under Harding was his finest hour.

To this day, Harding and Mellon's policies to deal with the economic crisis they inherited from Woodrow Wilson remain the outstanding example of how to bring an industrial economy out of crisis faster and more successfully than any other way. It should be called a textbook case except it isn't in any of the textbooks.

Harding and Mellon certainly didn't act like Barack Obama, Timothy Geithner, and Ben Bernanke when it came to their recovery policies.

They didn't do the 1920s equivalent of a QE II—a second round of quantitative easing (translated into simple English, that means pumping more money into the economy). They didn't spend their time blowing (stimulus) into a balloon with a big (trade deficit) hole in the other side. And they didn't scrap tariffs and jump into a World Economic Conference or create a new World Trade Organization, either.

Harding and Mellon retained the tariff. They refused to raise taxes. They also kept government spending under control. They could do this more easily because tariffs generate enormous income for the US government from the revenue they raise on all imported items.

A tariff in fact acts as a tax on imported goods. All the Republican conservative dinosaurs will roar in horror at that, not just because it's a tax but also because it can cause a little inflation as imported goods stop being so cheap. But the tariff simultaneously acts as a tax break and a huge incentive to domestic investors to invest their money in domestic US manufacturing instead. In that way, the higher a tariff is, the more high-paying domestic industrial jobs it creates.

And here's the punch line you will never read in Thomas Friedman— international investors love to invest in an industrial economy that is protected by tariffs.

Why should that be the case?

Because the revenue generated by the tariffs strengthens the government and its international credit rating. International investors don't care about free trade and they don't care about democracy. They care about making a profit and about the safety of their money. They want to invest in prosperous, expanding, and financially secure countries.

So if you refuse to raise taxes, as the Republicans now do, and if you refuse to cut spending, as the Democrats always do, you will drive away foreign investors and impoverish your own people.

What were the results of Harding and Mellon's policies? Business confidence recovered immediately. The US economy boomed. It did more than boom. It embarked upon its greatest period of expansion in history. It did this behind still-high tariff walls. And foreign investors loved it.

Harding didn't live to see it. He died of heart problems in 1923. He literally worked himself to death in the Oval Office. Poor Harding also was shattered by the discovery of massive corruption by his attorney general and interior secretary, who had stolen the strategic oil reserve of the US Navy. But Harding had saved the American people from the Great Depression of 1920 and put them back on the road to prosperity. And he did so through a low-regulation but strongly protected economy.

Even a casual study of US financial and diplomatic history during these years reveals more astonishing truths that confound the gospel of free trade and Thomas Friedman's endless preaching about the flatness of the world.

The United States did not retreat into selfish, irresponsible isolationism during those decades; the opposite was the case. Protectionist tariffs did not make the American people and the US government irresponsible or selfish. The United States peacefully settled its border differences with Canada and the British Empire in the 1890s. President Theodore Roosevelt won the 1905 Nobel Peace Prize for brokering peace between Russia and Japan to end their 1904–1905 war. After it was attacked in 1917 and 1941, the United States defeated Germany in two world wars and Japan in the second.

President Harding, the most cruelly lampooned and underestimated of American presidents, and his secretary of the treasury, Mellon, instead worked closely with the House of Morgan, the main banking power on Wall Street. Together they made sure that wealthy, prosperous America sent the impoverished nations of Europe a wave of low-interest massive loans to finance their rebuilding. It was comparable to the rightly praised Marshall Plan after World War II. The Harding-Mellon program, it should be noted, was not a naive, self-destructive altruism that would have cut the throats of America's own companies, as Thomas Friedman's panaceas invariably are. It was good business, just like the Marshall Plan.

America was the largest and most efficient industrial nation in the world; it earned more revenue from exporting its own goods to overseas markets than any other nation did. Therefore it made sense to maintain America's existing protectionist walls while simultaneously rebuilding the economies and purchasing power of America's biggest customers in Europe.

The Marshall Plan, launched in 1947, fulfilled the same function, and it resulted in a quarter century of record American exports to a recovering Europe.

Neither the Harding-Mellon plan of the early 1920s nor the Marshall Plan of the late 1940s required America's own tariff walls to be dismantled.

Nor did America's tariff walls discourage foreign direct investment. The opposite happened. International investment, most of all from Britain, flooded into the United States during the century 1865–1965. Throughout that century the United States remained by far the largest magnet for foreign direct investment of any country in the world. Indeed, it attracted more FDI in real terms than any other in the history of the world to that point.

This point needs to be stressed and restressed. It alone blows away the basic arguments of Thomas Friedman's world is flat Kool-Aid. And it also explains, of course, why China in 2010 outstripped the United States as a magnet for FDI per year, a condition it looks most likely to retain well into the twenty-first century.

Classical free-trade theory assumes that to protect an economy is a symptom of weakness and that it will drive away foreign investment. But this didn't happen during the great century of industrial America's supremacy. FDI flooded into the largest industrial economy in the world. It's easy to see where the two Friedmans and David Ricardo were wrong. International investors are rational. They want to make investments in prosperous, stable, and successful, growing economies. In other words, far from driving away foreign direct investment in an economy, sensibly scaled protection for domestic industry actively attracts it.

It is certainly true that the infamous 1930 Smoot-Hawley Act raised America's tariff walls far too high. It helped turn the already serious Great Depression into a national catastrophe. Even worse, it discredited the sound idea of more reasonable tariff levels for generations of American policymakers to this day.

Herbert Hoover was warned by hundreds of economists not to sign the Smoot-Hawley bill. An infallible genius in his own imagination, he then went ahead and did so anyway. Hoover even used special gold pens to sign the measure to underline his contempt for its critics.

For the next two years, as the Dow-Jones Index plunged in a death dive and the US industrial economy collapsed, Hoover only made things worse.

He froze wages and prices at their current levels, depriving the free market economy of its best natural self-correcting mechanism. He vastly increased taxes in 1933, and even worse, made them retroactive for 1932.

This was the real, usually forgotten reason for the great national banking crisis of winter 1932–1933. Conspiracy mongers have claimed that there was another "unseen hand" behind the crisis to propel Franklin Roosevelt into power and secretly socialize the United States. There was an "unseen hand" behind the crisis, all right. But the hand was Herbert Hoover's. The fool was sucking what little purchasing power was left out of the economy and triggering a run, forcing tens of millions of people to pull their last savings out of the tottering banks to pay their huge, new, unexpected tax bills.

Hoover was a Jonah president. Like George W. Bush and Barack Obama, he wrecked everything he touched as president.

Conservatives present the era as a golden age of minimum government regulation, even though, when Theodore Roosevelt became president in 1901, the life expectancy of the average American male was only forty-three—thirty-five years less than it is now. Liberals present that era as a dark age of industrial misery and legalized slavery for industrial workers, even though, in the Progressive Era, which really ran from 1896 to 1929, more human beings were raised to higher living standards across the United States than had ever happened in any country in human history.

There is truth to the simplified arguments of both the conservatives and the liberals. But the bottom line is this: industrial power generated wealth and profit on a scale never before imagined in any society in history.

A long struggle was eventually fought with partial success to bring the worlds of industry and finance under the regulation of the federal government. Safety nets for the poor and the elderly in society were not constructed until the 1930s as part of FDR's New Deal. A partial and very incomplete safety net for the sick—Medicare and Medicaid—was not constructed until the Great Society of Lyndon Johnson in the 1960s. Even in the half century since then, the United States has compared very unfavorably with every other industrialized democracy in the scale and cost-effectiveness of the health care it provides.

• • •

These are all familiar debates. But what conservatives and liberals alike all take for granted is that the industrial supremacy and wealth-creating capabilities of American society still exist and that they will continue forever.

They are blind to the supreme achievement of Industrial America in the century from the end of the Civil War in 1865 to the start of the Vietnam War in 1965. During those hundred years, America ceaselessly grew richer and stronger: it amassed the wealth and power to do everything that conservatives and liberals alike wanted. In the forty-seven years since then, the opposite has happened.

William Strauss, coauthor of *Generations*, wrote that the American people have gone from an economy that could do anything and a culture that could imagine nothing to the very opposite. Strauss was right: but he thought the basic reason for this was a dynamic of generations and a change of popular culture. In fact, there was a far deeper reason: it was the "unseen hand" that the neglected and marginalized British economic historian Ian Duncan Colvin had identified back in 1915. This "unseen hand" has been unerringly operating through the past 150 years of US history. And it has operated in direct defiance of David Ricardo, Milton Friedman, and the endless legions of free-trade true believers who blindly follow them.

From 1865 to 1965, regardless of whether the United States was at peace or at war, regardless of whether it was run by liberals or conservatives, that unseen hand ensured that the United States became and remained the dominant industrial nation on Earth.

That unseen hand was the power of protection and the maintenance of import tariffs.

It was America's ultimate secret weapon. It ensured the defeat of Imperial Germany in World War I and the unconditional surrenders of Nazi Germany and Imperial Japan in World War II. It ensured the ability to launch a Liberty Ship per day to defeat the U-boats in the Battle of the Atlantic and the building of twenty-four thousand B-24 long-range Liberator bombers and eighteen thousand long-range P-51 North American Mustang fighters to win the battles in the air over Germany.

It was America's industrial supremacy and vast potential that made possible the creation of the atomic bomb in 1945 and the hydrogen, or thermonuclear, bomb in 1952. It was America's vast depth in industrial resources and engineering that won the Space Race and the race to the Moon in the 1960s.

That industrial colossus is now gone. We could not go to the Moon in the next quarter century, however much resources we dedicated to the program.

The industrial resources no longer exist in American society, and no federal government could afford to fund the program. The new deep space rocket that NASA unveiled in 2011 will never fly unless America's broad industrial base is regenerated first. You don't have to be Albert Einstein or the Prophet Isaiah to work that one out.

There is a road back to space supremacy, however, and it is the same road that China is already wisely taking. That road is threefold:

First, reestablish protective import tariffs.

Second, reduce the burden of regulation and taxation on domestic American industry, giving it the incentive to revive in its continent-size market.

Third, the rise in tax revenues from the revival of industry and from taxation on imports through tariffs will restore the fiscal stability of the federal government.

These steps are essential to restore the broad industrial base, the widespread, secure economic prosperity, and the booming revenues for the federal government that are all essential if the US manned space program is ever to be revived.

That is what China has done over the past thirty-five years, starting from a condition of utter destitution in the mid-1970s. It worked for China. It will work for us.

All the debates between liberals and conservatives from 1865 to 1965 have to be seen in the context of America's protected industrial power. The triumph of democracy around the world from the death of Lincoln in 1865 to the death of Adolf Hitler in 1945, and through the death of Soviet communism in 1991, was not automatic or preordained. The world could see that American democracy provided a much better, more prosperous, freer, and fairer way of life for its huge and rapidly expanding population than old-fashioned Russian czarist tyranny, Nazism, communism, or any other competing form of government. America's mighty, booming economy continued to churn out the endless resources to prop up our friends and oppose our enemies around the world, wherever they might be.

It also helped that Thomas Friedman wasn't around yet during that Golden Century to endlessly lecture the American people how their world was flat.

As long as Americans correctly recognized that their world was round, they prospered. As soon as they bought into the free-trade delusion that their world was flat, they threw it all away.

Being stupid as well as shortsighted, the past three generations of Americans over the past half century never really minded as industrial jobs were lost by multiple millions, first to Japan and South Korea and then on an even bigger scale to China.

America's middle class over the past quarter century bought into Thomas Friedman's high-tech fantasy. They shared Friedman's blind faith that Intel, Microsoft, and their emulators would always create at least enough high-paying high-tech jobs to look after them. They kept to themselves the dirty little secret they all shared: all the descendants of America's generations of skilled industrial workers would be downgraded to flipping burgers—if they were lucky.

But over the past decade, India has started following China up the global economic food chain, and the Indians have started going after America's more skilled high-tech jobs. So the middle class started to feel the cold at last.

Thomas Friedman loves this development. He sings its praises endlessly in his books. He would, of course, sing a different song if his own multi-million-dollar-a-year income were suddenly to be offsourced to Hyderabad and Bangalore.

In fact, there is no reason why this should not happen. Why not outsource Thomas Friedman to India? It would certainly be far cheaper for the *New York Times* to do this. They could replace Friedman with new Indian columnists. The Indian writers would without question know more facts and be younger, smarter, and more energetic than Friedman is. A computer could recycle his clichés as well as he does. (His books, in reality, are probably typeset and turned into e-books in India, which is just the first step.)

Friedman has no time for the tariffs that protected America's domestic industries for so long. They served as an invincible magic suit of armor against all the attacks of the world for a hundred years. But in the 1960s, America's leaders unilaterally started to strip off that armor.

It started with the Kennedy Round of international tariff cuts to stimulate world trade in the 1960s. John F. Kennedy was the first of seven "Greatest Generation" presidents who led the United States for thirty-two years, the largest such generational cohort in history. They were the first presidents reared to the gospel of free trade, and with the exception of the underrated Gerald Ford they were all economic illiterates. They inherited the most invincible industrial economy the world had seen. By the time they were through with it, they were already running huge annual trading deficits with Japan, South Korea, and the other Asian tigers.

The Greatest Generation presidents naively thought that they were setting up their own country as China's "strategic partner." In reality they were just setting up their own country as "Uncle Sap"—they naively believed that giving China Most-Favored-Nation trading status with the United States was in their own country's national interest. Instead it set the seal on America's industrial suicide.

JFK started this rush of the Gadarene Swine over the edge of the cliff by slashing domestic US tariffs. His immediate successor, Lyndon Johnson, made things far worse by spending money like water. Johnson pushed through new waves of spending on his Great Society social programs, and he launched the Vietnam War. He even funded the Apollo program to the Moon all at the same time.

Some of these programs in fact were necessary, successful, and admirable. That was true of Johnson's epochal civil rights legislation, Medicare, Medicaid, and the Moon program.

It certainly wasn't true of the disastrous and fiscally ruinous Vietnam War. Vietnam set off fifteen years of inflation: this posed a mortal threat to America's middle class and responsible working class. It was finally broken by Paul Volcker when he was chairman of the Federal Reserve. We should note here that Volcker was appointed by President Jimmy Carter, though President Reagan backed him to the hilt. That was the kind of responsible, constructive bipartisanship America desperately needs today.

The Vietnam War was a huge bonanza for South Korea, Taiwan, and Japan. They sat on the sidelines. They started making their fateful inroads into the unprotected domestic US market. But they wisely kept their own economies heavily protected against American exports at the same time. The same unseen hand we've seen at work from the Hanseatic League of the Middle Ages to the rise of the British Empire and Abe Lincoln's industrial America was at work again.

Almost no one in the American ruling class recognized this at the time. Amid all of America's overpaid, pompous, and self-important journalistic elite, the only individual who recognized it clearly was the late David Halberstam, in his prophetic 1986 book *The Reckoning*, about the eclipse of Detroit by the Japanese and South Korean auto giants.

Halberstam, interestingly, took a very different view of the world from Thomas Friedman, his fellow *New York Times* contributor. Halberstam's heroes were the old-fashioned, industrial economy engineers who loved the consumer-durable products they made. His villains were Robert McNamara and his heirs, the MBAs from Harvard Business School and everywhere else. The McNamara MBA crowd was arrogantly proud of their ignorance of the basics of production, manufacturing, and engineering.

All they looked at was the immediate bottom line. They begrudged every penny that was invested into research and development and into making physical products better. That attitude has spread like a metastasizing cancer to devour all of American industry. Halberstam never bought into Friedman's delusion that a handful of software billionaires could generate a viable future to replace America's industrial economy.

I never met Halberstam. But I clearly saw that compared with Friedman, he was an old-fashioned, ponderous kind of guy. He wrote in the longest, most convoluted sentences you could possibly imagine. His paragraphs go on forever. Halberstam could never write or think in sound bites. The world of Twitter was anathema to him.

Halberstam died in a freak car accident in Menlo Park, California, in 2007. He led a personally happy and professionally successful life to the end. But no one paid him the slightest bit of attention on industrial policy. Even he never had a clear understanding of the crucial role of protectionism in the rise of Industrial America or how the abandonment of tariffs in the Kennedy Round had ruined his own country. As a classic 1960s liberal, of course, he thought JFK flew with a halo on angels' wings. Still, Halberstam stood alone as a voice in the American journalistic wilderness warning of disastrous consequences of the loss of industrial supremacy. But no one listened to him.

Richard Nixon was temporarily bothered when the annual US balance of trade moved into the negative for the first time ever in 1970. He made a big show of consulting all the big-name economists around. But Nixon's much-vaunted "genius" for foreign affairs didn't extend to any area of business or balancing the budget. He crippled the domestic US economy with a far greater burden of regulatory agencies and regulations than even Lyndon Johnson had ever dreamed of.

Nixon was finally pushed out of office in 1974 by the Watergate scandal. Then many liberals woke up to the realization that for all his ugly liberal-baiting, Nixon was the biggest expander of government in the private sphere that America had ever seen. He failed to tame inflation. Every one of his economic "solutions" proved to be a useless failure.

Nixon was replaced by Gerald Ford, one of the most decent men and honorable public servants ever to have graced the Oval Office. Liberals hated Ford for pardoning Richard Nixon. Conservatives hated him for not being Ronald Reagan. But compared with the presidents who preceded and succeeded him, the supposedly "stupid" Ford shines as a paragon of financial and economic responsibility. He was serious about cutting government spending. He vetoed courageously every spending bill that crossed his desk that violated his strict standards.

Ford's reward was to fail in his bid for election in his own name in 1976. His immediate successor, Jimmy Carter, became infamous for the combination of economic stagnation and out-of-control inflation (stagflation), soaring oil prices, and rising unemployment that made him, along with the Iran hostages fiasco, a one-term president.

Of course, compared to the economic records of presidents George W. Bush and Obama, even Carter's economic record would look impressive today.

Carter was succeeded by Ronald Reagan, who launched a nearly thirty-year era of prosperity and growth for the US economy, but on terms very different from the boom eras of the past.

Reagan inherited a defenseless domestic economy whose traditional tariff walls of protection had been gutted by the Kennedy Round and JFK's equally idealistic successors. Reagan never thought to reimpose them. He brought two new breeds of so-called conservatives into power, both of whom were really just traditional liberals wearing new labels. They were the neo-conservatives and the libertarians.

The two groups hated each other like poison and still do. Libertarians want America to pack up its global presence and bring all the troops home. They want minimum government on everything. Neoconservatives want to go to the other extreme in foreign policy. They never saw a nondemocratic country they didn't want to bomb—or rather, get the US Air Force to bomb for them.

But the libertarians and the neocons all marched in identical lockstep with each other when it came to leaving the US industrial economy open to being swamped by unfair competition from other countries around the world.

By insisting on the vital importance of free trade and by ridiculing and smothering any platform to present the case for economic protectionism, they have ravaged their own country's economic defenses and destroyed its prosperity. They have left America wide open to be weakened and destroyed by economic foreign competition and all the social pathologies that follow from destroying the prosperous jobs of tens of millions of people.

Remember that none of this had to happen; it is a lie to claim it was inevitable.

The problems didn't come from the Soviet Union, America's ideological competitor in the Cold War. They didn't come from the nations of Continental Europe, either. They came from America's closest allies in northeastern Asia—Japan, South Korea, and Taiwan, three nations that owed their safety and their very survival to the US military presence protecting them.

As long as China was America's sworn enemy for most of the rule of Mao Zedong, China could do the United States no harm. But after a succession of US presidents embraced China as America's sworn ally, it was awarded Most-Favored-Nation trading status, and that left the US economy wide open to being swamped by far cheaper Chinese goods. Presidents George Herbert Walker Bush, Bill Clinton, George W. Bush, and Barack Obama—two Republicans and two Democrats—all let this dire state of affairs get worse and worse. None of them raised a finger to stop it.

Those four presidents all believed that the world was flat. They all blindly believed that free trade was a win-win game, not a zero-sum game. They all passively allowed China to maintain huge tariff walls to US exports while it wooed US Foreign Direct Investment at the same time.

I once spoke at a seminar where Thomas Barnett, author of *The Pentagon's New Map*, praised George W. Bush for "getting China right." Barnett was invited to endless Pentagon seminars before and since to give this advice and more like it. That's where your tax money is being wasted. It helps explain why the Pentagon can't win any of its wars anymore.

Bush I, Clinton, Bush II, and Obama all believed Friedman's nonsense—and Thomas Barnett's. They all believed that America was investing in the democratic future of China by running up enormous trade deficits with it. But as I've explained in chapter 2, on China's rise, democracy in China is seen as a threat by the middle class and by the poor and working classes.

This view is not based on stupidity and ignorance: it is rooted deep in China's historical experience. The Chinese people know that division and weakness lead them straight into dictatorship, civil war, anarchy, chaos, and communism. Those were the lessons of their experience from 1840 to 1980.

The only thing Thomas Friedman's advice to the last three presidents, mindlessly echoed by Thomas Barnett and so many other "clever fools" (as my mother sensibly called such people), has done is to weaken the United States of America, the great locomotive for democratic change in the world, and to strengthen the most populous dictatorship that has ever existed.

Friedman is famous for stating as a "law" the principle that the higher the price of oil rises, the stronger dictatorships become around the world, and vice versa. There is indeed quite a bit of truth to this proposition. (Even Thomas Friedman can't quite get *everything* wrong, though he certainly comes close to it.)

The dark 1970s of soaring oil prices were accompanied by despair and loss of confidence in the future of the democratic system in the United States. Jimmy Carter and Henry Kissinger both shared this pessimism. Then in the 1980s, President Ronald Reagan created a highly successful alliance with the royal family of Saudi Arabia (a subject I explore in my earlier book *The Politically Incorrect Guide to the Middle East*). Global oil prices plunged, the US economy boomed, and the Soviet Union collapsed.

But then successive US presidents ran up record trade deficits with China. Thomas Friedman praised them all for doing it. Yet this move drove the US economy into inevitable crisis. Now the collapse of domestic industry is driving America toward collapse in the twenty-first century. And Thomas Friedman remains ignorant of what I shall call Sieff's Law, which states that the prestige and strength of democracy around the world is directly dependent on the economic prosperity and optimism of the major democratic nations.

Therefore, the stronger China's industry becomes relative to US industry, the more China's influence will rise in the world and that of the United States will shrink. That is Sieff's Law.

Therefore, by weakening the United States and strengthening China, Thomas Friedman's free-trade, flat-earth gospel has strengthened the forces of dictatorship around the world. It has ruined the prospects for spreading global democracy in the twenty-first century. Unless the United States restores protectionist policies to rebuild its industrial economy, this process is necessarily irreversible throughout this century.

We see the proof of Sieff's Law everywhere today in our real round world. China is now the most influential nation and largest trading partner with the nations of sub-Saharan Africa. It has eclipsed the United States entirely on that continent. It is eclipsing the nations of the European Union as well.

China is rapidly rising to similar eminence within Latin America. It is eclipsing the United States in the two economic giants of that continent, Brazil and Argentina. I've documented in chapter 2 some of the key deals Beijing has pulled off with both those nations. And it's rapidly moving in the same direction with Mexico as well. It shouldn't be a surprise that after advocating for decades policies that have impoverished America's working class and ruined his own country at the expense of China, Thomas Friedman should now be suddenly much more impressed by China's dictatorship than by America's democracy. But if the United States woke itself up and imposed sensible tariff policies to protect its own domestic industries, these negative trends would be immediately reversed.

Of course, both the Democrats and the Republicans would have to get their acts together and grow up at long last. Or they would have to be replaced by a successful third party that could appeal over their heads to the American people. The odds against this happening are admittedly appalling.

People such as Thomas Friedman and Arianna Huffington like to say that a big part of the problem is education. But they seem to believe that all we need is to magically wave a wand and invest in broadband and PCs for every school in the country, and that as long as America's kids are computer-savvy, the future prosperity of the Republic will be assured. Well, as we liked to say back in my native Ireland when I was a boy, "Pull the other leg, it's got bells on."

Thomas Friedman, Michael Mandelbaum, Arianna Huffington, and Richard Haass, the head of the Council on Foreign Relations, all insist that we invest more money in schools and education as the solution for our problems. None of them ever mentions the need to protect domestic US industries from unfair foreign competition. They don't know what they're talking about.

They are putting the cart before the horse.

I live in Montgomery County outside Washington, DC. Washington, DC, had one of the worst school systems in the country. Mayor Adrian Fenty, one of the best mayors the city has ever had, appointed a lady named Michelle Rhee to clean up the school system. The Washington, DC, system spent more money per student than almost every other school system in the United States and it was still one of the worst—poor test scores, outraged parents, and high dropout rates. Rhee came in with a mandate for change, and make changes she did. She closed useless schools. She tried to fire useless teachers. The teachers' union, of course, fought Rhee tooth and nail, but she got them to agree to wholesale firings in exchange for a sizable merit raise. She got far too little help from parents, who griped about losing their favored teachers and principals (good or bad), expected miracles, or didn't like the way she opposed giving their kids an easy ride for getting passing grades they hadn't earned. In the next city elections Mayor Fenty was beaten in the Democratic primary, which is the real race to pick DC's mayors.

The victor and current mayor, Vincent Gray, was a typical old political operator. Rhee was squeezed out. She jumped before she could be pushed. She left a cheating scandal in her wake that will forever obscure whatever important lessons the nation could learn from her short tenure.

DC schools reverted at once to their useless old ways. Polls showed that Washington voters claimed to be shocked about how lazy, incompetent, complacent, and self-indulgent Gray was as mayor. He stuffed his administration with unqualified, useless old cronies. Quite simply, the Washington, DC, voters shouldn't have been so stupid as to vote for him in the first place.

This story can be told a thousand times over in school districts across the United States. Throwing money mindlessly at a corrupt, incompetent system is just going to be a waste of more money. Ignorant and selfish parents and other voters have far too much influence on school curricula. This should be a job for the federal government. It needs to mandate nationwide far higher standards. But the current crop of Democrats and Republicans are simply too stupid to even think of doing such a thing.

But there is a deeper problem and a deeper solution.

Parents and their kids aren't interested in learning practical subjects because there is no future in industry or manufacturing anymore in the United States. But make no mistake: there is no alternative to them.

There are still more than 310 million people in the United States of America. They all want and need homes, air conditioning, steel, refrigerators, clothes, television, and so much else. If companies in the United States don't manufacture those goods, other countries will. But soon we won't be able to afford to pay for them. We've already lost our great manufacturing base. But it doesn't have to be gone forever. The US government and Congress need to learn the right policies to get it back.

What are these policies? Is it even possible to rebuild Industrial America?

• • •

We could discuss regulatory burdens, entrenched unions, the rising costs of health insurance, and more, but other countries that are beating us face many of the same challenges. Above all, then, the US government needs to manipulate its national currency the way China does its own currency. It needs to give tax breaks to companies that create jobs within the United States and strip tax breaks from American companies that instead hire people abroad. (That would be bad news for former Utah governor Jon Huntsman. His company hired five people outside the United States for every one it hired within the United States over the past decade.)

Most of all, the US government needs to do what every Republican president did from Abraham Lincoln to Dwight Eisenhower: it needs to restore tariff protection for American companies producing goods within the United States.

Once those things happen, the quality of schools across the United States will start rising overnight. It will especially start rising in mathematics, chemistry, physics, and engineering.

Why will that be the case?

Because of the good old-fashioned laws of supply and demand. Industry will actually need more skilled workers: millions more of them. Once the demand for jobs appeared, people will compete to get them. And they will try a lot harder to get the skills they need to get those jobs.

Understand this if you understand nothing else in this book: there is only ever going to be one job in IT for every thousand people who read Thomas Friedman's books and try to make a career in IT.

IT is a capital-intensive field. It is not labor-intensive. You simply don't need many programmers. Under current US tax and trade laws, most of them are soon going to be outsourced to India anyway.

Now, outsourcing our lawyers to India would be a real improvement. I guarantee you that all our legions of lawyers would turn protectionist overnight if all their secure, fat-cat jobs suddenly started flowing down the tubes to Hyderabad and Bangalore.

And as I've said before, outsourcing Thomas Friedman and his friends to southern India or to southeastern China would be the best move of all.

It's perfectly feasible to do this: the literacy and intellectual standards of English-language journalism in India are head and shoulders above those in the United States. The *South China Morning Post*, published in Hong Kong, is one of the world's greatest English-language newspapers. Its business, industrial, and financial coverage puts Rupert Murdoch's *Wall Street Journal* to shame.

The US educational system a century ago had no trouble at all turning out the largest and best-trained, most enterprising, innovative, and high-quality industrial workforce the world has ever seen. Once the demand for those skills revives, the pressure from parents, local communities, and their politicians for the school system to get its act together will rise overnight.

Appearing on television to try and reassure the American people, President Obama flatly lied and said it didn't matter because the United States was still a triple-A nation.

Writing in his web column on August 10, 2011, after the US government had been downgraded from AAA to only AA by the credit agency Standard & Poor's, Peter Morici of the University of Maryland, former chief economist for the US International Trade Commission, spelled out in clear language the fatal price America was still paying for failing to protect its domestic manufactures:

> The Yuan is undervalued by at least 40 percent, and its intrinsic value increases at least 6 percent each year because of Chinese productivity growth. With Chinese inflation exceeding U.S. inflation by only 3 percentage points, it is hard to see how Chinese inflation will provide any relief.
>
> Decisive action is needed now to counter currency manipulation by China, Japan and others—these could include U.S. counter intervention in currency markets, currency conversion taxes and licensing currency transactions to offset similar practices by those mercantilists.
>
> All this requires major shifts in U.S. policy, and for the President to articulate a clear path for Congress to support and for his Administration to implement.

Morici spelled out clearly the shocking scale of the currency imbalance between the United States and China. It's something you never read in Thomas Friedman's endless flow of books and columns that blame American workers and business owners for being destroyed by forces Friedman will not let them defend themselves against.

"To keep Chinese products artificially inexpensive on U.S. store shelves, Beijing undervalues the Yuan by 40 percent," Morici wrote. "It accomplishes this by printing Yuan and selling those for dollars and other currencies in foreign exchange markets. Presidents Bush and Obama have sought to alter Chinese policies through negotiations, but Beijing offers only token gestures and cultivates political support among U.S. multinationals producing in China and large banks seeking business there," Morici continued.

He recommended that "The United States should impose a tax on dollar-Yuan conversions in an amount equal to China's currency market intervention divided by its exports—about 35 percent. That would neutralize China's currency subsidies that steal U.S. factories and jobs. It would not be protectionism; rather, in the face of virulent Chinese currency manipulation and mercantilism, it would be self-defense.

"Cutting the trade deficit in half, through domestic energy development and conservation, and offsetting Chinese exchange rate subsidies would increase GDP by about $600 billion and create at least 5 million jobs," Morici concluded.

Following Morici's policies could turn around the US economy and put the country on the road back to renewed prosperity in zero time. It wouldn't require a wholesale plunge into isolationism (though pulling out of hugely expensive and unwinnable wars would certainly help us, too). And it wouldn't even require us to leave the World Trade Organization. After all, China, Japan, and South Korea remain respected member states in the WTO, even though they manipulate their own currencies and internal regulations to protect their domestic markets from US competition.

China, Japan, Taiwan, and South Korea are not being evil in following these policies, and I have no intention of demonizing any of them. Their governments are being sensible. They are looking after the self-interests of their own people. Why can't the United States have leaders like that?

NINE

The Fools Who Lost the Secrets

How Al Gore and the 111th Congress Destroyed Thomas Jefferson's System That Kept America the Most Advanced Technological Nation in the World for 220 Years

President Barack Obama has a Strategy for Innovation to renew American industry. Did you know that? You will find it at http://www.whitehouse.gov/innovation/strategy. Reading it is an education. But not the way the president and the White House think.

There is not a scintilla of honest or original thought and not a grain of common sense in that strategy. Thomas Friedman must love it. It reads as if it were distilled from his books and columns. In fact, we know it was. *Time* magazine has listed two of Friedman's books, *The World Is Flat* and *Hot, Flat, and Crowded*, as two of the books Obama read during his first years in the White House.

Sure enough, Obama's Strategy for Innovation is a mindless echo of Friedman's timeless words of wisdom: There is the usual empty rhetoric about restoring America's traditional role as the innovating nation of the world. There is a lot about Friedman's favorite clichés of investing in green technology, transportation, and energy systems—a sure way to ruin. There is nothing about coal, oil, or fracking for natural gas.

Most of all, there isn't a word about rebuilding America's old, traditional industries—the industries of heavy engineering, steelmaking, mass-production cars, consumer durables, or shipbuilding.

There isn't a word in it to acknowledge the threat of unfair foreign competition. The Obama strategy, like that of George W. Bush before him, takes its geography straight from Thomas Friedman. Both presidents drank Friedman's Kool-Aid about a flat free-trade world. The new strategy therefore doesn't raise a finger to protect American industries from unfair foreign competition. It chases pots of gold over the horizon. It pays no attention to the real needs of American industries, small businessmen, industrial workers, and inventors now.

Because it chases pots of gold over the horizon, this isn't a strategy for innovation in the real world. It's a strategy for leprechauns.

The strategy for innovation doesn't say a word about industrial espionage, either. But anyone who talks to FBI agents dealing with these issues knows that they take it very seriously indeed. They take the threat as seriously from our "ally" India as they do from China. But the FBI and the embattled industries of America get no help from Congress or the White House on this central issue. It doesn't matter whether they are controlled by Republicans or Democrats, as we're going to see.

Here was what President Obama had to say about the need for innovation in twenty-first-century America. His first three sentences are right on the ball: "History should be our guide. The United States led the world's economies in the twentieth century because we led the world in innovation. Today, the competition is keener; the challenge is tougher; and that is why innovation is more important than ever."

Then, however, the president starts swallowing his Kool-Aid. Innovation, he continues, "is the key to good, new jobs for the twenty-first century. That's how we will ensure a high quality of life for this generation and future generations. With these investments, we're planting the seeds of progress for our country, and good-paying, private-sector jobs for the American people."

One of the mains sections of the strategy has the inspiring title "Invest in the Building Blocks of American Innovation." Except, of course, there is nothing whatsoever in the strategy about investing here in any products that people really need and would pay money to buy in a world of seven billion people. The subtitles of this section are enormously revealing—unintentionally. Not one of them was written by a real engineer or businessman. They were all written by lawyers and political hacks who'd just Googled the books and columns of Thomas Friedman. They are all about excuses to pour more money into the American education system, into hidebound government bureaucracies, and of course they are obsessed with broadband and IT. There is not a word about heavy industry—the real source of profit, job creation, and innovation for China and Germany. There is not a word about reviving the once world-beating US industries of steelmaking, television, refrigerators, electronics for consumers, and so much else.

This new strategy might be a very good strategy for the island city-state of Singapore, or even for the tiny nation-state of Israel. Singapore is small enough to base its economy entirely on international finance and cutting-edge, high-tech innovation and incremental improvement. Even little Israel is a bit too big for that to work for everyone.

Thomas Friedman imagines that sitting behind a PC and doing nothing but work on developing clever software can produce enough decent-paying jobs and profits to sustain a continent-wide society of 310 million people. That idea is simply infantile.

The Obama strategy (virtually ghostwritten by Thomas Friedman) assumes against all the evidence of the past fifty years to the contrary that the only kind of education that matters is American-style college education. It doesn't give a hint about the need for young people to learn practical engineering experience in the industrial workplace.

Here are most of the subsection titles:

- "Educate Americans with 21st-century skills and create a world-class workforce."
- "Improve America's science, technology, engineering, and math education."
- "Reform elementary and secondary education."
- "Restore America to first place in the world in college attainment."
- "Strengthen and broaden American leadership in fundamental research."

Then the Strategy for Innovation gets really silly. It calls for

- "A new transportation vision with high-speed rail."

Next, the strategy for innovation includes a section so irrelevant to restoring America's industrial power that its architects must have been confident that no one would bother reading it:

- "Develop the next generation of air traffic control."

A laudable goal, no doubt, but it hardly belongs here. What were they smoking?

Then the architects of Obama's Strategy for Innovation get into what really floats their boat: "develop a nationwide, state of the arts, communication network" and "expand access to broadband."

You can just see them imagining how the "great philosopher" Thomas Friedman would sagaciously nod his head and commend their wisdom for *that*.

At the beginning of 2011, we saw the most dramatic confirmation of my thesis that President Obama listens blindly and trustingly to the false prophet Friedman: Obama appointed Jeffrey Immelt, the chairman and CEO of General Electric, as the chairman of his jobs creation panel, the President's Council on Jobs and Competitiveness. Thomas Friedman loves Immelt: he breathlessly, worshipfully quotes him in his books as often as he can. Now Obama listens to Immelt because Thomas Friedman did. But what did Immelt actually do at GE? He closed down thousands of American plants and axed hundreds of thousands of American jobs.

To put this man in charge of job creation strategies is like giving Al Capone the job of keeping Chicago free of beer in the Roaring Twenties.

As Shahien Nasiripour wrote in the *Huffington Post* on January 21, 2011, "Immelt's firm stands as Exhibit A of a successful and profitable corporate America standing at the forefront of the recovery. It also represents the archetypal company that's hoarding cash, sending jobs overseas, relying on taxpayer bailouts and paying less taxes than envisioned."

Immelt's record of destroying the American industrial base is clear. As Nasiripour documented, "As the administration struggles to prod businesses to create jobs at home, GE has been busy sending them abroad. Since Immelt took over in 2001, GE has shed 34,000 jobs in the US, according to its most recent annual filing with the Securities and Exchange Commission. But it's added 25,000 jobs overseas.

"At the end of 2009, GE employed 36,000 more people abroad than it did in the US. In 2000, it was nearly the opposite."

The other members of Obama's "jobs creation" panel come with comparable, appalling records in destroying American jobs. As Alana Semuels reported in the *Los Angeles Times* on October 9, 2011: "Just days before the president appointed Kenneth I. Chenault, chairman and chief executive of American Express, to the council, the company announced a massive restructuring that closed a facility in North Carolina and eliminated 550 jobs, or about 1% of the company's workforce. At the same time,

American Express announced it had made $1.1 billion in the fourth quarter of 2010, up 48% from the same period the previous year."

Ursula Burns, chief executive of Xerox, destroyed 4,500 jobs in her company in the first half of 2011 before President Obama named her to his jobs creation board.

Jim McNerney, chief executive of Boeing, axed 1,100 American jobs in January 2011 and has since eliminated many more in Arkansas and Kansas, Semuels wrote. Yet Boeing remains highly profitable. Semuels noted that its profits soared by 20 percent, to $941 billion, in the second quarter of 2011. In the seven years from 2004 to 2011, Antonio Perez, chief executive of Eastman Kodak, eliminated 9,200 jobs in Rochester, New York, alone.

The people Obama has chosen and honored to create new jobs are directly responsible for the destruction of hundreds of thousands of American families and millions of lives by their selfish, immoral, and cynical policies.

What have Immelt and his board not tackled? So far, they have not raised a finger to reduce the endless jungle of government regulations that strangle start-up industries and businesses in the United States. Even Thomas Friedman and Michael Mandelbaum admit that these regulations now total more than 114,000 pages.

Am I being far too hard on President Obama and his handlers and ghostwriters? Just look at what a real businessman from New York State told Thomas Friedman's parent company, the *New York Times*, about how wonderfully the entrepreneurial climate has improved in the three and half years (at the time of writing) of the president's administration.

It took Neil Blumenthal fifteen years just to get a Small Business Administration loan. He was turned down by fifteen banks before he finally found one that would approve a $200,000 loan to his company. He had to sign so many documents, he said, that his hand hurt. He had to promise not to open a zoo, a swimming pool, or an aquarium. Although his company was already profitable, those fifteen banks wouldn't touch it because it didn't already have two years of tax returns under its belt.

Very revealingly, Blumenthal told the *Times* it was his understanding that a majority of new and recent entrepreneurs were either foreign-born immigrants or hadn't received US college degrees at all.

Here let me tell rising businessmen, from pizza deliveries to high-tech IT start-ups, a simple piece of advice: if you want to hire real talent, shut down your Human Resources Department and fire every member of it. If your company is small enough, vet every significant new hire yourself. As your company grows, make sure only your most successful managers vet their own and select their own deputies themselves. Sieff's Second Law applies here: people hire people like themselves.

So if you have hardworking, hard-driving, energetic, competent managers, they will generally hire people like themselves who also will be competent, energetic, hardworking, and hard-driving. Mediocrities will only saddle you with more mediocrities.

I saw this repeatedly in my years as a senior editor at United Press International. First-class editors and managers hired first-class people — not always, but almost always. Nonentities and passive parasites hire more nonentities and passive parasites every time. And all the nonentities — the people who are simply worthless at everything else, go into Human Services: everywhere.

That is a crucially important reason why the bigger an American corporation is, the less truly creative it is as well in actually manufacturing anything: when you surrender the crucial power to hire talent to people who lack any talent themselves, they are never going to hire any real talent for you. They won't be able to ever recognize it and they'll hate and fear that talent when they do recognize it.

General Matthew Ridgway, one of the greatest American generals of the twentieth century, said that when he was chief of staff of the US Army in the 1950s the most important and difficult challenge he ever had was what he called "protecting the mavericks" — the truly creative people — from all the nonentities who wanted to smother their work and break their spirit.

When I was a senior editor at UPI I found that was my most important and difficult job, too.

Anyway, what we have in America today is a risk-averse society filled with scores of millions of cautious, mediocre bureaucrats who believe everything Thomas Friedman has to say. And then they are surprised when everything goes wrong.

The president's own rise and background are of crucial importance to understand the true nature of modern America, for President Obama is not some sinister "wolf in sheep's clothing." He is an entirely typical member of our ruling class, our meritocracy (depending on how you define merit), what Russians call the *nomenklatura*. So is Thomas Friedman, of course.

Columnist Frank Rich of the *New York Times* has acknowledged the contrast between the hopes Obama aroused in his many admirers and his failure to deliver them.

Rich wrote back in August 2010 that Obama "came to office with both a first class intellect and a first class temperament" and described him as "the smartest guy in every room." But he acknowledged, "If he's so smart and so sane, why has he fallen short of his spectacular potential so far?" Rich then acknowledged that "the biggest flaw in Obama's leadership" is that "he is simply too infatuated with the virtues of the American meritocracy that helped facilitate his own rise."

Who were these meritocrat geniuses and how were they chosen? Rich answered, "Almost all had advanced degrees from Ivy League schools, proof that they had aced standardized tests and knew the shortcuts to success exploited by American elites."

Another admirer of the president, Jonathan Alter of *Newsweek*, agreed with this assessment. He wrote in his book *The Promise: Barack Obama: Year One* that the president "suffers from a cultural class myopia. He's a patsy for glittering institutions that signify great achievement for a certain class of ambitious American."

Yet Alter also admitted that none of Obama's "brilliant policy mandarins knew anything about what it was like to work in small business, manufacturing, real estate or other parts of the real economy."

This is a revealing and highly significant comment. For Obama far more than Bill Clinton represents the triumph of the so-called meritocrats in American politics, business, and society. They all tend to see themselves and their successes as entirely the product of their own brilliance; they are deserving, and anyone else who has not achieved their level of success must not be. They flatter themselves as creative and independent when usually the opposite is true. They tend to live in an arrogant, unreal bubble that allows for little questioning of common wisdom and little acknowledgment that there are other worthwhile paths in life beyond the ones they have taken.

The problem is much wider than Harvard or Yale. It comes down to an almost universal ignorance among the college-educated classes of the crucial importance of manufacturing to maintaining a decent standard of living for most of the American people.

Instead, the specialized protective, arrogant, unreal bubble world of American academia, standardized testing, and government bureaucracy has produced a new race of decision-makers. And none of them knows how to run a business or a farm, or operate the cash register at a 7-Eleven.

And so, over the past sixty years, America has gone from being the wealthiest, most prosperous nation the world has ever known to the most

spendthrift and feckless one. Its great domestic industries and their scores
of millions of well-paying jobs have vanished. Its big businesses have fled
overseas to escape the crushing burden of endless, ever-increasing government regulations. Its smaller businesses have simply been crushed to death
beneath those burdens.

Now President Obama, with much fanfare, has announced his intention
to plow $447 billion into infrastructure renewal in the United States. At
first glance, this sounds wonderful. Thomas Friedman supports it enthusiastically. He and Michael Mandelbaum note that US federal government
investments in national infrastructure were crucial to creating new eras of
American growth and prosperity in the past.

As this book has documented, that is certainly true. But as always with
Thomas Friedman, even an apparently truthful and helpful insight turns
out to serve only as a wrapping to hide a very different and destructive truth.

As ABC News has documented, much of the new investment infrastructure is going to Chinese corporations and other East Asian ones. *It isn't
going to revive American industry and manufacturing at all.*

According to ABC, the restoration of the Alexander Hamilton Bridge in
New York is directed by China Construction America, a subsidiary of the
China State Construction Engineering Corporation. The better paid parts
of the project including engineering and design work were kept for Chinese
experts, the report by Chris Cuomo, Joseph Rhee, and Linh Tran said.

Of course, the profits from the project won't stay in America: they'll all
go back to China, too.

Cuomo, Rhee, and Tran document the same story in Alaska, where the
sections of the new Tanana River Bridge will be manufactured outside the
United States. That project has outraged the American steelworkers who'll
be starved of the jobs that Obama is supposedly spending the money on the
project to create.

The same story is being repeated thousands of times around the United
States. The Obama administration, like the George W. Bush administration
before it, is not raising a finger to ensure that the contracts for the projects
it is funding first and foremost create jobs for American workers inside their
own country. The entire American ruling class now lacks the moral commitment, the moral drive, and the simple education and competence to
look after the interests of its own people.

Among the many things that this current American ruling class is failing
miserably at is the crucial need to protect the US Patent Office and patent

system from being dismantled. That process began under President Bill Clinton, though the driving force behind the disastrous "reform" of the Patent Office then was Vice President Al Gore.

In the name of "reforming government" and of "transparency"—two of his favorite slogans—Gore made the patents filed into the Patent Office far more accessible to the general public than they had ever been before. He took special pains to get Patent Office information listed on the Internet, his pride and joy.

But this must be a good thing in our flat world, right?

We'll maybe it is in Alice's Wonderland. But as this whole book is laboring to show, the round world of the twenty-first century is a dog-eat-dog place of growing international competition to control and develop scarce resources to feed and satisfy a record human population of seven billion people.

What Gore and his reforms really did was something very different. They allowed foreign governments and corporations to plunder all the crown jewels of American research and development as soon as they were filed. The process began under Gore. On March 29, 2000, while the Clinton administration was still in office, the Patent and Trademark Office (PTO) was transformed into the US Patent and Trademark Office (USPTO), a performance-based organization (PBO) under the American Inventors Protection Act of 1999. Gore was the driving force behind these changes. In March 1996, he created the concept of the PBO along with his National Partnership for Reinventing Government. The US Patent Office was only the second federal agency in history to become a PBO, after the Education Department's Office of Student Financial Assistance. The Clinton administration defined a PBO as "a results-driven organization that delivers the best possible services to its customers." It also, crucially, said a PBO "commits to accountability for results by having clear objectives, specific measurable goals, customer service standards and targets for improved performance." This apparently innocuous and admirable goal of "accountability" translates into a crucial abandonment of security for new patents. One of Gore's most cherished innovations was imposing "transparency" on the US patent system. New websites were created that gave the details of new ideas and inventions recorded with the patent office. This was tantamount to putting all the latest cutting-edge secrets of American technology and innovation on an open table, to be freely plundered by computer-savvy companies and corporations around the world. From the mid-1990s, at Gore's incessant urging, two new open Internet websites containing details of patent filings were set up by the US Patent Office: they were PatTF and AppFT. PatFT contains issued patents from 1790 to the present, and AppFT contains published applications from 2001 forward. Ironically enough, op-ed writers at the *Wall Street Journal* have complained in recent years that even these websites were not open enough to outside searchers.

China has already developed an industrial espionage and rapid response system that takes advantage of Gore's so-called achievements in Patent Office transparency with stunning efficiency. Professor Dan Breznitz, at the Georgia Institute of Technology in Atlanta, and his student Michael Murphee document this in their new book *Run of the Red Queen*. They spent three years in China researching it. They have produced the best book I have come across in English on how China's economy actually suc-ceeds. They smash every cliché about green, innovative China that Thomas Friedman ploddingly recycles.

As respected Israeli business analyst Shlomo Maital wrote on August 15, 2011, in the *Jerusalem Report* magazine, "Focusing on China's technology companies, Breznitz [and Murphee] smashes the myth that countries must invent new things in order to prosper."

How can that be?

China's real genius, Breznitz and Murphee document, is focused on what they call "incremental innovation." Maital explains that this means "making things in new and better ways rather than inventing better things."

To put it another way, Breznitz and Murphee say that China leads the world in second-generation process and product innovation. They say that China's companies don't actually do any new cutting-edge research and development themselves. They let universities and companies in other nations do it for them. Then they move with lightning speed to snap up the fruits of that innovation before the slow-moving remaining megacorpora-tions and monster federal and state bureaucracies of the United States can do anything with it themselves.

Maital sums up Breznitz and Murphee's discoveries succinctly: "Chinese firms offer 80 percent of global best quality at half the cost: For instance, Apple engineers design the iPhone in America. Within three weeks Chinese engineers know how to make it—faster, cheaper, better."

Now, Thomas Friedman and every free-trade economics theorist in America will smile condescendingly at you if you tell them this. They will all slowly and painstakingly (out of "respect" for their questioners' "unintellectual" stupidity) explain that this kind of growth cannot be sustained. It's a point Friedman himself never tires of repeating: China must transform along the green and democratic lines Friedman himself always tells them to; otherwise its growth engine will run out of fuel. Without innovation it can't go anywhere.

What is the answer to this endlessly repeated catechism? To use Friedman's own preferred form of argument: "Wrong! Wrong! Wrong!"

Here is what Breznitz and Murphee found: China's per capita Gross Domestic Product rose by an average rate of 7 percent every year from 1961 to 2005. During that forty-four-year period, it rose from $105 income per person in 1961 (at the depth of Mao Zedong's Great Leap Forward—one of the most destructive famines of all time) to $1,400 per person in 2005.

Breznitz told Maital that China's biggest and most successful corporations don't succeed by striving to invent things themselves *but by rejecting government pressure that they do so*!

"Chinese companies have been doing wonderfully by being on the cusp of the latest available technologies developed elsewhere and then being able to work on them," Breznitz told Maital. "It's a strategy that is basically against the central government's push for product innovation."

But that strategy, one of the real secrets behind China's industrial success, flies in the face of President Obama's beloved Strategy for Innovation, too, doesn't it? After all, Obama, like Thomas Friedman, says the United States has to focus on innovation above everything else; otherwise, China will totally eclipse us. But neither of them really knows anything about how China's successful companies really grow. Breznitz, who does, says that his research has led him to exactly the opposite conclusion: he predicts that the new drive to produce products "invented in China" will clash with the established success of the "Made in China" policy.

In other words, it's more important to make products cheaply and well than to invent them.

It's more important to steal good ideas from other companies around the world, especially in America, than to come up with them yourself.

It's more important to protect your own research and development from being stolen than to actually do it.

And it's more important to steal the research and development secrets from other countries than to come up with it yourself.

In other words, the US government and the remaining few major US industrial and high-tech corporations need to invest more in industrial espionage, and protecting their own secrets from it.

The metaphors of American football as played in the National Football League explain these principles perfectly.

A champion-level NFL team has to be able to seize the football from the other side: that is the mission of industrial espionage—a crucial field where China now leads the world. Then the team has to protect its football. That is the mission of tariff policies and of intellectual copyright laws, which we used to call patent laws. No NFL team can win a game without an offensive line to protect its quarterback and football. No NFL team can win a game without a good defense to block the attacks of the other side and strip the football from it through interceptions and other turnovers. Every decent coach in the NFL knows these basic truths. So do millions of football fans who watch the games every Sunday. So why don't the president and Congress of the United States, the greatest minds of the Republican and Democratic parties, and the economics and business schools of the great universities of America, know it, too?

If Thomas Friedman ever had to write or talk about the strategies of football he'd be revealed as a laughingstock overnight.

Clearly Al Gore never took the basic strategies of American football seriously. He would not have unwittingly destroyed America's historic R & D supremacy if he had.

Thomas Jefferson's old US Patent Office system jealously safeguarded these crown jewels of American research and development for two centuries. Gore's "transparency in government" reforms of the US Patent Office stripped them away.

The rate of response that allowed China to strip even the secrets of the iPhone from Apple in lightning time would not have been possible twenty years earlier. It was made possible only by Gore's government reforms and the stripping of confidentiality and secrecy from the operations of the Patent Office.

This story has been repeated a hundred thousand times over the past decade, and America has lost every time.

The story is not even an original one. It has happened again and again throughout history.

Nations that have grown wealthy and powerful through protectionist policies then use their wealth for successful industrial espionage: they simply buy, spy, or steal the advanced industrial secrets of other countries and use them to better advantage themselves. That was how the Ottoman Empire learned the secrets of military gunpowder technology from Spain in the early sixteenth century and used them to conquer all of the Balkans and southeastern Europe.

It was how France under Minister of Finance Jean-Baptiste Colbert in the 1670s stripped Venice of the secrets of glassmaking technology. It was how the United States in the 1950s and 1960s took Britain's pioneering work on the jet engine, jet airliners, hovercraft, and even mainframe computers (a concept developed by British cryptographer Alan Turing breaking German codes during World War II) and developed them for vast marketing and financial success for the rest of the century.

Now China is doing the same thing to us. And as Breznitz and Murphee have documented, it's been working for them.

President George W. Bush was blind to the damage.

Now President Obama, with the bipartisan support of the Republican and Democratic majorities in the 111th Congress, is making things even worse. He is going to approve a proposed patent law reform that is backed by all the big multinational corporations, especially the ones that have "outsourced" (translation: destroyed) millions of American jobs overseas.

Small-businessmen and actual inventors fiercely oppose the reform. But it is going through anyway. Our big, fat-cat universities of course love it. Bureaucrats everywhere love it. The reform will bring US patent law into line with that of most countries around the world, we are told.

That is absolutely correct. And it's the source of the problem. For the real reason why US research and development beat the rest of the world for 220 years was that it wasn't the same as the patent laws of the rest of the world.

Thomas Jefferson made sure of that. He personally revised the patent laws when he was secretary of state in 1793.

But as we'll see, everything that Thomas Jefferson built then is now being dismantled by Al Gore and his successors.

Patent laws are crucial to encourage an atmosphere of invention and innovation. You can have all the White House strategies in the world that you like. But if inventors and innovators believe that their great ideas and improvements are going to be stolen from them, they aren't going to really invest in bringing their invention to market.

Or they'll sell their inventions to other companies and countries that will pay them a better price for their ideas.

US patent law lay behind all the discoveries of applied electrical technology by Thomas Edison and Nikola Tesla. It lay behind the founding of the modern steelmaking industry by Andrew Carnegie, the oil industry by John D. Rockefeller, and the modern mass-production auto industry by Henry Ford. (Ford lost his global supremacy in automobiles to General Motors because he choked up-and-coming talent in his own company. Then his best engineers jumped ship to General Motors under the more innovative and management-savvy Alfred Sloan.)

From the very origin of this country, the Founding Fathers and the framers of the Constitution of the United States recognized the crucial importance of rewarding scientists and inventors. The first patent law was passed by the first US Congress in 1790, less than a year after it had been elected. That Patent Act gave the power to grant payments to only three heads of the great federal offices of government: the secretary of state (who was Jefferson at the time), the secretary of war, and the attorney general. In those days, patents were granted for an initial period of fourteen years. Like any piece of legislation, and like tariffs during their long history, the Patent Act has been repeatedly amended or replaced. It seems that once you get a good idea, the lawyers who have always infested Congress can't resist the temptation to tinker with it. Very rarely, better minds have improved on the original intent. The original wording of the first Patent Act didn't satisfy Jefferson. In 1793 he changed the wording to more carefully define a patent as "any new and useful art, machine, manufacture or composition of matter and any new and useful improvement on any art, machine, manufacture or composition of matter."

Jefferson's change worked. In the first three years that the act was in force, only 55 patents were granted under it. That's an average of just over 18 per year. But over the next forty-three years, 10,000 more patents were approved, an average of 233 per year.

Until 1836, you had to reside in the United States and be a citizen of the country to file a patent here. But immigrants were flooding in, and lots of British, German, and French citizens were having good ideas too as the Industrial Revolution gathered speed. So these restrictions were withdrawn.

For thirteen years, weirdly, control of the Patent Office was given to the State Department. But that didn't seem to do any harm. After all, the State

Department wasn't receiving campaign contributions from some multinational corporation based in India or China. In 1849, control was moved to the jurisdiction of the Department of the Interior.

Interestingly, popular hostility to patents always peaked when the United States was going through its worst periods of prolonged economic depression. This happened during the Cleveland Depression of 1893–1896. This negative attitude revived during the Great Depression and, much more briefly, after World War II. But whenever things got better, the traditional American generosity and optimism toward regarding the fruits of invention reasserted themselves.

The modern structure of US patent laws was set under President Harry Truman in 1952. Remember, those were still the golden days of protectionist industrial America. The tariff walls of industrial America came tumbling down in the 1960s. Then free trade was artificially grafted onto the tree of orthodox conservative beliefs by Ronald Reagan in the 1980s. But US patent laws continued to protect and encourage innovation and enterprise.

Finally, Gore's "reforms" blew an enormous hole in the protective castle of US tariff laws, as I documented earlier in this chapter. And we can see the results over the decade that followed. The rate of loss of manufacturing and industrial jobs to East Asia only accelerated under President George W. Bush.

According to the End of the American Dream website, the United States has lost a staggering 32 percent of its manufacturing jobs since the year 2000, and more than forty-two thousand manufacturing facilities in the United States have been closed down since 2001.

In August 2011, the British Broadcasting Corporation reported that in the first decade of the twenty-first century, under both presidents Bush II and Obama, the United States did not create a single additional job beyond the total that existed in 2001.

This catastrophe happened not because Bush II and Obama didn't swallow Thomas Friedman's flat-world gospel. It happened because they *did*.

The one great breakthrough in American innovation in the past decade, the development of fracking technology to cheaply extract natural gas from clay shale, didn't require any significant new patents at all. Old-fashioned US engineers and miners, getting their hands dirty, upgraded a universally overlooked technology that had been in use for at least six decades.

George Mitchell was the legendary wildcatter who so successfully used horizontal and hydraulic explosive mining techniques in the Bakken clay shale formation of North Dakota. He was nearly ninety years old at the time. He was a self-made mining billionaire. He was one of the last classic wildcatters. He had been shaped by the tough, two-fisted engineering culture of the Texas oil fields in the 1920s. All that innovation investment in broadband, universities, and air traffic control that President Obama and Thomas Friedman love so much had nothing to do with it.

In other words, tough old industrial and mining America was coming to the rescue of twenty-first-century kinder, gentler, green America when green America's smart-suited, soft-handed, impeccably polite, and deferential new generation of leaders didn't have a clue what to do. Harold G. Hamm, the sixty-six-year-old discoverer of the vast Bakken oil and gas field in Montana and North Dakota and CEO of Continental Resources, comes from the same world as George Mitchell.

This amazing development came as news to that prophet of doom for the US energy industry Thomas Friedman. In *Hot, Flat, and Crowded*, published in 2008, Friedman claimed that the US energy industry was the most backward in the world when it came to his favorite bugbear—research and development into clean energy.

"When was the last big breakthrough in clean energy production in the United States?" Friedman asked. "Answer 1957—with the opening of the world's first central station commercial nuclear reactor. . . . That's right—we have not had a scale breakthrough in clean energy since the days of filterless cigarettes and segregation."

Now, of course, during those fifty-one years from 1957 to 2008, the US mining, coal extraction, and oil extraction industries remained the most cost-effective, cleanest, and technically advanced in the world. But oil and coal didn't fit into Friedman's neat, tidy, laptop keyboard-pressing idea of what clean energy should be.

Old-fashioned oil field, gas field, and mining engineers such as wildcatter George Mitchell never appeared on Friedman's mental radar screen. Like the intellectual snob he is, Friedman never tires of dropping the names of his IT and corporate friends such as Jeffrey Immelt, the Suit who was then the chairman and CEO of General Electric. But Immelt never saw the Fracking Revolution coming, so of course Friedman didn't, either.

This is a very important point to understand—people such as Thomas Friedman and his "genius" friends have no idea of what makes an industrial economy run. They have no idea of what kinds of heavy industry are vital to produce an industrial civilization and a high, sustainable standard of living for countries of fifty million or three hundred million people. And they have no idea of where industrial innovation really comes from.

Paul O'Neill, first treasury secretary of President George W. Bush, was the last strong voice for the realities of maintaining America's economic prosperity in a twenty-first-century world of seven billion people. O'Neill was scorned by the neocon, Cato Institute, and *Wall Street Journal* crowds (and that's just from his own party) from day one. Eventually he was ridden out of Washington, DC, on a rail because he was a manufacturing guy who had been chairman of the Pittsburgh-based Alcoa Corporation.

O'Neill wasn't the usual slick-talking ignoramus on heavy industry and manufacturing, he was a world-class business leader in those fields. He lasted less than two years with George W. Bush.

In an administration largely characterized by reckless incompetents, O'Neill was a Cassandra figure: he was a prophet telling hard truths who was denied every honor.

O'Neill opposed the rush to war in Iraq. In 2001, he predicted a coming international financial crisis. He warned that the United States needed a 66 percent tax rise; otherwise it would soon be running a $500 billion-a-year federal budget deficit. (President Obama, of course, *wishes* he were only currently running deficits like that.) O'Neill expressed pessimistic concern over the vast global stampede into unregulated financial derivatives. This was universally seen as the product of his intellectual backwardness. He was a financial fuddy-duddy. The September 2008 Wall Street meltdown proved he was right.

Industrial innovation, as Paul O'Neill clearly understood, doesn't only come from universities, or from clean, antiseptic IT suites of laboratories and offices. In fact it almost never comes from them at all. It comes instead from the electrical, physical, and chemistry laboratories of major corporations.

This is a reality of which President Obama remains in total ignorance. He doesn't believe that well-paying industrial and manufacturing jobs are possible or even desirable. He focuses all his efforts on Thomas Friedman's will-o'-the-wisp fantasies of innovation, green energy, and broadband highways.

However, the industrial magnates of China understand the truth of where industrial innovation really originates very well. So do Dan Breznitz and

Michael Murphee. They discovered that China's main industrial region, Guangdong Province (what used to be known in the West as Canton), in the Pearl River Delta, also generates the nation's main innovation and high-tech industries. Guangdong alone generates 19 percent of all of China's own innovating patents and 37.5 percent of its entire high-tech exports.

The Pearl River Delta, they write, "is the only region [in China] where one can discern growing industrial clusters in form, fortune and capabilities."

In other words, China's most advanced high-tech industry grows directly out of its massive low-tech industrial base.

So industrial innovation can come only from an industrial base. *If you don't have an industrial base, you aren't going to get any industrial innovation.*

This principle applied to the best news America's energy industry has had in more than a century.

The Fracking Revolution transformed the world of global energy economics the way nothing had since the 1973–1974 oil embargo. It was the biggest liberating breakthrough in global energy possibilities since Spindletop erupted in Texas on January 10, 1901. It was already starting when Thomas Friedman wrote his sneering condemnation of energy industry research and development that words I quoted above. Fracking was already transforming the world within a year of Friedman's book coming out. And he had no clue it was coming.

In fact, Friedman prophesied only a year before the Fracking Revolution really took off in 2009 that it was impossible. He predicted that the US clean energy industry was the worst in the world at the very time it was about to become the world's leader.

How could that be? Didn't Friedman prove that "total investment in research and development by electrical utilities in the United States in 2007 was about 0.15 percent of total revenues"?

"In most competitive industries," he continued, "the figure is 8 to 10 percent."

Well, the fracking breakthrough didn't come from any research by electrical utilities. It came from hands-on, old-fashioned, hard-engineering tinkering by industrial America–type mining engineers led by George Mitchell.

• • •

Are the lessons of the Fracking Revolution being learned and implemented in President Obama's new Strategy for Innovation? Of course
not: in the fall of 2011, new legislation to complete the destruction of
US patent law protections swiftly and smoothly made its way through
Congress with bipartisan support, and President Obama enthusiastically
signed it into law.

The US House of Representatives approved the new bill by an overwhelming vote of 304 to 117. As the vote indicates, there was bipartisan support for it.
The US Senate passed similar legislation in March 2011. Both bills contain a
potentially momentous change: they would give a patent to the first person or
company that can file an official patent application. For more than two hundred
years, the patent has gone to the person who actually comes up with the bright
idea for the new invention. You can imagine how this tilts the playing field from
Joe Blow Machinists of Tinyville, Ohio, to the patent filing department of a
multinational working on a similar solution. Advocates say the change would
simplify procedures and reduce litigation. But it just assures the big corporations
will always beat the individual and the small company.

Microsoft is passionate about pushing the new legislation through—and
no wonder. Microsoft spends around $100 million a year just defending its
own patents and procedures from patent challengers.

The major multinational corporations support the big change, too.

The new act is, of course, given a rousing patriotic name. It is called the
American Invents Act (AIA). It would more truthfully be called the We're
Going to Stop Americans Inventing Act.

Congressional leaders delayed the approval of the legislation, but for
the wrong reasons. Like pigs feeding at the same trough, they couldn't see
beyond their own pork barrel.

They were really only concerned that the legislation might weaken
their procedural grip on controlling the federal budget. They insisted that
Congress continue to monitor and control the revenues generated from patent fees. Once that issue was resolved to their satisfaction in the usual kind
of arcane Capitol Hill legal compromise, they had no trouble agreeing to
push the bill through.

Senate Majority Leader Harry Reid of Nevada and his fellow Democrat
Senator Patrick Leahy of Vermont have of course claimed that the legislation would create two hundred thousand new jobs. That is as empty a piece
of hype as anything Newt Gingrich and Bill Clinton promised on behalf of
the North America Free Trade Agreement (NAFTA) back in 1994.

Republican representative Lamar Smith of Texas pushed the bill through, too. This should reassure you about America's future, dear reader. When it comes to making suicidal, catastrophic decisions for the future of the American people, the Republicans and the Democrats can still agree just fine.

The US Chamber of Commerce and President Obama both love the legislation. But quite a lot of high-powered and serious critics have been sounding warnings about this obscure act.

Henry N. Nothhaft, chairman, president, and CEO of Tessera Technologies in San Jose, California, wrote a major critique of the bill that was published on March 31, 2011, in the august pages of the *Harvard Business Review*.

Nothhaft acknowledged that "Representatives of some of the largest companies in the world testified that the new patent reform bill will enhance job creation in America." But he then presciently noted, "Yet the one and only group that actually creates all new job growth in the U.S. and could challenge those claims—i.e., startup entrepreneurs and small businesses—was not invited to speak."

That was "Too bad," Nothhaft continued. "Because if only Congress and the American people could hear the voices of entrepreneurs, they might learn how key elements of this new patent reform bill will in fact enrich the giant technology multinationals at the expense of American job creation."

"The problem with replacing 'first to invent' with 'first to file' is not simply that it tramples upon the core American belief in merit, which holds that the person who actually invents something first ought to own the rights to it. This measure will also reduce a patent system expressly designed by the Founders to serve small business inventors into one in which Big Business has the advantage and entrepreneurs are shut out," Nothhaft wrote.

"This cannot help but stifle job creation and undermine U.S. technological and economic leadership in the world," he warned.

How could this be? It is because "as multiple studies old and new confirm, only small startups create new industries and the millions of jobs that go with them. Indeed, over the last century, virtually every new industry was launched not by a big established firm but by entrepreneurial innovators," Nothhoft wrote.

Analysts Chris Gallagher and Kevin L. Kearns made similar points writing in the Congress Blog of the influential and respected Washington, DC, specialist newspaper *The Hill*, which covers Congress.

• • •

In their March 24, 2011, article titled "Reality-Based Patent Reform," Gallagher and Kearns note that in the "open innovation" world of the high-tech twenty-first century, wealth-producing invention or innovation "most often emanates from public and private transfers of technology through licensing and the collaborative interactions of universities and smaller start-ups, spin-outs, and research firms.

"This new, open-innovation dynamic is gradually replacing the formerly dominant, internal 'closed innovation' efforts of large companies. The scientific innovation model of our smaller firms, universities, and research consortia and the incremental innovation model of the large market incumbents both contribute to our world-class innovation," Gallagher and Kearns wrote. However, they continued, the proposed new legislation "ignore[s] the needs of the fast-developing independent start-up model."

Gallagher and Kearns criticized the new bill for "promoting the unwieldy 'first-to-file' procedure, which eliminates inventors' critical 'grace period' protections. This and other provisions will cripple early-stage innovation by 'harmonizing down' our first-class patent system to the inferior systems of other countries, which should be persuaded to 'harmonize up' instead."

Gallagher and Kearns clearly recognized that the new patent law will end a 220-year legislative tradition that has kept American R&D the greatest in the world.

Instead, they say, the proposed changes will Europeanize "our system for the filing convenience of global multinational firms—that overwhelmingly practice the internal, 'closed innovation' approach." And this change, they say, "will cripple today's innovation evolution with costly procedures while curtailing the beneficial 'creative destruction' inherent in technological progress."

What will the results of this epochal change be? Gallagher and Kearns are very clear about what will happen next. "Forcing the American economy into a single, narrow innovation model favoring outsourcing, offshoring global giants will stamp out the local jobs generation capability of smaller firms," they warn.

In other words, the new legislation will not create a new golden age of invention, innovation, and high-tech job creation the way President Obama, Senator Reid, and their Republican partners are proclaiming it will.

The legislation will certainly be a giant step toward creating the "flat world" that Thomas Friedman has preached for so long. But that is because it will demolish one of the last remaining walls protecting American inventors from having their ideas stolen by big international corporations and governments before they—and the American people—can get any benefit from them.

Gallagher and Kearns have very clear-cut advice on what the members of the House and Senate should do about the new bill if they really care about the future of the great nation they claim to serve.

"Congress should not intervene to distort the technology economy's continued evolution by crippling the open, independent innovation efforts of small businesses, our nation's leading job creators, at the very time we can least afford it," they conclude.

The new legislation will make the world a lot more flat, all right. More accurately, it will tilt the global playing field in China and East Asia's favor.

The author of the Book of Ecclesiastes in the Bible famously wrote that "the race is not always to the swift, nor the battle to the strong."

But in answer to that Scriptural wisdom, the famous wit Damon Runyon, author of *Guys and Dolls*, memorably replied that when it came to identifying the swift and the strong, "that's still the way to bet."

For more than a hundred years, in the era of tariff-protected industrial America, it was American companies that were the biggest, richest, and best in the world. Over the past fifty years, the pendulum has remorselessly swung that wealth and power away from us. Ian Duncan Colvin's unseen hand didn't just operate remorselessly in English history, as he recognized nearly a century ago. It also has been operating in ours.

A study published in March 2010 by the Ewing Marion Kauffman Foundation in Kansas, using US Census Bureau data, dramatically confirmed the crucial role of small and new businesses in job creation.

This study, *The Importance of Startups in Job Creation and Job Destruction*, used data compiled by Business Dynamics Statistics, a US government dataset compiled by the US Census Bureau. The BDS series recorded the annual number of new businesses (start-ups and new locations) in the United States over the twenty-eight-year period from 1977 to 2005. It defined start-up companies as less than one year old.

The Kauffman Foundation study revealed that for all but seven years between 1977 and 2005, existing companies destroyed jobs, they did not create them. Established companies axed one million jobs net per year across the United States.

By contrast, in their first year, new firms added an average of three million jobs.

Here we see again the totally stifling and destructive role that the rule of the MBA bottom-line bean counters and the Human Resources Departments play in preventing America's large, established corporations from finding and hiring the energetic, can-do talent they really need to upgrade their products and revive their companies.

Small start-ups, by contrast, can't afford to hire all those consultants and Human Resources Department bureaucrats. That's why they aren't stifled and choked by them. Start-ups still have MBAs. They just don't have people they pay a fortune to who don't believe in getting their hands dirty. Nothing is worth less than advice, even when it's good. I'll take an accomplishment over that any time.

Small start-ups also create the wealthy supercorporations of the future. And even on a small scale, they contribute more to job creation than all the statist, quasi-socialist efforts of the federal government and state governments combined.

By contrast, the US Department of Commerce announced in April 2011 that multinational corporations had moved about 2.9 million jobs outside the United States over the past two decades.

So let's get this straight. Small, new start-up businesses created almost all the new jobs in America over the past thirty-four years. Big multinational corporations terminated and sent overseas millions of jobs at the same time.

Yet the patent laws reform that Republicans and Democrats cozily agreed on in the current Congress strip small businesses and individual inventors of their protections. Instead, it gives far more clout to the big corporations. It gives them the power to steal from and snuff out the work of America's own inventors.

No wonder entrepreneur Neil Blumenthal told the *New York Times* that he had no hope that either Congress or the federal government had a clue how to really encourage entrepreneurship in this country when they couldn't even manage to maintain a decent credit rating for the US government.

None of this bothers Thomas Friedman, of course. "India and China may take a few American jobs with cheaper labor, but these are transient advantages," he writes airily in *Hot, Flat, and Crowded*. No need to worry then. (Friedman is fond of telling you not to cry over your soon-to-be-spilled milk, even as his hand is still on the glass.)

But India and China are two heavily protected rising Asian superpowers with a combined population of 2.5 billion people: that is more than eight times the population of our own rapidly deindustrializing United States. And in neither *The World Is Flat* or in *Hot, Flat, and Crowded* does Friedman write a word about how to protect American innovation after the patent laws system that has nurtured it for so long is finally destroyed. As we saw in chapter 1, he and coauthor Michael Mandelbaum retain that invincible ignorance in their new book *That Used to Be Us* as well.

Friedman does have something to say about patent laws reform. Typically, he's all in favor of it. Also typically, he relates it only to the cyber universe. Anything made of steel, magnesium, aluminum, or any other real metal is as alien as the surface of Mars to him.

Once in a while Friedman will allow a confused, sloppy, always casual reference to sanity and fair play to appear in his voluminous writings. In *The World Is Flat*, he quotes IBM chairman Sam Palmisano (Does Friedman know *anyone* who *isn't* a billionaire, multinational IT fat cat?) that "We must protect the interests of individuals and companies that create truly new, novel and useful inventions."

Well, yes, of course. But after those few words, do either Friedman or Palmisano offer a single hard, practical, sensible suggestion about how to protect these precious individuals and small companies? Not a single one.

When it comes to the right kind of patent laws to protect America's future, I've got Thomas Jefferson on my side. Thomas Friedman has Al Gore, Harry Reid, and their Democratic and Republican fellow fools. The choice is clear.

Epilogue

The American people do not have to despair of their future. There are reasons for bright optimism that no one dreamed of only five years ago. The future is full of opportunity as well as of danger, true hope as opposed to false promises.

The American people can still regain their old bright optimism and real hopes for a better future. But to grasp these opportunities and make the most of them, Americans have to reclaim their identity: they have to remember who they were—and who they are going to be again.

The knowledge of science and engineering, the ability to organize large-scale corporations, the learning of the lessons of history will not come without effort to tens of millions of Americans. But they are vital.

Americans have forgotten who they were. They have become ignorant of their own history. They despise it.

Americans, the wonder of the world for three hundred years as the most pragmatic and adaptive of peoples, are now trapped in a web of theories and pretentious, useless ideologies and false teaching. They are blinded by their ignorance of history, stripped of their industries and wealth by their ignorant reverence for free trade, isolated by their miserable lack of knowledge of the real reasons for the success of other nations. And they are amazingly naive and pathetically uneducated about the iron laws of chemistry and energy on which their entire way of life and very survival depends.

The pundits, the supposedly wise men and women who are meant to lead and educate the American people, have failed totally in their responsibility.

Their ignorance and incompetence have been compounded by their cowardice and laziness. They endlessly recycle old clichés. Whether they pontificate about spreading democracy, the joys of free trade, or the fools' gold to be gained from IT and broadband, it is all the same: they do not know what they are talking about. The collapsing standard of living of 310 million Americans mutely testifies to all their failures.

The American media have failed to educate the American people about the dangers we face and the resentments we have generated with other major powers. Our political leaders of both parties are woefully ignorant of them.

Americans have to recognize that they need at last to start defending their economic borders just as they need to beef up the neglected defenses of their land borders, especially to the south.

Most of all, the American people need to relearn what were the industrial policies, philosophies of life, and society that made this country so great for so long.

They need to know that there is no alternative to coal, oil, and natural gas to produce the cheap energy they have taken for granted for so long.

They also need to know that they are sitting on far greater energy riches than they dreamed were possible only five years ago.

They need to know that only manufacturing industry and heavy industry can generate the scores of millions of well-paying jobs they had enjoyed for so long.

They need to know that their great heritage of invention needs to be revived and protected. It will not survive by itself.

They need to throw the snake-oil solutions of the MBAs, the business consultants, and the free-trade newspaper pundits into the trash can of history where they belong.

This book has documented the real track records of protectionism versus free trade through eight hundred years of global economic history. It has documented the great opportunities for energy independence that the American people now enjoy thanks to revolutionary new technologies to extract oil and natural gas for generations to come.

And it has exposed the economic illiteracy of our past half century of leaders and pundits who were blind to the erosion of American wealth, prosperity, and global power that their own policies made inevitable.

Thomas Friedman and Michael Mandelbaum were right about one thing at least. Americans as a people need to rediscover and revive the qualities that defined them for so long, the qualities "that used to be us." But the childish, ridiculous fairy tales they offered were not solutions. They were silly dreams for Hobbits. They will only guarantee that the American people continue to complacently sleepwalk down the road to irreversible ruin.

In contrast to Friedman and Mandelbaum, this book does not peddle pessimism or fatalism. It teaches that what was lost can still be found.

New industries can arise to replace the old ones if the crushing burdens of federal regulations can be lifted or eased, and if future presidents and congresses commit themselves to protect these new industries the way generations of leaders did from 1861 to 1961. A nation that recognizes the importance of protecting its energy reserves and its heavy industries will also rapidly relearn the principles of courage, practicality, and can-do achievement that inspired it for so long.

In a thirty-year period from 1939 to 1969 the American people defeated the Great Depression. They defeated Nazi Germany and Imperial Japan. They armed and fed their allies in the Grand Alliance of World War II. They developed television. They exterminated polio and smallpox. They put twelve Americans on the surface of the Moon 240,000 miles away and returned them safely to Earth — an achievement no other nation has come near to matching. They did all these things, and so much more, while creating the highest standard of living for the largest number of people ever known in human history. We did all these things for hundreds of years in the past. And we can, and must, do them for hundreds of years in the future.

That used to be us. That still should be us: and it can be — again.

Acknowledgments

This book owes its entire existence and originality to Eric Nelson, my ideal editor at Wiley and to Krista Goering, a shining treasure among literary agents. My deep thanks also to John Simko, my production editor at Wiley who performed prodigies of efficiency in the great can-do traditions of Industrial America. And taking the opportunity, thanks as well to Clio's captains, my wonderful teachers of history. At Belfast Royal Academy: J. L. Lord, Bill Maguire, Jimmy Paul, George McConnell, Charles Winston Breen, and Ken Hawton. And at Oxford: Greig Barr, Walter Eltis, Hans Schenk, William E. Leuchtenberg, John Maddicott, and Isaiah Berlin.

"From all my teachers have I gotten wisdom."

Index